W9-CPE-145

THE HIDDEN CHILD

THE LINWOOD METHOD FOR REACHING THE AUTISTIC CHILD

JEANNE SIMONS AND SABINE OISHI, PH.D.

WOODBINE HOUSE • 1987

Copyright © 1985, 1987 by Linwood Children's Center, Inc.
All rights reserved under International and Pan-American Copyright Conventions.
Published in the United States by Woodbine House.

Library of Congress 86-050459

ISBN 0-933149-06-9

Cover Design: Carol Schwartz
Book Design: Wordscape, Inc.
Photographs by Dan Rosenberg

Manufactured in the United States of America

The Library of Congress has cataloged the first printing of this title as follows:
Simons, Jeanne.
    The hidden child: the Linwood method of reaching the autistic
child/Jeanne Simons and Sabine Oishi.
250 p., 17 cm.

    Bibliography: p.
    Includes index.
    ISBN 0-933149-06-9 (pbk.) : $17.95
    1. Autism.   2. Autistic children—Rehabilitation.
3. Linwood Children's Center. I. Oishi, Sabine.
II. Title.
RJ506.A9S54 1987   87-50459
618.92'8982—dc19   CIP

2 3 4 5 6 7 8 9 10

For information about institutional purchases and about other Woodbine House
books, please send for a free catalog:

    Woodbine House
    10400 Connecticut Avenue
    Kensington, Maryland 20895
    or call TOLL FREE: 800-843-7323

To the staff of Linwood.

Table of Contents

Acknowledgments

This book about the work done with autistic children at the Linwood Children's Center, was begun in October of 1983. However, over the years, there had been several attempts to present an account of the Linwood method, so that by the time I was entrusted with the project a large amount of material had accumulated on which I was able to draw to enrich and substantiate my own observations and research. In introducing this book, I would therefore first like to acknowledge those people whose interest and active participation over the years sowed the seed that eventually blossomed into *The Hidden Child*.

In 1968 Dr. Kathryn Schultz, medical director of Linwood from 1962 to 1975, submitted a grant proposal to the Meyer Foundation of Washington to finance a publication about Jeanne Simons' work. The money was forthcoming, but illness and the pressure of work prevented the project from getting off the ground. Nevertheless, a lot of material was generated, including hours of taped conversations about aspects of the work done at Linwood between Jeanne Simons, Dr. Schultz, and Dr. Joseph Slavin with whom Jeanne Simons had started work with a first group of autistic children at Children's House in Washington in 1949.

Years later, Dr. Slavin's son, Dr. Robert Slavin and his wife, Dr. Nancy Madden, who as students had worked at Linwood, tried to revive the book idea. They taped and transcribed lengthy interviews with Jeanne Simons around specific topics. Again, other commitments interfered and the project remained in the planning stages. However, it was through Bob and Nancy Slavin that I was introduced to Jeanne Simons. Their intimate knowledge of the subject, advice, and editorial assistance have been invaluable and is gratefully acknowledged.

Jeanne Simons herself had published only a few pieces over the years, but she had written down relevant anecdotes illustrating typical aspects of autistic functioning, as well as several full length case studies and recollections of the founding of Linwood. The immediacy and intensity of these first person accounts illuminate the treatment approach in ways no analysis, however detailed, ever could. They also convey the unique flavor of the therapeutic relationship that is the basis of all progress. These personal recollections by Jeanne Simons appear in the text in italics. Additionally, Jeanne Simons was, of course, intimately involved in every phase of the book. Beginning with accounts of events predating the foundation of Linwood, to wide ranging discussions of the methods developed over thirty years, to a line by line scrutiny of the manuscript, Jeanne Simons and I worked closely together in our attempt to put on paper what before had only existed in practice.

When I first approached the task of organizing and analyzing the existing material about the Linwood method and of identifying and describing the underlying concepts, it became clear to me that in addition to working closely with Jeanne Simons, I also needed first hand experience with the daily routine of the children, the educational programs and the treatment philosophy I was to write about. Consequently I spent four months at Linwood, observing the children, getting to know them, appreciating their uniqueness, and eventually participating in activities with them. I quickly felt at home at Linwood. I was extended the hospitality of every classroom and was guided, instructed, and involved in the daily routine as much as possible. My endless questions were patiently answered in whatever spare moment was available, and various staff members also read and critiqued sections of the manuscript and were otherwise active on behalf of the project.

As part of my research I also contacted many parents of present and former Linwood students and a number of Linwood graduates all of whom shared with me their memories, thoughts, feelings, and hopes. They added an invaluable perspective to my understanding of the problems that face families with autistic children and confirmed the importance of an early diagnosis, support, and treatment in an atmosphere of warmth and acceptance for the whole family.

Linwood has an active Board with many members not only committed to the Center, but beyond that to the cause of autistic children and adolescents in general. The Board's interest and the active support of individual board members was instrumental in getting the project under way and extended to all phases of its execution.

Without the acceptance and cooperation of staff, parents, students, and board members this book would not have been possible in its present form. Since they are too numerous to mention by name, a general vote of thanks has to suffice to all of them who together constitute the living fabric of Linwood past and present.

As an author, my personal, heartfelt thanks go to our editors, Terry Rosenberg and Marshall Levin whose enthusiasm about the book was encouraging and whose light editorial hand made the final phases of preparation for publication as painless as possible.

Sabine Oishi
Baltimore, June 1986

Foreword

Bertram A. Ruttenberg, M.D.

In the mid-sixties my staff and I visited Linwood to observe the already legendary Miss Jeanne Simons and her staff in action. The word had spread among the early workers with autistic children that here was someone with an uncanny ability to understand what the autistic child was trying to communicate and the origins and the meaning of his particular behavior patterns.

We found Miss Simons in the old house she had set up for her children. There she had assembled a devoted and attentive staff. They were low-keyed and respectful of their charges—children who, in their own way and time, however obliquely, were trying to reach out, to show and tell. Somewhere in the anxious outbursts and the strange behavior of the children was a message which would bring understanding of how they could be helped.

Suffusing Linwood's atmosphere was the presence and strength of purpose of Jeanne Simons. We felt at home—this was our kind of place; there were our kind of children. We too had started our center in 1955 specifically to develop methods of assessing and treating this type of children that Dr. Leo Kanner had delineated. Though we were coming from a different conceptual framework—that of psychoanalytic child development as defined by Beata Rank and our founder, Mitchell Dratman—we seemed to have arrived at the same basic approach of meeting the child at his level and in his mode of functioning. If we could devote enough empathetic attention, the autistic child could be engaged and the message carried in his unique behavior deciphered.

Jeanne Simons came to her educational therapy approach as a devoted teacher and almost singlehandedly developed basic tenets and techniques by putting herself on the line, taking over the total care and responsibility for her charges. Pioneering is a lonely business. What an exciting discovery to find another place that did what we did, but twenty-four hours a day and with a depth of understanding that left us in awe. We felt supported, validated, and no longer alone. Miss Simons extended us the same acceptance and basic respect that she gave her children. We left enriched by our visit.

Perhaps now is the time to reveal a well kept secret. In 1976 we reported a longitudinal study of the comparative therapeutic effectiveness of eight different settings. What seemed to make a "good" program was sensitivity to the behaviors and needs of the children, skillfully implemented by a dedicated and attentive staff, regardless of the therapeutic orientation.

These eight settings were never identified by name. One was described as having "the relaxed, pleasant, informal air of a democratically organized family. Reinforcement principles were used flexibly as they seemed appropriate for a given child. The staff expressed their ideas freely." That setting, as described by our graduate student raters, was Linwood. After the study was completed, and quite apart from it, we asked the raters informally to rank-order the eight settings in terms of where they would prefer to send an autistic child. Linwood ranked the highest; our own center ranked second.

Linwood and our Center for Autistic Children both were founded in 1955, specifically to address the needs of autistic children. They remain among the few devoted exclusively to this population. Jeanne Simons, however, brought to her founding of Linwood five years of prior outpatient experience with autistic children at Children's House, who were in danger of being segregated as untreatable in state hospitals. She obtained permission to work with these non-verbal children. "Parents cared and I cared," she told me. Perhaps that short statement contains the essence of Jeanne Simons. "The parents needed relief." Linwood resulted. Her empathy for parents of autistic children was profound and almost unique at that time.

I hope that this highly personal account will serve as an introduction to the spirit of *The Hidden Child*. The book is an invaluable statement of one center's basic understanding of and successful therapeutic approach to autistic persons. Linwood was and will be, in many ways, inseparable from Jeanne Simons, but the test of a method is that it can be described and set down in a way that can be passed on to others. This book accomplishes this goal.

Basic to the Linwood method is an affirmation of the humanness and respect for the worth of the autistic person as an individual; neither the parents nor the child is judged. The child is accepted and engaged as he is, with emphasis on the identification of areas of healthy potential in his unique behavior patterns in all aspects of his daily life, which are then slowly directed and molded into useful and socially functional activities.

The child is met at the level of his functioning with humanity and respect and, above all, with incredible patience and gradually increasing expectations, based not on a predetermined plan or pace, but in response to the therapists' understanding of the origins and meaning of his behaviors. Relations developed on this understanding build bridges to modified and new behaviors.

In this book, we are first introduced to autism and its range of unusual sensory sensitivities through beautiful, detailed descriptions. The book is filled with clinical vignettes and presents an approach to autism in simple language, described in real life encounters. This alone renders an invaluable service. It shares a lifetime of personal experience with, and understanding of, facets of autism through these one-to-one encounters—a veritable handbook of "how to." You learn how to observe and regard autistic persons, how to understand and shape relationships, how to shape behavior and motivate the disinclined child. The question of reward and punishment is examined. The "how tos" and "not tos" of setting limits are explored. The approach to the autistic child's need for sameness and associated compulsions and manipulative traits is outlined. Also described is the use of operant conditioning tempered with the understanding that the behaviors are expressions of inner need and anxiety.

A lengthy chapter on the nature of the disorders in language and thought process follows. Underlying brain dysfunction that interferes with both communication and interaction through blurring of self/other differentiation is postulated. The dearth of imagination and fantasy is described. We are led to consider the autistic child's basic problems in social and emotional development, which include the inability to relate the impact of environment to his own inner experience and the disjointedness and fragmentation which result from a lack of self concept. We are shown the development of a pool of positive emotional memories, the emergence of jealousy and possessiveness as a sign of progress, and sharing which signals a beginning sense of self vis à vis others. We follow this evolution through the detailed account of the successful treatment of one child into adulthood.

The Hidden Child concludes with an account of Linwood's current programs and new directions. Outcome for the first eighteen years is presented (we await eagerly its updating to the present) and a summary statement of the Linwood philosophy.

For years my colleagues and I have thought about putting down our experiences, ideas, and approaches to the understanding and treatment of autism. That no longer is a pressing need. It has been done for us. We workers in the field, parents, and all autistic children owe Jeanne Simons and Sabine Oishi a lasting debt of gratitude for this invaluable contribution.

Bertram A. Ruttenberg, M.D.
Medical Director
Center for Autistic Children

ONE
◆ ◆ ◆

An Introduction to Autism and to Linwood

"Sabine's french fries," the boy seated next to me said softly, looking out of the corner of his eye at the half-empty carton in front of me. His own tray was empty. He had wolfed down his food, head bent, as if eating was an all-important and difficult task requiring full concentration. He didn't seem to pay attention to anything going on around him at the fast food restaurant where I was having lunch with him and his teacher. But his comment showed that he was very much aware of his immediate surroundings.

Though his statement sounded like a straightforward comment rather than a request, I responded as I would have to any other child asking me for a share of my uneaten portion. I pushed the rest of my fries over to him and he dispatched them with the same speed, the same lack of visible pleasure with which he had attacked his own food. He had to be reminded to say "thank you," just as earlier when we were introduced he had had to be reminded to look at me. "Hi," I had said, "What's your name?" "Mark," he mumbled, his hand limp in mine. "Ask her what her name is," his teacher had urged. Mark, his gaze sliding past my left ear, had responded with "What's my name?" He had twisted his body away from me while shifting his weight from one foot to the other. "Your name is Mark," I said, "My name is Sabine." I released his hand and he quickly stepped away from me, mumbling softly to himself. I didn't think that he had heard me, but I was wrong. "Sabine's french fries." He not only remembered my name, he pronounced it correctly, and despite his confusion over pronouns, he clearly knew the important distinction between "yours" and "mine."

For a child who had not started to use speech for communication until he was well into his teens, Mark had come a long way. At the time I

1

met him, he was about nineteen years old, the oldest of the students at the Linwood Children's Center in Ellicott City, Maryland which I was visiting for the first time that day.

Mark, like most of the children at Linwood, is autistic. At nineteen, his body is that of a young man, heavy-set, with wide shoulders and a slight pot belly. Teenage acne and blond fuzz seem out of place on his soft-featured face, which is that of a much younger boy. Most of the time, Mark walks around with a dreamy half-smile, head cocked, as if listening to an inner voice, seemingly oblivious to what goes on around him. When he is addressed, his expression changes to an anxious frown, and in the midst of other children milling around, he seems to shrink into himself. He often mutters to himself as he goes about his business, and has to be prodded to look people in the face and to speak in more than one-word sentences.

Mark had been a breech birth. From the beginning, there were indications that all was not well. One of the worrisome symptoms was Mark's head-banging, which became more pronounced over time to the point where he was putting holes in the wall with his head. Though his early physical development was reportedly normal, his speech development was delayed. By age two he had a vocabulary of sorts, but he stopped talking by two and a half, becoming increasingly withdrawn, rocking, and crooning to himself, running around aimlessly, flapping his hands. He also became self-aggressive, biting his arms and hands, and hitting his head and face.

When he entered Linwood at age six, he was clearly afraid of people, especially younger children. He was nearly mute, at most mumbling to himself in a low voice. The eye contact he made was no more than fleeting. His hands were deformed and scarred from biting himself.

Today, Mark's arms and hands are healed. He still has occasional outbursts of temper, during which he hits a wall or rips at his clothing. But he is part of a group of boys who are socially advanced enough to leave Linwood for trips to restaurants and shopping malls or to go to public school or to outside work sites. Mark is taken to a volunteer job at the county library several times a week. At Linwood he helps with routine office work, such as copying and collating. He is slow and plodding but dependable, and he obviously enjoys the tasks he is given. The lunch at which I joined him and his teacher was one of a number of privileges accorded to the more advanced children at Linwood. In Mark's case, it was the reward for a week during which he had not had any major upsets and had fulfilled all of his obligations.

The handicaps that Mark has in large part overcome, are all typical of autistic children and clearly distinguish them from other developmentally impaired children.

WHAT IS AUTISM?

Autism, as a separate syndrome, was first described in 1943 by Dr. Leo Kanner a child psychiatrist at the Johns Hopkins Medical School. In its classic form it is characterized by:

- *Early onset—possibly from birth, but certainly before age two and a half.*

- *Social and emotional impairment—often shows up almost at birth.*

Babies retreat from physical contacts, cannot be comforted, do not develop eye contact, do not reach out in any way and do not react to verbal or nonverbal cues, such as facial expressions.

The children do not exhibit appropriate emotional responses, such as crying with tears, smiling, or laughing. They seem to lack the ability to recognize themselves as members of the human race and often fail to make distinctions between their animate and inanimate environment, treating people as objects.

Autistic children do not seek consolation from others when they hurt themselves and often do not even seem to notice that they have been hurt.

- *Communication disorders—encompass both the development and the use of speech.*

In some children speech never develops or else comes to an abrupt end around eighteen months of age. Other children do develop language, but do not use it appropriately in social situations. Speech does not acquire meaning for them and consists mainly of the repetition of sounds, words, or phrases they have picked up and which they imitate.

Preverbal and nonverbal behavior also differs from the norm in these children. They do not use gestures to communicate, they do not respond to body language, and they do not copy facial expressions or gestures, such as hand waving, clapping, or pointing.

- *Retardation or deviance in cognition—with approximately 60 percent of people with autism having measured IQ's below 50, 20 percent between 50 and 70, and only 20 percent having IQ's of 70 and above.*

These numbers are hard to interpret, since autistic children often cannot be tested with conventional, standardized tests. There seems to be a correlation, however, between intelligence level and treatment outcomes for autistic individuals.

Typical of autistic functioning is the extreme variability in different areas of cognition. Autistic children perform most poorly on tasks requiring abstract thought, conceptualization, symbolism, and logical reasoning. Both their thinking and their play lack imagination.

On the other hand, they often excel at tasks requiring rote memory, mechanical mathematical manipulations, and visual-spatial skills. Some of them are able to retrace routes they have only traveled once or to draw detailed scale maps of their environment, a room, the playground, or a freeway system.

In addition to these major distortions of basic psychological functioning, autistic children usually also exhibit several other unique behaviors and characteristics. Among these are:

> • *An excessive need for sameness—with autistic children usually reacting to changes in their environment with great distress.*

They hold rigidly to routines and also exhibit compulsive attachments to certain objects. They engage in rituals and stereotypical movements, such as twirling sticks or flapping strips of paper. They are also fascinated by spinning objects.

While their food intake may be limited to only one or two items, they resist any attempts to change or expand either their diet or their circle of activities.

> • *Abnormal responses to sensations—with these children often being overly reactive to sensory stimuli.*

Autistic children are often extremely sensitive to certain sounds, light, touch, or taste. Conversely, they may appear deaf, oblivious to extremes of heat or cold, insensitive to pain, and generally nonreactive to sensory stimulation.

There are a number of *nonspecific symptoms* that are also frequently observed in autistic children.

Many of them are *hyperactive*. Some children also have *abnormal* sleep patterns or display *strong fears and phobias*.

Delays in self-help skills such as toileting, dressing themselves, or developing acceptable table manners are frequently encountered with these children, along with *difficulties with balance and fine motor coordination*, though many parents report normal or even precocious early motor development.

Many autistic children have *violent temper tantrums* during which they become destructive or *self-aggressive*. At times their hitting, slapping, biting, and scratching of themselves is mistaken by doctors for the self-mutilating behavior typical of the Lesch-Nyhan syndrome.

Today it is generally accepted that there may be several causes of autism, each producing similar symptoms. Among these are untreated phenylketonuria, rubella, celiac disease, and chemical exposure in pregnancy.[1] Progesterone, taken by the mother during the early months of pregnancy to prevent premature delivery, is among the substances suspected as possibly being correlated with autistic symptoms.[2] Speculation also centers around hormonal imbalances in the brain and brain damage incurred before, during, or after birth. This could be caused by intrauterine bleeding,[3] or a variety of other complications of pregnancy, such as infectious or viral diseases, poisoning, or toxicosis.[4]

Autism occurs either by itself or in conjunction with other disorders that affect brain function.[5] A number of autistic children have epileptic seizures or develop them during adolescence, and common causes for both disorders might be assumed.[6] Twin and sibling studies suggest a possible genetic component.[7,8]

No known factor in the psychological environment of a child has been shown to cause autism, though institutionalized babies who have suffered severe maternal deprivation sometimes exhibit autistic-like behaviors.[9] To distinguish it from other forms, this type of autism could be defined as "superimposed." This has also been reported in rare cases of extreme stress.[10] Other forms of autism have been observed following an encephalitic illness. In many of these cases, the symptoms have shown themselves to be reversible.[11]

In all, speculation leans strongly toward a biogenic explanation and autism is no longer seen as a psychogenic problem.[12]

Autism has been found among children of all racial, ethnic, and socio-economic backgrounds all over the world. It is four times more common in males than in females. In its classic form, as described by Dr. Kanner, autism occurs in approximately five out of every 10,000 births, but the occurrence is three times as common if a broader definition includes children with autistic-like symptoms who need special educational and therapeutic programs.

Early infantile autism is considered a lifelong disorder. It ranks among the most severe childhood disturbances, and for many years autistic children were counted among the "hopeless" group of patients with mental disorders for whom little could be done. Since their behavior often made it impossible to keep them at home, they ended up in institutions, locked away by a system that had no key to their illness.

Progress in treatment is slow and is measured in tiny steps. The average stay of children at Linwood, for example, is five to seven years. Even after years of treatment involving every aspect of the children's lives, many of them will never be able to live on their own or support themselves.

There are former Linwood students — about one in four — who have been mainstreamed from Linwood and have eventually attended regular schools. A number of them have even gone on to universities. Many hold independent jobs as library workers, taxi drivers, secretaries, accountants, and other skilled or semiskilled occupations. Many maintain their own apartments. A few are married. But, on the whole, complete "cures" are rare and even successful autistic adults continue to struggle with the remnants of social and emotional difficulties.

Hopefully, research will one day uncover all the causes of autism and lead to increased possibilities of prevention and drug treatment. In the meantime, ideas about causation, as well as about what goes on within autistic children and about the best way to help them, remain informed conjecture and depend to some extent on trial and error.

The earlier a diagnosis can be made and treatment started, the better are the chances that the child will not develop some of the more extreme destructive and self-aggressive behaviors that complicate therapy. Early treatment also helps the families cope better with the challenges presented by these children so that the children can be integrated into the family routines without being allowed to dominate everybody's life.

Even with treatment, however, it is almost impossible to keep some autistic children at home. Their obsessive insistence on sameness and the many compulsions and rituals to which they cling with passionate obstinacy often disrupt family life to the point where a normal existence is impossible.

Some children may insist on having the house arranged in a certain way and will not tolerate even the slightest adjustments. One child, for example, had to have all the furniture piled on the kitchen table. If something had been moved while he was away, he would scream and go into a tantrum, and the screaming would not stop until everything was put back. Another child had to have everything upside down and he moved all the objects he could reach into that position while the parents were asleep. Everything fragile had to be removed or it would be destroyed. Another child would gobble down his food and not allow anybody to eat after he was finished. And one family had to live in constant gloom because their child insisted on having all the blinds, shutters, and curtains in the house closed.

The parents often feel totally helpless in the face of their children's needs and demands. They are afraid of the temper tantrums that may be brought on when the children become upset. Neighbors may complain about the frequent screaming. In fact, parents of autistic children even have been reported to the police for suspected child abuse.

In some cases the children become destructive when their routines are interfered with; in others, they turn severely self-aggressive so that the parents are afraid that their children's health or even their lives may be in danger. Most autistic children cannot be left unsupervised for more than a moment. Their environment has to be protected from their destructive urges as they themselves must be protected from the risks they tend to run. They may dash out into traffic because they have no concept of danger, or burn or cut themselves for the same reason. Some children escape from their rooms at night or go to sleep only if somebody is standing by their door. There are few baby sitters able (or willing) to deal with autistic children, so that many parents are unable to go out or have any kind of private life while their children remain at home.

Only relatively recently have families of these children been able to get help and find appropriate placements for them. In the forties and early fifties, autism was still virtually unknown, even among professionals. Autistic children were variously diagnosed as deaf, retarded, schizophrenic or brain damaged, and there were no centers or institutions that specialized in treating them.

A VISIT TO LINWOOD

At first glance the children presently at Linwood exhibit none of the more extreme, disruptive, or distressing behaviors described above. On a sunny day, all but the youngest group of Linwood students are out in the spacious, well-equipped yard. Their activities seem to be those associated with any group of youngsters playing out of doors. But closer observation quickly dispels this impression of normality.

With the exception of one delicate, little girl, the group consists of about twenty boys who look to be from eight or nine years old into the midteens. Normally, a group this size would generate a lot of noise. One would expect to see children playing ball together, racing each other around the yard, wrestling or talking together, or perhaps competing for the playground equipment.

This group, however, is strangely static and quiet. Most of the observable activity is initiated not by the children themselves, but by the large number of adults spread through the area. Their role, clearly, is not to keep a bunch of exuberant youngsters under control but, on the contrary, to activate and connect a group of children who seem out of touch with each other and their environment.

Only a few of the children play together, and when they do, their contacts are fleeting, superficial, and lacking imagination.

One short, pudgy fellow in a baseball cap and glove catches a ball thrown to him by a bigger boy, but their exchange is short. Soon his partner, a curly haired, snub-nosed, handsome boy charges off with a yell to capture one of the swings. The fellow with the ball doesn't seem to mind. Smiling imperturbably, he aims his ball at one of the counselors who partners him for a brief game before moving on to another youngster.

Talk between children is practically nonexistent, and only a few address the adults spontaneously. Some of the children hum or talk to themselves, often repeating phrases or jingles without any apparent connection to anything that is going on around them.

Only one boy, slight, with honey-colored hair and a pale, angelic face, keeps up a high-pitched chatter, endlessly repeating the same information and insisting on responses from the various people he happens to meet.

"It was raining last night, it was raining, Miss Bessie, it was raining hard, it was raining. . ." or, "The leaves are falling down, Bill, say, the leaves are falling down, they are falling down. . . ." His slightly nasal, droning chant rises and falls relentlessly, but none of the other children take any notice of what he is saying.

Now and then a child uses speech to communicate, but it is rare and their utterances are usually in the form of brief requests and are couched in one or two word sentences, like a boy on the swings who commands, "Push Gerry!"

Near the gate stands a freckle-faced youngster with luminous, grey eyes. His head is covered by a cloth hat over which he has pulled the collar of his jacket. His arms are crossed over his head and his hands are curled into fists and hidden in the sleeves, so that it looks as if he were strapped into a kind of straightjacket. Every so often he breaks into a little trot, darting toward the gate, then turns away again and stands, swaying slightly, his gaze flicking restlessly from side to side. When a counselor approaches, the boy mumbles, "go home." He is told that he will go home on Friday, which seems to satisfy him momentarily, but the same exchange is repeated at regular intervals.

Some of the children, while not communicating themselves, obviously understand what is said to them and respond appropriately to requests or suggestions that are made to them.

Near the fence, a boy lies on the ground, knees drawn up, eyes closed, and thumb in his mouth. A counselor tells him to get up, since the ground is still damp. She talks to him softly, chiding him good-naturedly for being such a lazybones. Chin on chest he glances at her from under lowered brows. His eyes twinkle in lazy amusement. Led in a walk around the grounds he drapes his arms around her and hangs heavily from her shoulder. She deposits him on the merry-go-round, where he promptly curls up on the seat, closes his eyes, and sticks his thumb back in his mouth. As the merry-go-round picks up speed, he is told to hold on to the bar. Without a change in expression and without opening his eyes, he reaches out and grabs it. As soon as the motion stops, he retrieves his hand and puts his finger back in his mouth again.

Many of the children ignore adults when they are addressed by them and continue their activities as if they were alone, or they move away if someone intrudes into their space. The impression that many children move within invisible boundaries is reinforced by observing them over time. Many have a set space in the yard where they sit, stand, or play, and they ignore or resist attempts at getting them to move or to interest them in a different activity.

One sturdy, blonde boy invariably stands in one corner of the fence. Around his neck he wears a necklace he sucks on most of the time. Mostly, he stands quietly, observing the activity around him out of the corners of his eyes. If anybody comes too close, he stiffens and presses himself further into the corner. Now and then he makes a silent foray along the fence, almost touching the counselor who usually stands there. But if children approach him, his otherwise placid face becomes agitated and he calls out in protest, "sooofa," with an ascending screech on the first syllable.

The intensity with which some of the children engage in an activity seems to cut them off from any awareness of their surroundings outside the narrowly prescribed circle of their preoccupation and contributes to their isolation.

In the sandbox a blond-haired boy intently and rhythmically throws up handfuls of sand. When most of it has dribbled through his fingers, he chucks the remainder toward an invisible mark and simultaneously and accurately aims gobs of spit through a gap in his teeth at the same spot. He can be engaged in other activities, but as soon as he is free, he returns to the sandbox and resumes his sifting, throwing, and spitting.

While some autistic children seem insensitive to pain and to the extremes of temperature, others exhibit an extreme skin sensitivity. This may be the reason why they take off their clothing, especially shoes and socks, at every opportunity, demand to have their backs scratched, or have lotion put on their faces, hands, or bodies. Some children also seem to have an unusual sense of smell and bizarre taste preferences. At times they try to smell the hair, clothing, or skin of other people, and some sniff or lick at any object they come across.

By the steps to the porch a thin-faced boy, with intense, prominent eyes and a crest of brown hair is down on his hands and knees, sniffing the ground. Stretching to reach the drainpipe, he flicks out his tongue and licks the metal. Edging around the fence, he bends over every so often, touching some objects in his path with his tongue. Standing, he licks the backs of his hands, then rubs his hands and forearms across his face and upper body in a graceful, sinuous movement that resembles nothing so much as a cat cleaning itself.

Despite some distinctly odd behaviors, a low level of play activities, and a lack of communication, these children do not strike an observer as retarded. One or two gesture or move in ways that might suggest some neurological impairment. But their faces are neither flat and empty like those of severely retarded children, nor distorted by emotions like those of children with some emotional disorder. Many look serene, though abstracted, sitting or standing quietly, or engaged in mechanical, repetitive activities. As a group these are attractive children. Many of them are well-built and fine-featured. But there is something of the sleepwalker about many of them. Others remind one of absent-minded professors, cogitating upon some abstruse point oblivious to the conversation eddying around them. It seems that at any moment they could wake up, or step out of their abstraction and pick up the normal activities and conversations they seem capable of. But the spell holds and is hard to break.

It takes patience, persistance, and an unusual kind of vision to take on the task of trying to reach these special children. In 1949 Jeanne Simons was working at Children's House in Washington, a treatment center for emotionally disturbed children. There she encountered a number of children who did not seem to fit any of the standard diagnostic categories. She was particularly struck by some of the unique features they seemed to have in common. She noticed, for example, that many of these children set up invisible boundaries for themselves beyond which they rarely moved. All of the children also exhibited some compulsive behaviors and often only engaged in a single, repetitive activity.

None of these children used speech to communicate. Though some had a limited vocabulary they applied it mechanically at odd times throughout the day or repeated whatever they heard without apparent comprehension.

The most striking characteristic was the apparent social and emotional isolation of the children. They either ignored each other—and often the staff—completely, or if someone invaded a child's space or interfered with some compulsive activity, he would simply be removed like an unwanted object.

Jeanne Simons worked with these children not knowing that their distinctive behavior had been described and labeled six years earlier by Dr. Leo Kanner. In 1950, still not knowing anything about autism, Miss

Simons agreed to treat Lee, a boy who had been diagnosed autistic by Dr. Kanner himself.

Lee was a unique human being who also exhibited many of the typical, often mysterious characteristics of a true autistic individual and the severe symptoms that make this type of child so difficult and yet so fascinating to work with.

Jeanne Simons' work with Lee foreshadows much of the philosophy and the techniques that evolved into the treatment approach described in this book. The story of Lee, as Miss Simons has written it, is therefore the best possible introduction to the subject of working with these special children.

THE STORY OF LEE

I met Lee in 1950. He had been diagnosed as autistic when he was three years old and had been living in private residential institutions for seven years. His parents took him home for vacations as often as possible, but as he became older he became more and more unmanageable. He was extremely self-destructive, with scars all over his face, forehead, and hands from his own scratching.

His parents brought Lee to me for an interview, hoping that I could help them during the month he would be home. They told me that Lee communicated only with garbled language and had constant temper tantrums. He also suffered from seizures and had frequent asthma attacks that were so severe that they required hospitalization.

During the interview, Lee walked up and down, back and forth in an awkward way, moving a key chain from one hand to the other. He seemed unaware of where he was and did not seem to register my presence. He was extremely thin and too small for his eleven years. He had a handsome face topped with curly black hair, but his head seemed too big for his frail body.

As his mother talked about Lee's temper tantrums, his compulsions, and about how difficult he was, I looked at him and said, "Lee, we are talking about you. Your mother would like me to help you." He did not give any sign of hearing me. His mother said that he could not understand what I was saying to him and that he had no awareness of other people. Nevertheless, as we continued our conversation, I reminded Lee from time to time that we were talking about him.

My heart went out to this deeply troubled, helpless child

and his desperate parents. I looked again at Lee's scratched and scarred face and arms, and I promised to see him as often as possible. A few minutes after he had left, his mother brought him back. He had become upset as soon as he was out of the door and had insisted on coming back in again. He didn't look at me, but just stood there, clawing at his face. I put my hand on his head and said, "Try to show me what upsets you." He kissed me and mumbled, "I want you to be my mother." I replied, "I will try to be a good friend to you, Lee." He smiled and walked out without another look.

During that month I saw Lee as often as possible during afternoons and weekends. Sometimes his parents called me late at night because he was so upset. Somehow I was able to reach him and to quiet him down a bit, although I never understood what he was upset about. As the month went on, I found I could understand some of what he was saying in his garbled way of communicating, and I found that I could set some limits on his severe compulsion to endlessly play records very loudly. I was also able to reduce the frequency and intensity of his temper tantrums. Finally the end of the month came and Lee's family was preparing to send him back to his institution. The day before Lee was to leave he came up to me and told me in his awkward way that he wanted to live with me.

I don't know what came over me. After talking to Lee's parents, I rented a big farm house with lots of land around it and moved into it. I also arranged to have a medical student and his wife come to live with us to help with the farm and with Lee, and I managed to get Lee into a small group with one of the therapists at Children's House in Washington where I was working at the time.

As soon as I had everything set up, I panicked. I still knew next to nothing about children like Lee and I had no idea what I'd gotten myself into. I went to talk to Dr. Leo Kanner at Johns Hopkins University, who was the first to describe autism and was the foremost expert on autism.

Dr. Kanner had diagnosed Lee as autistic, and I went to him hoping to get his blessing for the task I was about to undertake. When I told him what I had done, he looked at me in disbelief. He thought for a moment, puffing on his huge cigar and finally he spoke. "It's worth a try," he said. I felt as if a great weight had been lifted from me. I'll never forget the support and advice Dr. Kanner gave me during that incredible year.

Shortly afterward, Lee moved in. Almost immediately I got

a taste of what was to come. He found an old bell and ran through the house ringing his "freedom bell"—freedom from the institution he had been in, freedom from people he was afraid of. I showed him his room which opened into my own. When he saw it, all traces of happiness disappeared from his face. He stared at the door leading to his room. Then he clawed at his face and forehead, bit his hands, screamed, and hit the door with his head. I asked what was wrong, but he didn't seem to hear me; he just scratched, clawed, bit, and hit himself even harder. I looked at the door to find what was upsetting him so. The color? The knob? It was just an ordinary door. Then I saw the keyhole. Was he afraid of being locked up? I told him that there was no key, that I could not lock his door. His attacks on himself became still more violent. He stared at the keyhole. I was right, he was afraid of a key. I racked my brain for a way to reassure Lee, and finally came up with a foolproof solution. That afternoon we sawed the door in half so that it worked like a dutch door. This gave us both an illusion of privacy but it assured Lee that I could never lock him in. Years later Lee told me that this incident was crucial in gaining his trust.

When it was time to go to bed, Lee took about twenty different objects into bed with him. One was a key chain that he never parted with. The other things varied from some broken down teddy bears to a number of small beads. The next morning it was difficult to get him going. He had an elaborate series of rituals he had to go through to get dressed. When night came again and he was ready to go to bed, he looked in his room and immediately fell apart. He screamed, banged his head, and gagged. I realized that one of his objects must be missing. I looked everywhere, crawled on the floor, under the bed, behind the radiator. At last I found the little lost bead. I was exhausted, and I also realized that Lee could make me more compulsive than he was. I knew that I would rather search for hours to find what he had lost than to live through his screaming and self-aggression.

The next morning I took all his objects and arranged them neatly on his dresser. Before Lee went to bed that night I told him that those objects were not mine, that he was responsible for them. For a few mornings I helped him line up all his objects on his dresser so that they would not get lost. After a while he no longer lost anything and I was gradually able to help him reduce the number of objects he took to bed with him.

From the first day Lee lived with me he demanded every

minute of my time. He endlessly babbled about whatever was on his mind, asked me for help, and flew into a rage if I could not give him immediate attention or if the telephone rang and I had to answer it. I knew that I would be drained of all mental and physical energy within a week if I allowed things to continue this way, and I knew that if Lee was ever to adjust to life at home again he would have to be able to occupy himself and to live in a more normal environment. We set up one room in the house where Lee could discuss his problems and where I would be his therapist. During this time he had my full attention, and no interruptions were allowed. However, at other times and in the rest of the house I was Lee's friend, not his therapist. Lee accepted this. He called me "Miss Simons" during the therapy sessions, but between sessions he called me by my first name.

Lee had an extreme compulsion about birthdays. He had to know everyone's birthday. He even stopped strangers in the street to ask them about their birthdays, and he became very upset and self-aggressive if people did not answer him. He was such an expert on birthdays that he had a built-in calendar in his head. If anyone told him their age and their birthday, he could tell them the day of the week on which they were born. He was never wrong. However, he never told anyone his own birthday. If anyone asked, he would often fall to the floor and stretch out, rolling his head from side to side and gagging. Lee's obsession with dates was so extreme that he would pick up newspapers out of the trash can or even out of open fires just to read the dates on them.

It was several months before I understood Lee's compulsion about dates and birthdays. He began to tell me stories that he wanted me to type for him. He talked in a monotone, very rapidly, never stopping between words. He asked me to type his stories. When he dictated to me, he spelled the words out instead of saying them. He spelled faster than I could type, and he never made a spelling mistake. I asked him to slow his spelling down so that I could understand him, and he did so. Later, he decided on his own to say the stories in words. But every sentence was one long word.

Lee's stories were all very concrete memories from his early childhood. They contained minute details of peoples' clothing, knocks at the door, conversations, names, and so on. One of the first stories was about crying. Lee remembered that he had cried and cried one day when his grandmother was looking after him. His grandmother thought that he cried because his mother was gone and tried to console him by saying "your mother will be back." Lee said, "I had to cry much more. Can you imagine, Miss Simons, how it feels when your mother will be BACK?" and he put his hand on his back. Obviously, the only meaning "back" had for him was as part of his body.

I asked him to tell me the dates of his stories, and he had no trouble giving me exact dates. However, I noticed that the stories took place earlier and earlier. Sometimes he would refuse to give me a date at all, saying it was too long ago. The dates he did give me had him remembering things from when he was two, eighteen months, even one year old. If I asked him if he was sure, he would wring his hands, roll his head back and forth violently, gag, and scratch his forehead open with his fingernails. I stopped asking for dates, but I was puzzled—I didn't know that anyone could remember from such an early age, but Lee was never wrong about dates.

One day, Lee dictated a story that consisted mostly of babbling and a few baby words along with sounds of doors closing, a train going by (he lived next to railroad tracks as a baby), and the words adults make when they see a baby. During this story Lee gagged and his breathing became labored. I was afraid that he might be about to have an asthma attack or a seizure, and I told him to stop his story and save it for later. But he refused to stop. He continued the story, becoming more and more agitated. Finally, he mumbled the date when the events were supposed to have taken place. It was before Lee was born! I knew that I had a real problem.

I immediately set up an appointment with Lee's father so I could ask him about Lee's birthday. The father seemed very upset, and demanded to know why I was so interested. I told him that I felt that Lee's compulsion about dates might have something to do with his own birthday. "Miss Simons," he said, "No one knows about this except Lee's mother, his grandmother, and me." He told me that when Lee was about three, the family moved to a neighborhood where no one knew them. Because Lee was so tiny and thin, they told everyone that he was only eighteen months old so that no one would ask what was wrong with him. So Lee was really 13 instead of 11!

The next day I told Lee about his birthday. He did not say much. He did wonder if he had "lost" two years, but on the whole he seemed relieved and said in a pleasant voice, "Now I am 13 years old." Lee almost immediately lost his intense compulsion *about dates and birthdays. He still asked people their birthdays, but did not insist on an answer. He also enjoyed his next birthday very much for the first time. I later realized that Lee's date compulsion must have arisen from the fact that his was the only birthday in the world that did not fit in his built-in calendar. His parents told him the day of the week on which he was born, but it did not square with his calculations for that year. When he found out he was really thirteen, his birthday finally fit.*

One night while getting ready for bed, Lee said suddenly, "Miss Simons, I am one-and-a-half years old."

"Do I have to carry you, or can you walk, Lee?" I asked.

He laughed. "No, I cannot walk yet, but I am really one-and-a-half years old." A few minutes later he said, "Miss Simons, I am six months old."

"Then I really have to carry you, Lee."

"Are you strong enough for that?"

"Yes, Lee, I am."

"If I were six months old I would have to have a crib. I would fall out of the bed I sleep in now." This came after he had dictated a story about sitting on the lap of a friend and being scolded because he was too big for that. "Do children sit on laps?" he asked. I told him that it was all right to sit on a lap even for an eleven year old.

"You are in so many ways still a little boy, Lee."

"When am I a little boy?"

"Often, Lee. For example, you still like to take all your animals and your favorite objects to bed. Little boys like to do that."

"I want to be a little boy. One day that will be off my mind, but not yet."

"Do not hurry getting it off your mind, darling," I said, and I kissed his black curls. Lee snuggled under his covers. I tucked him in and fifteen minutes later he was sound asleep.

In addition to dates and birthdays, Lee had many other compulsions. One of them was his extreme preoccupation with intravenous needles. He often carried some needle-like object around with him, and in any doctor's office he wanted to see the needle. He talked about wiping off his arm and about the smell of alcohol. He did not seem to fear needles, but often looked at them with something like tenderness. It took almost a year before I got a clue to this puzzle.

One day Lee had found a doll's feeding bottle. He wanted to see a real baby bottle, so I bought one. He was very excited and wanted to know whether he could have some warm juice in it. I partly filled the bottle. He ran upstairs with it and lay down on the bed. Drawing his knees up and putting one hand under his head, he started to suck from the bottle. "Is that the way babies drink the bottle?" he asked.

"Do you remember how you drank the bottle, Lee?"

"Yes, my mother gave it to me in my crib." Lee put his head on the pillow and held the bottle in both hands.

"Sometimes babies are taken on the lap."

"Why?" he wanted to know.

"Babies like it, Lee. It's comfortable and soft."

"Not for me. They gave me the bottle in my crib." He emptied the bottle, made baby sounds, and played with the nipple. "Can I have some more?" I refilled the bottle and Lee drank it in a relaxed way. Then he asked me what to do with the empty bottle. He watched attentively while I cleaned it then asked, "Can I have this bottle again?"

"Yes, Lee, when we have lots of time."

"Can I keep the bottle with me?"

"No, you can have it when you need it during our time together. Big boys like you don't drink out of baby bottles, but you may have it once in a while."

"Yes," he said, "It's like typing stories. Things go off my mind that way. Will the needle go off my mind?" He seemed far away, rolling his head back and forth and making occasional baby sounds.

After a few minutes he gave a sigh. "Miss Simons, I do not have to talk about intravenous needles anymore. I feel so relieved. It's off my mind."

I asked him what he meant by "off his mind." He explained that things that worried him used to go down there—pointing to his stomach—and had given him hurt feelings and seizures, but since I had been working with him, many things were now really off his mind. He did not know where they went, perhaps out of the window. He jumped up and down on his bed happily.

Very shortly after the intravenous needles went off his mind, another compulsion disappeared. From the first day Lee had been with me he often stretched out on the couch of the living room endlessly playing the first few grooves of a record. With a faraway smile on his face he would fondle his key chain, rolling his head back and forth, oblivious of his environment.

He would announce that he was going to play a record a cer-

tain number of times. The number was always in the hundreds. Then he would play the beginning of the record over and over and over again until he got to the number he had specified. I began to count to see how close he got, and found that he was always completely accurate. If something interrupted him before he had reached the full count, or if he was asked to add another repetition or two, he got very agitated, often scratching himself and insisting in a barely audible voice that he had to play it the exact number of times, say 239, though the numbers varied somewhat from one time to the next.

After several months I asked him about the significance of these numbers. He became very anxious and gagged, but then mumbled softly, "The drops came out of a bottle through a needle in my arm. Do not ask the date—I was in a hospital." I found out that Lee had to spend much of his first two years at Hopkins because he would not eat and had to be fed intravenously. The number of times he played his record seemed to correspond to the number of drops of fluid he had been given.

Although Lee usually woke up in the morning with a cheerful "good morning," he had to go through countless rituals before he could get dressed so that getting up took nearly an hour. One day Lee seemed upset when he woke up. He would not talk, but wrung his hands and banged his head. It took him much longer than usual to get dressed and he stayed upset for most of the rest of the day.

A few months later, he woke up in the same state of mind again. Since I was a little short of time that morning, I picked him up, put him on a chair and dressed him. I had expected him to be upset, but instead he gave a big sigh and mumbled, "You should have done this 15 minutes ago and you should have done it on November...."

Years later, Lee solved this puzzle for me when I visited him at home one day. He asked whether I knew why I had done the right thing in getting him out of bed on March— Then he told me that every night he had either good or bad dreams. It took him as long to "get away" from a good dream as from a bad one, but on those dates in November and March he had a dream that was neither good nor bad and he had needed my help to get away from that dream.

When Lee came to live with me he did not know how to relate. He had no eye contact and did not want to be touched. As time went on, we established a good relationship, although he never did develop proper eye contact with me or anybody else and still disliked being touched.

I wanted to give him a chance to be the only child and to enjoy my company without having to share it with anybody. No friends visited me at home, though I went out occasionally to see somebody, leaving Lee with the couple that shared our house.

When Lee had established a good two-way relationship with me, I decided that it was time for him to share me with my friends, so I invited a couple I knew to spend the weekend with us. When Lee heard about this, he became upset and wanted to spend the weekend at home, but I did not let him do that. Then he started questioning me. "Will they like me?" he asked. "I do not know Lee, but we like you." I told him.

"Will you go out with them alone?" he wanted to know. I told him that if we decided to go out he would come with us and that we would all decide together where we wanted to go, and that as long as he lived with me this was his house too.

Lee seemed satisfied and even mildly excited about the forthcoming visit. The day before my friends arrived, I prepared a dessert. Lee came into the kitchen and sat down on the floor. He was very pale, his eyes rolled back and he gagged. He looked as if he might have a seizure. "Miss Simons, I am very sick. I am going to die."

"Don't die on the kitchen floor, Lee." I told him. "Why don't you stretch out on the couch in the living room. I'll be with you in a minute. Do not go upstairs. You are too sick to climb stairs."

Lee sat straight up. His color came back, and I felt that the danger of his getting a seizure was over. When I came into the living room he was on the sofa, playing a record. I sat in a chair next to him. After ten minutes he mumbled, "What was that awful feeling I had?"

"Maybe you are jealous."

"Is jealous a feeling I get when you make pudding for your friends?" He did not seem to need an answer.

Years later he told me how jealous he had been when he saw me making a dessert for my friends. But once my friends were there and he felt part of the family, he had not been jealous any more.

During the time Lee was living with me, his compulsions gradually diminished. His seizures disappeared, as did his asthma, his tantrums, and his self-aggression. After a year in the farm house, he returned home, and I moved back into an apartment. At first he had a difficult time readjusting to his family, and I saw *him at least once a week to help him through his transition period. Later Lee was a frequent visitor at my apartment. He learned to live comfortably at home, and his parents were even able to take him on a trip to Europe.*

When he was twenty-one, Lee moved to a village for the handicapped where he adjusted quickly. He learned how to bake bread and was very proud of his skill. He often came home for holidays and usually came to see me, often reminiscing about his stay with me. Five years later Lee died suddenly and inexplicably of a brain hemorrhage, still looking much younger than his age.

BEGINNINGS

Through Lee, Miss Simons became acquainted with Dr. Kanner. Her experiences with Lee and with her group at Children's House convinced her that autistic children could be approached and helped. At the same time it became clear that only early, intensive, and prolonged intervention could hope to overcome the severe handicaps under which these special children labored.

Having experienced firsthand how difficult they were to live with, as well as talking with parents and visiting their homes, Miss Simons also began to appreciate the urgent need for a program that would offer relief to the beleaguered families of autistic children. The disruptions that their compulsions and tantrums produced, the inordinate amount of time, attention, and energy their care demanded, the need for ceaseless vigilance and supervision drained the parents of all energy, seriously affected other family relations, and impaired the quality of life of the whole family without benefitting the children themselves.

As she observed the positive effects of an experimental day program at Children's House in Washington, Miss Simons became convinced that what was needed was a residential program. For the children this would offer opportunities for consistent, focused, and individualized treatment in an environment designed and structured to accommodate their particular needs. For their families it would provide breathing space, an uninterrupted period of time to live normal lives and experience normal family interactions.

The idea for a special place took root and in 1955 after a long, frustrating search for a house that was big enough, safely tucked away without being too isolated, and with ample grounds that could be enclosed and secured, the ideal house was found. It was an old mansion at the end of a country road, yet only ten minutes' drive from shops and recreational opportunities. It had been occupied for many years by a family with eleven children, most of whom were grown and had moved away. The house had become a burden to the original owners who were eager to move into smaller quarters. They agreed to a down payment of only five hundred dollars, a modest amount for such a property, but nevertheless straining the resources of the founder.

In those days, education for developmentally impaired children was not yet federally funded, and only some parents were able to pay for the cost of having their children in residence. Miss Simons had to continue working elsewhere to earn enough money to run Linwood and to pay a pittance to the faithful staff that had accompanied her from Children's House.

The house itself, while suitable for a family, presented numerous problems for use as a home for autistic children. Eight open fireplaces not only proved inadequate to heat the large rooms, they were also extremely dangerous. In one room there was a large grate that the children could lift. Below it was a slide that went right down into the furnace room. Antiquated and dangerously exposed wiring also posed dangers and many of the lights did not work at all. Peeling paint and deteriorating masonry needed immediate attention.

The early days were a constant struggle to keep one step ahead of disaster and only the fact that the whole staff pitched in wherever they were needed made it possible for the venture to survive and prosper. Tales of life at Linwood during those early days reveal the total dedication and single-minded determination as well as the sense of humor necessary to cope with the never-ending difficulties. Following is a personal account by Miss Simons of some of the problems she and her staff faced in coping with the chronic lack of money and with the shortcomings of the physical facilities while caring for the first group of children.

At the end of our first week, inspectors from the health department and the fire department came. They were horrified. They stood and shook their heads as I began to tell them about our goals and the difficulties that we faced in working with our children. I was so enthusiastic that they decided that they would help us. We had an incredible list of things to fix. They came back month after month, shaking their heads each time, but as long as we were able to show them that we were working on the problems they had identified, they were willing to give us time to take care of things one by one as best we could.

Simply getting water was a major trial. Every so often the faucets would start to dribble water and then the flow would stop altogether. I discovered the old well in the backyard had an antiquated cover that did not fit properly anymore. The well was about eight feet deep, and the water level was so low that the only way to clean out the floating sticks and leaves was to climb down into the well.

There was only a narrow space between the pump and the wall. Since I was the thinnest, it was my privilege to be lowered into the well by two staff members every time the pump got clogged and to clean it out and get it going again. The children were fascinated by the whole process. Finally, we installed a new heavy cover, hoping to prevent the problem, but despite this, debris somehow managed to get into the water and the pump continued to get stuck.

I noticed that one of the children who had been especially interested in the clean-up operation spent a lot of time in the corner near the well. Though there was a fence between him and the well, my interest was aroused and I investigated the corner. Hidden in the grass I found a long stick. Intrigued, I hid behind a tree before the children came into the yard. Promptly Billy went to his corner. When he believed himself unobserved, he maneuvered the stick through the fence, quickly lifted off the well cover with it and threw sticks and leaves into the well. The pump promptly seized up. Then he lowered the cover again and secreted his stick in the grass for future use.

Even without Billy's "help," the pump broke down on the average of three times a week. We were told that the pump should not have standing water in it. So Caesar, the handyman, and I dug a trench and installed clay pipes to drain the pump. But our troubles were not yet over. As the water level got lower, the well went dry. We had to borrow water from neighbors or carry it from a creek about a half mile distant.

The exercise we got carrying water during the summer only slightly prepared us for managing the heating during the winter. We found that the furnace and eight fireplaces provided very little heat. Open fires were much too dangerous to be used while the children were present. Instead we installed Franklin stoves in a few rooms and carefully screened them off from the children. The stoves were fueled with coal, which was delivered with a great cloud of coal dust. We had to go down to the basement and fill our two small buckets, and then carry the coal back up to the first, second, and third floors. Caesar cared for the stoves during the day, but I had to do it after he left in the afternoon. The stoves had to be fed every four hours, even in the middle of the night. We could only afford the most inexpensive coal. It had large stones in it that had to be cleaned out of the stove each time it was refilled. There were the Franklin stoves, open fires upstairs in some of the offices, and the kitchen stove, which was fueled by wood, to keep going.

I also cleaned the house, and this caused a sensation more than once. Several times people came asking for the director. I would be cleaning the bathrooms or filling a stove, and was found with a toilet brush or a bucket of coal in my hand. After a year of this drudgery someone donated money to install oil baseboard heat and the open fireplaces could be closed off and the Franklin stoves became legend.

During the first heavy rain we made another discovery-the roof had twelve leaks. We put pots and pans under them every time it rained and were glad to discover no further leaks after the next few rain storms. One day when it was raining and our pots were all in place, Mrs. Goodwin, our nurse, stood in the hallway and said, "Miss Simons, there is another leak." I looked up to the third floor landing, and there was the most beautiful little boy urinating right down. It was the first naughty thing he had ever done and we were both delighted with his progress despite the fact that his aim was perfect and he was hitting Mrs. Goodwin right on the head. "Don't worry," I said, "that leak will stop soon," and we both went laughing under the stairway.

The financial and physical hardships did not deter Miss Simons or her staff, and somehow Linwood continued to function.

We started with nothing. We had no furniture, no dishes. We used orange crates for tables and shelves, and made do without most things. Then different groups began to make donations. We got stacks of glass plates and china, and I put them all up in the attic, out of the way. We then began to get small monetary donations, and we kept going little by little. As people began to hear about Linwood, they would come to visit. All of us were often in one room, with things looking pretty chaotic as people arrived. I talked with generous groups who visited, telling them about our goals and plans. I once overheard a group say as they were leaving, "Either she is crazy or she really has something to offer. We better give her a thousand dollars just in case."

Initially I had to do most things, including the bookkeeping. I had no idea how to do it so I went to the dime store and bought regular ledgers. Usually we had to spend more money than we had, so most of the entries were in red. I got tired of this, and switched colors after a while so that more would be in the black. When the accountant saw this, he could not figure out what had happened until I showed him where I had switched the colors. Fortunately, Mrs. King soon took over the bookkeeping.

We started with eleven children, but Linwood grew very quickly. Within the first year, nine were in residence. The first night we had them, they didn't go to bed. I didn't know what to do. We stayed in the yard to see what would happen. One child climbed on top of the swing, one was in the sandbox, and another sat on the grass. I just sat. It got later and later. Ten o'clock passed, then eleven, and then twelve. They were still awake. Then at one o'clock, the one on top of the swing fell asleep still sitting there. We took him down and put him to bed. Gradually the others also fell asleep and by two o'clock they were all in bed and asleep for a little while. I sat on top of the stairs to see that they would not run out. There was very little sleep.

Later I moved a cot to the foot of the stairs to make sure that none of the children could escape and get into trouble when everybody was asleep. It was only when we could afford a regular night staff that I was able to relax at night.

Once in a while the children were so difficult that I didn't think that we could go on any longer. Nothing was safe at first, and the children's inventiveness and their total disregard of danger sometimes produced frightening situations. One child was once found standing on a third floor windowsill urinating out of the window. When asked what he was doing, he answered quite seriously, "My wee-wee wanted some fresh air." Another time a strong feeling of unease made me return prematurely from a meeting to Linwood. There I discovered that one of the children had managed to climb up onto the roof and was balancing along the edge. He was pulled to safety before anything happened.

On another day we missed a child and could not find him anywhere even though we were sure that he could not have left the grounds. Linwood has beautiful old trees and one, a huge spruce, is taller than the house itself. I remembered that I had last seen the child near the tree. When I investigated I saw him sitting way at the top of the tree where it curves over the house. There he sat, rocking on the limb and paying absolutely no attention when he was told to come down. He acted deaf and just continued rocking. I changed into blue jeans and started climbing the tree. On my way up I talked to the boy and told him that he would have to stay indoors if he didn't come down immediately. That got through to him. He loved the outdoors more than anything and the threat of being confined in the house motivated him to start coming down. So I didn't have to go all the way out of the limb to get him. I don't think that it would have held us both. All of this happened on the day of the monthly board meeting and the board sat gaping in horror at the sight of us in the tree.

Yet another child discovered that he could get between the walls and between the floors and the ceilings through a narrow winding back stairs. We could hear him, but we couldn't find him until we realized that he was not in a room but between rooms. I had to crawl after him and in the pitch dark follow him by the noise he made. Eventually I was able to grab him by a foot and pull him out.

THE LINWOOD METHOD

Linwood owes its existence in good part to Lee and to the first group of autistic and autistic-like children Jeanne Simons worked with at Children's House in Washington. From these first, intense experiences, and out of almost thirty years of work at Linwood, there evolved a view of autism and of treatment techniques that will be presented in the following chapters.

The model we are presenting does not pretend to answer all questions or to be correct in every way; but it incorporates a lifetime of experience and is backed up by the contributions of Linwood graduates who "made it," and who became able to verbalize some of the thoughts and emotions that were inaccessible, inexplicable, and inexpressible at an earlier stage of their development.

Basic to this model is the belief in the worth of the individual in all of his manifestations, and respect for the healthy potential that exists in even the most handicapped human being. The approach described in this book aims at helping autistic children develop as total human beings in an environment in which every aspect is an important treatment component. Specific symptoms, such as mutism or lack of eye contact are never treated in isolation, nor are there set priorities or predetermined schedules that are applied equally to all children. Every child is accepted as the individual he is, and treatment starts at the point at which he is when he joins the program.

It is the belief of the staff at Linwood that the only lasting change is that which occurs as an integral part of an overall development. Furthermore, everything a child is taught has to connect to something that comes from within the child himself so that it can eventually become a meaningful part of his everyday life. As long as learned behavior is merely a mechanical response to drill and training, he will not be able to use it independently, expand on it or generalize it in a way that will make it a natural part of his behavioral repertoire. Also, symptoms such as compulsions that are attacked in isolation before their meaning to the child is understood or before he has developed a more varied set of behaviors to fall back on, either persist or are simply replaced by other similar behaviors.

Following is a summary of the basic tenets that define the Linwood approach to the treatment of autism and provide the underlying structure of the method:

1. The child is accepted in his totality.

When a child first enters Linwood, he is accepted as he presents himself. At no time is his behavior labeled as either good or bad. It is assumed that a child acts the way he does because that is the only option he has at that particular time. While a child's environment is structured in ways to encourage change, to diminish dangerous or inappropriate behaviors, and to develop more appropriate ones, his need to behave in a certain way is always respected and accepted.

2. The focus of treatment is on the health in the child.

Treatment is aimed at identifying behaviors that can be worked with rather than at suppressing symptoms that may interfere with learning. Any behavior a child exhibits spontaneously, no matter how limited or bizarre, can be used to make contact with him and can eventually be expanded into more varied and functional activities. It may also become a means to sustain the child's interest in new activities that add to his behavioral repertoire.

3. All education is therapy, all therapy is education.

At Linwood, therapy is a way of life. The focus is on educating the total child in an environment designed to make all experiences therapeutic. Though children with special needs receive individual attention from educational specialists and all children work on particular skills during scheduled activities, the main emphasis of *educational therapy* is not on academic content. *What* is being taught is viewed as less important than the *atmosphere in which learning takes place.*

Social and emotional awareness is fostered by experiences within the group and with various staff members in many formal and informal settings. Standards of behavior are demonstrated by those who live and work with the children and the children are invited to adopt them when they are ready.

To generalize the effects of treatment, the staff works closely with parents and with teachers and supervisors at schools and jobs the youngsters may go to outside of Linwood.

4. Therapy is flexible.

Expectations, rewards and limits are geared to each child's developmental level, rather than to his chronological age. The overall treatment goal is to help the children come out of their autistic isolation and become functioning members of society. But the route by which this goal is reached varies for each child. Rather than setting priorities that apply equally to all of the children, therapy at Linwood follows the child's lead.

TREATMENT ELEMENTS

The first step in working with these children is to carefully assess their level of functioning. The next step is to help the children become aware of their environment by establishing contact with them. First relationships build bridges between the children's isolation and the outside world and they also help to mediate the inevitable stresses and frustrations the children face as they are helped to learn and grow. And finally, therapy consists of initiating changes in a child's behavior that will gradually make it more varied, more socially acceptable, and more functional.

These three elements — *observations*, *establishing relationships*, and *changing behaviors* — run through the whole course of therapy. They are closely interrelated and often overlap but in the interest of clarity they will be presented in separate chapters.

TWO
✦✦✦

Observations

INTRODUCTION

Observations provide the information on which all education and therapeutic interventions are ultimately based. In therapy, "Know the Child" is the first principle. Before any interventions are attempted, one has to know what a child is ready for. The correct timing of interventions, a critical part of therapy, is totally dependent on accumulated information about the functioning of each child. Detailed observations are therefore the most useful tool of therapy with children whose limited behavior often yields only the faintest behavioral clues.

Visitors are always impressed by the fantastic wealth of detail the staff sees in children who to an outsider may seem passive or unresponsive. They quickly come to understand that this is due to the fact that each child is closely monitored and observed throughout the time he spends at Linwood.

Observations play a role in any type of therapy, but they are basic to an individualized therapy approach that is designed to be responsive to each child's daily needs, within a framework of goals that are determined by his specific deficiencies and developmental level. The Linwood staff observes a child at intake and continues doing so throughout all phases of treatment. The observation process will be alluded to in every chapter of this book. The following sections are designed to give specific examples of the kind of information careful observations can provide and of the ways this information influences therapy decisions.

THE DIAGNOSIS

Autistic children usually cannot be tested with standardized instruments to arrive at a diagnosis or to ascertain their potential. Because of their lack of communicative speech and connectedness, they perform poorly in any formal evaluation and often end up being labeled as severely retarded, even in cases where later development reveals normal or even above normal intelligence levels.

Where standardized tests are used, it is often only possible to give those subsections that deal with visual-spatial skills, such as matching designs with blocks. The Merrill Palmer intelligence test as well as the Wechsler Intelligence Scale for Children (WISC) are sometimes used in this fashion with younger or more impaired children. With higher functioning children tests that assess language functioning and social skills may also be used. There exist a number of diagnostic checklists, such as the PEP (Psycho-Educational Profile, developed by Dr. Eric Schopler)[13], which are especially good for identifying emerging skills of lower functioning children. The information from such lists provides a behavioral profile and identifies patterns of functioning in various areas.

The information gathered from such tests and checklists, as well as from observing the children, allow a diagnostician to distinguish children with predominantly autistic features from those with other types of impairments.

There are some behavioral abnormalities in mental retardation, for example, that are similar to those seen in infantile autism, such as rocking, stereotypical movements, and lack of focused attention. A differential diagnosis is usually possible by looking at indicators that are unique to autism.

One is the unevenness of autistic performance in various cognitive areas. Retarded children usually perform at a low level across the board. They tend to comply with instructions but fail test items because they are unable to understand what is asked of them, because their attention span is too short, or because a task is generally too difficult.

Autistic children, on the other hand, may resist testing or ignore instructions as well as the instructor and test materials. They may even systematically avoid giving the correct solution to a specific task. Their performance on tests is uneven, with low scores on items that test language or deal with abstractions and concepts. On the other hand, they may excel in tasks calling for visual and spatial skills or for the manipulation of numbers.

Physical characteristics also tend to differ. Many autistic children are agile and show good motor development. Apart from a tendency to roll up their eyes, their facial features generally strike an observer as normal. Often, they are even exceptionally good looking. This contrasts with a tendency toward slack facial features and impaired physical agility in the retarded population, though some autistic individuals are awkward in their movements or posture or display some spasticity.

It is also possible to distinguish the typical lack of communication in children with autism from other types of language disorders. Children with other serious developmental language disorders generally make eye contact, which is lacking in autistic children, and will often try to communicate by means of gestures, whereas there is a pervasive lack of responsiveness in autism. Autistic children often respond to sounds inconsistently, distinguishing them from hearing-impaired children.

Odd behaviors, bizarre responses to the environment, and repetitive routines are related to the autistic child's insistence on sameness or to a compulsive attachment to certain objects. They do not display the hallucinations, delusions, or incoherence typical of schizophrenia occurring in childhood.

Most diagnostically significant, however, is the lack of social and emotional connectedness that characterizes a majority of autistic children and that is rarely found in the same pervasive form in any other group of impaired individuals.

At Linwood, information on which a diagnosis is based comes from several sources. Most of the children have a history of previous examinations, many in Speech and Hearing clinics. Results of formal testing which usually rule out hearing impairment, brain damage, and other medically assessible conditions and a tentative diagnosis of autism from another agency are often available on the children that are sent to Linwood for assessment.

THE INTAKE ASSESSMENT

All of this background information may suggest the presence of autism or autistic-like behaviors. To confirm the diagnosis and to determine the severity of the syndrome as well as its specific manifestations, each child is examined and observed during a structured yet informal intake examination.

One of the aims of this procedure is to determine whether the child is suitable for placement at Linwood. Children who are accepted are those with well-defined autistic characteristics. Children with multiple handicaps, serious neurological disorders, or those who seem primarily retarded are sometimes accepted for temporary placement to alleviate autistic symptoms, giving them a better chance to adjust and function in other institutions.

Not every autistic child can be accepted at Linwood, since there may not be room for him in an appropriate group. Any given group can only absorb one or two children who are hyperactive, self-aggressive, destructive, or who have compulsions that are especially disruptive, such as prolonged screaming. The membership in a group must not only not interfere with the needs of an individual child, but should ideally enhance his opportunity to learn to develop. Wherever possible, a mute child would, therefore, be placed in a group in which at least one child uses speech in some form. The optimal composition of a group is one in which the children are at similar levels of development and therefore profit from the same over-all structure and teaching. However, the children also have to be different enough so that they do not all have the same needs at the same time.

In addition to assessing a child's suitability for the program, the in-take examination is, in a way, the first step in the therapy process. It gives the therapist a chance to observe the child's characteristics, deficiencies, and areas of strengths on which treatment can capitalize. A child who shows some awareness of his surroundings, for example, uses some speech, or is able and willing to imitate the examiner, is at a higher level of function-ing than one who runs around aimlessly or engages only in compulsive behaviors.

In the assessment of children suspected of being autistic, the most tell-ing diagnostic indicator is how aware they are of their environment and how they relate to people. Normal or retarded children, for example, usually react with some distress if their mothers leave the room, whereas autistic children rarely protest. This is often an indication that the child has failed to establish a normal relationship with the mother.

A very small percentage of autistic children want one or both parents in the room during the assessment. They may even insist that the parents stay in a specific position. This is usually more an indication that they cannot tolerate change than a sign of true attachment, and their seeming dependence may actually be a way of controlling the environment. A child's extreme clinginess may also be a symptom of the parents' inability to let go. Some parents cannot bear the idea of a possible separation from their child, even though the child's behavior at home overtaxes their strength.

During the assessment, the therapist attempts to engage the child in a series of tasks that involve a few simple materials, such as a Montessori pegboard with graduated cylinders, simple puzzles or form boards, pic-ture books, blocks, a ball, crayons, and paper. A great deal can be deduced about a child's social, emotional, and cognitive function by the way he ig-nores, resists, or follows the evaluator's example and instructions.

The most impaired children are those who seem to pay no attention to anything. They run around aimlessly, touch things at random, flap their arms, spin, or simply sit in a corner, sometimes holding on tightly to some object. They do not react or change facial expression when they are ap-proached. When the adult touches something they are holding, they either drop it or walk away without being visibly upset. Children who hold on to an object, or even try to pull it out of the adult's grasp, are usually less impaired, since they show at least some awareness of what they want.

Also typical of autism is that most autistic children actively avoid eye contact, to the point of rolling up their eyes until only the whites show.

Sometimes a child who appears to be oblivious to his surroundings can be caught watching something out of the corner of his eyes. Many autistic children have especially well developed peripheral vision. Some do not respond to speech. They may even stop up their ears or hit them rhythmically and hum in an attempt to shut out outside sources of sound.

Even with children who seem to pay no attention to their surroundings, careful observation will usually reveal some awareness, however minimal, or a fleeting, almost involuntary interest in something that is happening during the thirty to sixty minutes of the intake assessment. For example, children who otherwise seem totally nonresponsive may react to music. They may stop their roaming or turn their heads when they hear it, or walk toward the record player or music box when the music stops.

Another child may spontaneously touch or start playing with something, such as spinning the wheels of a toy truck. The examiner may then try to spin other objects within the child's view to see whether he takes any notice or even imitates him. Some children will tolerate such activities at close range, others will move away but take up an object the moment the therapist has put it down and has walked far enough away so that they feel unobserved. A less withdrawn child may reach out for the hand of the therapist and guide it toward an object in an attempt to have him continue an activity or get something that is out of his own reach.

If there are observers in the room during the intake examination, the truly autistic child simply ignores them. He brushes past them to get a toy or reaches around them as if they were inanimate objects. If they happen to hold on to something the child wants, he may push off their hand without looking at them and treat the hand as if it were not attached to a person, but was simply an obstacle between him and a desired toy. Dr. Kanner's "acid test" for autism was to prick a child with a needle on the back of the hand. A few children did not react visibly to the pin-prick. They acted as if they did not feel it. The majority attempted to brush away the needle without touching the hand that guided it or looking at the person who was inflicting the prick. They did not seem to make the connection between the needle and the intent of the adult, but treated it as they would any other object they happened to come in contact with.

A more advanced level of awareness is demonstrated by a child who actively resists demands made on him during the assessment. Some children will try out every position of a puzzle piece except the correct one. By their selective avoidance they will betray the fact that they not only know what is expected of them but would be able to do the task if they chose to. It also becomes clear that they are not only uninterested in demonstrating their expertise but are actually bent on hiding it, thus protecting themselves against interference from the outside.

Another form of this kind of negativism can be seen in children who already have some speech. The examiner may take a crayon and say, "that's green." Instead of repeating "green," the child might say that the crayon is red. Rather than correcting the child, the examiner continues to draw and after a short time takes up the green crayon again, saying "red." If the child then insists that the correct color is green, it becomes evident that he knows his colors, but is very negative.

In the course of this kind of interaction, the examiner never corrects the child when he gives a wrong reply, nor does he praise him for a correct one. For one thing, the aim at this point is simply to find out what a child knows and can do. For another, any kind of reaction only makes negative children more negative. How to deal with this kind of problem will be discussed in a later chapter.

On the whole, such negative children are easier to work with and are usually further along than those who do not react to anything and fail a task either because they are unaware of what goes on around them, do not understand what is asked of them, or lack the basic skills to comply with a demand.

The way a child fails a task may also reveal something about his level of development. If he cannot complete a puzzle, for example, but at least tries to place some puzzle pieces, or uses them constructively in some way, such as stacking them and building something with them, he is likely to be better off than a child who simply throws the pieces around, chews on them, sniffs them, attempts to spin them, or flaps them against his fingers or cheeks.

During the initial assessment the evaluator will also look for signs of spontaneous play, such as rolling a ball or riding a tricycle, and for evidence of specific skills, such as speech, the ability to understand and follow instructions, or physical agility and coordination. The children are also tested for the level of their cognitive skills, such as counting, recognizing pictures, familiarity with colors, the ability to match colors or shapes, and, with older children, reading, writing, and speech and reading comprehension.

For example, Gerry was asked to draw a cake. Unhesitatingly he wrote "c-a-k-e." When asked to add arms and fingers to a picture he had drawn of his mother, he quickly spelled out "a-r-m-s" and "f-i-n-g-e-r-s." His reaction is typical of the concreteness with which autistic children often interpret instructions.

The intake examination may reveal other typical autistic ways of dealing with language. Children may repeat words they hear without any understanding of what is being said to them. Or they may use phrases inappropriately that they may have been taught in a different context. Asked how old he was, Gerry answered readily, "I'm fine, please."

A characteristic of autistic cognition is the confusion of self with other. Asked to scratch his back or touch his nose, an autistic child with a fair amount of understanding of language will often comply by touching the examiner's back or nose. Some children, even older ones, may follow instructions correctly, but remain mute themselves. It is usual to find that their *understanding* of language (receptive vocabulary), is more developed than their *ability to use words* (expressive vocabulary).

If a child reacts negatively to a task, the therapist usually changes to something else, but he may return to the original task several times to see whether a child can be induced to comply with instructions or whether he gets upset when he is pressured. During the assessment the therapist will also try to see whether and how a child can be motivated to complete a task. Sometimes he will stay with it if he gets occasional help and sometimes it is possible to keep him going by interspersing the activity with something the child shows special interest in, such as playing a few bars of music or blowing soap bubbles.

While a child is never intentionally provoked, more pressure is usually put on him during the assessment than once he enters the Linwood program. Observing his reactions to a certain amount of frustration may reveal a lot about the way he reacts to people, the way he handles himself, and the things that stimulate, soothe, or upset him. This may provide pointers for ways of working with him later on.

Staffers whose group a child might qualify for are usually present during the initial examination. This gives them an opportunity to observe how the child performs with someone else in a relatively structured situation and alerts them to certain typical behaviors. The staff does not read a child's record until they have worked with him for some time. This ensures that they are not influenced by any previous diagnosis or label attached to a child.

Sometimes a typical and definitive symptom may escape casual observations during the intake examination because of a child's unusual facility in one or another area of functioning. One child, for example, impressed the examiner as performing at such a high level in the assessment tasks that autism seemed out of the question as a tentative diagnosis. It was only upon reexamination of the videotaped session that the therapist was struck by the characteristic way the child had failed to react to observers in the room. During the course of the session a ball had rolled under an occupied chair. The child pushed the person's legs away as if they were blocks and reached around them without once looking up or giving any sign whatsoever that there was a difference between the observer and the chair on which he sat, or other objects in the room.

On the other hand, one little boy was initially deemed unsuitable for

Linwood because he related quickly and easily to people and seemed affectionate and "cuddly," rather than cut-off and remote. It was only when his echolalic speech and his difficulty with even the simplest abstract concepts became more clearly apparent that he was reevaluated and found to have a number of autistic characteristics that had been masked by his atypical social behavior.

INTERVENTIONS BASED ON OBSERVATIONS

Once a child has been placed in an appropriate group, he is restricted as little as possible. Instead, he is closely watched to assess his way of functioning in the new environment. It often takes prolonged observations before it becomes clear at what level a child is functioning or what meaning one or the other of his behaviors may have. A particular behavior, such as an obsessive attachment to a toy truck may have a different function for different children and for the same child at different times or in different situations.

As we will discuss in some detail in a separate chapter, such a compulsion may be virtually the only voluntary behavior a child has. Spinning the truck's wheels and holding on to it may be all he is interested in. Taking away his truck in an attempt to make him do other things, even if it is just for a short while, may have serious consequences. A child whose exclusive compulsion is interfered with is likely to either fall apart or to latch on to another equally engrossing compulsion.

At a later time, the same child may have learned to use the fact that people are careful not to upset him by making him give up his truck. He may place it in the middle of the room and scream any time another child comes near it. In this way, he can control the whole room and dominate the activities of the group. At this point the child has obviously become aware of other things besides his compulsion. He is interacting with others, even if it is in a negative way, and it is likely that he has also developed in other areas. He may still put up a fight if limits are set to his use of the toy truck, but he will be able to tolerate some restrictions and profit from them by developing other interests and skills.

Another child may have a strong attachment to a toy truck too, but though playing with it may be his favorite activity, it is not his only one. In such a case, the compulsion can be used to motivate him to develop new skills, by using play with the truck as a reward for working on some other task.

Intervention techniques differ depending on the function of a certain behavior, on the ability of a child to understand speech, on his ability to control his behavior, and on his personal style and characteristics. The various approaches to work with specific problems will be described in the following sections. The important thing to remember is never to take any action or interfere with any behavior until or unless its meaning to the child is clearly understood. The child also has to have developed to the point where he has other activities to fall back on while one particular behavior is being dealt with.

It is not necessary to understand the causes for a particular behavior pattern to be able to work with it, nor is it useful to give interpretations of his behavior to the child. The important thing is to be as certain as possible what the child's strengths and limitations are, and at what level he is functioning, so that any interventions are timely and appropriate. It is especially important to know when a child begins to become more aware of his surroundings and is ready for his first interactions and relationships. The following example illustrates how a child's observed behavior can alert the therapist to the fact that a child has developed a new awareness of his environment.

> *Larry was initially totally oblivious of other people. His world was narrowly circumscribed by invisible boundaries within which he played with a single toy. What he really liked was to hide in a box. Whenever there was a box available he would take his toy and hide under the box with it.*
>
> *When he began to occupy a little more space in the room, he would carry the box with him, pulling or pushing it along. Occasionally the therapist would put her foot in his box, to test his reactions. Without looking at her, he would simply remove the foot as if it were an annoying obstruction, and then continue to play near her.*
>
> *After some weeks of this, the therapist happened to put her foot in Larry's box again. He removed it as usual, hesitated, then moved the box out of reach and returned to the therapist. For the first time he looked her straight in the face, then, quick as a flash, he scratched her furiously. He had clearly made the connection between the person and the interfering foot.*
>
> *From that time on, Larry showed a marked preference for the therapist's hand whenever he needed something that was out of his reach. The therapist had obviously ceased to be just another object.*

Familiarity with a child's habitual behavior enables the staff to note minute variations or a break in behavioral patterns which often signal a general readiness for change. It is at those times that intervention is possible and has the best chance of success.

A child who has seemed blind and deaf to anything going on around him may be observed one day to briefly focus his eyes on a toy another child is playing with. Another child may be a severe feeding problem. Instead of eating his food he will throw it around. By and by he may dump food less frequently, a possible first indication of a growing interest in food. A child who accidentally drops an object he compulsively clings to without immediately picking it up, may be ready to be interested in a different toy. Only continued observation and careful experimentation can determine the significance of these minute changes.

Sometimes, especially when there has been relatively rapid progress, a child reaches a plateau of growth where he seems to stagnate. Or there may even be a temporary loss of gains made over a period of time and a regression to earlier behavior patterns. Such fluctuations may be indications of several things. They may be caused by factors in the environment, such as a change of routine, loss of a counselor, familial tensions, or changed family constellations, all of which can be stressful. Or they may be the sign that the child needs a period of rest to consolidate the gains he has made. In fact, a period of regression sometimes precedes an important change or another growth spurt.

After three years in treatment, Larry had a long period of extreme anxiety. He returned to the compulsive play with a bottle top which he had given up over a year earlier. For days in succession he would cry, or throw himself against any hard surface in the room. He wanted to be cuddled one moment, the next moment he would scratch and kick the person holding him. Since he had had brief periods of regression before that were always followed by definite gains, Larry was watched especially carefully for any indications of what it might be he was struggling with.

Up to that time Larry had only eaten baby food but around the time he began to regress it was noticed that he would take sandwiches, smell them, then throw them away. He would himself choose his jar of baby food, but as soon as he had it, he would smash the jar. His behavior suggested to the therapist that he was ready for a change in his diet. It was decided to try him on solid food. A little bit of food was put into his mouth. He resisted, but didn't kick or scratch, —his usual forms of protest. After a little while, he chewed and swallowed.

Every day he came and indicated that he wanted regular food, and every day he showed the same initial resistance when he was fed it, but in the end always ate it. One day he spat out the mashed potatoes he had been accepting for several days.

When it was pointed out to him that he seemed to have liked mashed potatoes before, he spontaneously picked up a spoon and ate them by himself. From that day on he ate solids and did not need to be fed anymore.

INTUITION

Outside observers who are not atuned to the therapy process and who are unaware of the wealth of information that determines every therapeutic decision are often struck by the way interventions catch a child at just the right moment in just the right way to produce visible, sometimes dramatic, changes. These interventions may be tried and true techniques or seemingly spontaneous reactions to a certain situation. At times there doesn't even seem to be a trigger for the therapist's decision to intervene at that particular moment. When recounting the course of treatment the therapist may say, "I *felt* he was ready . . ." suggesting that he was guided by intuition. But when pressed or closely observed, it becomes evident that there were a number of indications that convinced him, often without thinking about it, that the time was right for a change.

Having a "feel" for what a child needs or is capable of at any point in time and acting upon it at the correct moment is what distinguishes an inspired therapist from one who simply applies standard techniques. Yet much of what a superior therapist seems to know intuitively can be learned.

Intuition can be defined as the insight a therapist gains from objectively observing a child's behavior over a period of time without consciously analyzing it. After a while, the accumulated observations begin to form a pattern which suggests the form and the timing of the therapist's moves.

Understanding the importance of observations in therapy helps demystify the therapy process. This does not mean, however, that anybody can work successfully with these children. Practice and experience are essential for the gathering of meaningful observations. The accumulated observations have to be analyzed and interpreted. Then, based on the information gained in this way, the therapist has to come up with creative interventions.

Most outstanding therapists are excellent observers. They are also patient, flexible, open, secure in themselves, and respectful of others. And they have the ability to remain nonjudgmental and objective while caring about each child as an individual. Taken together, these characteristics and skills suggest that work with autistic children is at least partly an art and that successful therapists are artists as much as artisans.

As we have seen, observations give therapists and educators many of the tools they need to work with. However, therapy is not a one-way process. Successful therapy requires the active participation of the patient. To bring about meaningful and lasting changes in an autistic child's behavior, he has to be helped out of his isolation and has to be motivated to get in touch with the environment. The child cannot find the way into the outside world by himself. Therapy has to build bridges for him in the form of relationships that provide both meaning and structure for the child. The building of relationships is one of the important, ongoing tasks in the treatment of autistic children, and is the subject of the following chapter.

THREE
✦ ✦ ✦

Relationships

INTRODUCTION

The most significant characteristic of autistic children is their inability to relate, which results in what has been called their "autistic aloneness." Many of the most striking manifestations of autism, such as the absence of communicative speech and eye contact, compulsive activities, and stereotypical self-stimulation are part of this lack of human connectedness.

The deficiencies in their social and emotional functioning differ from the types of relationships observed in other severely disturbed children. In schizophrenia, for example, existing relationships may become distorted as the child loses touch with reality and enters a world of bizarre fantasies. Autistic children, on the other hand, rarely develop relationships because they do not voluntarily enter the world we call real. In an emotional sense they could be described as "not-yet-born."

Despite increased research efforts, the causes of autism have not yet been found. Whether because of an hormonal imbalance in the brain or because of structural brain damage before, during, or after birth, the sensory apparatus of autistic children seems unable to cope with the impact of sensations and emotions. These children appear not merely "thin-skinned" or "high-strung," they seem to experience most stimuli as unpleasant or even painful. It is as if their organism lacked the capacity to isolate, channel, filter, or process sensory input. This holds true for physical sensations such as touch, sight, and sound, but the most striking aspects of the syndrome are deficits that relate to an apparent inability to deal with social stimuli, including language.

To protect themselves from being overpowered by confusing or painful sensations and emotions, autistic children erect barriers against the outside world. Depending on the degree of their disability or possibly on its

41

etiology, these barriers may be "porous" and admit some outside stimuli, or they may be practically impenetrable. Correspondingly there is a wide spectrum of children with autistic symptoms. At one end of the scale are the children who are severely handicapped. Often retarded, and with little or no communicative speech, they are hard to reach. At the other end are those who are highly verbal and whose deficiencies lie mainly in the area of social interactions, especially with peers.

To speak of children as "protecting themselves" against the intrusion of sensations or emotions may give the impression that they are in conscious control of the kind or the amount of sensory stimulation that reaches them. This may be true of older children who can be observed actively avoiding interactions or sensory stimulation. Rather than looking at people directly, they may peek at them out of the corners of their eyes, or they may even roll their eyes all the way up until only the whites show. When addressed, some children cover their ears or start humming or droning to themselves to close out the outside source of sound. There are also children who insist on wearing earmuffs or keep hats or hoods pulled down over their ears or eyes to avoid contact. Many children do not allow themselves to be touched, run away when they are approached, or start screaming when they are asked to talk.

The defense mechanisms in the newborn and the very young child, however, are probably closer to involuntary reflexes. How the organism manages to exclude sensory input is less important then the fact that it does so to the point where children may appear deaf, put things in their mouths indiscriminately, and seem immune to extremes of heat, cold, and pain. Many young autistic children do not even react with reflexive blinking to unexpected loud noises, and deafness is often the first suspected cause of their lagging speech development. While clearly not blind, they look at objects and people without seeming to take them in or make distinctions between them. Their faces are masks over which expressions sometimes flicker like lightning, without apparent connection to outside events. Many of these children look years younger than their chronological age, their features unmarked by experiences or emotions.

If they allow themselves to be held, picked up, or carried, autistic children do not mold their bodies to that of the adult, but hang in their arms like a rag doll or a sack. But mostly they actively avoid any kind of physical contact. The void left by shutting out external stimuli may be filled by internal sensations produced by self-stimulation, such as rocking, spinning, rapid finger flapping, or high-pitched humming. These stereotypical activities may also be part of the barriers that insulate the child against the intrusions of outside stimuli. When asked whether he remembered why he compulsively flipped sticks as a child, one autistic adult recalled that he did it "Because I liked it. It made me feel good. It made me feel safe."

When they are forced to deal with the physical world, these children put all their energies into making it as predictable as possible. Autistic children prefer objects to people, possibly because objects can be manipulated and will stay put, while people move in unpredictable ways. An unvarying routine in a static environment reduces the possibility of having to deal unexpectedly with possibly uncontrollable situations or sensations. Also, repeated stimuli tend to desensitize the organism so that sensations triggered by repetitive sounds, routine activities, and familiar sights become muted. Any change in a stimulus, on the other hand, produces fresh sensations. This may be another reason why interruption of a routine, changes in the physical arrangement of the environment, and the slightest variations in sights, sounds, or tastes often provoke extreme reactions by autistic children.

Autistic children also tend to retreat into themselves if they are faced with emotional reactions from others. While their own emotions remain undifferentiated, they are extremely sensitive to those of the people around them. Looking back to an earlier time in his life one autistic boy said that he never felt that he had problems he couldn't handle except once, when he was afraid he would go crazy because he saw his mother cry.

Autistic children are alone in their world, but they do not seem lonely. They do not suffer the pains of emotional deprivation which neglected children might feel, possibly because one cannot miss what one has never had. They do not reach out and actively avoid attempts by others to draw them out of their isolation by resisting the emotional and physical intimacy which is part of a normal nurturing relationship. They avoid being stroked, cuddled, or kissed, or at best receive such expressions of affection and encouragement with stony indifference. Praise and other verbal interactions either don't register or produce paradoxical, negative results. Efforts to engage an autistic child in a relationship can therefore lead to avoidance as the child slips farther and farther away. If he is pushed too insistently, he may eventually erupt in desperate fury, as often directed against himself as toward the environment.

How, then, is it possible to tempt a child out of his isolation and give him a fair chance at a normal life? How can he be motivated and learn to trust people to guide him safely into a world that confuses and frightens him? This chapter is about establishing relationships with autistic children as a first step toward the process of rebirth through which they must go before they can develop the skills they need to function in society.

The following case study told by Jeanne Simons highlights some of the stages one little girl went through in developing a relationship with her in the course of therapy.

THE STORY OF CATHY

Cathy was delivered by Caesarian section after a twenty-four-hour labor. She did not breathe immediately and required stimulation. From birth on, Cathy was a feeding problem. She seemed totally uninterested in food and had a great deal of difficulty adjusting to her formula. Her early development was slow, on top of which she had an acute illness at twenty months, suggesting poliomyelitis. She made a satisfactory recovery, but by the time she was three and a half, her mother was seriously concerned about her.

Physically she had an awkward gait, poor coordination, was unable to feed herself, and lacked vitality and initiative. Her speech was poorly developed and consisted mainly of repetitious fragments used without apparent comprehension. Her mother had Cathy tested, and a thorough neurological examination and psychological testing suggested brain damage and possible retardation. The parents were told not to push her, but to let her develop at her own speed. So Cathy was enrolled at a private nursery school, while the mother devoted herself to "helping" Cathy.

Instead of making progress, however, Cathy became more and more apathetic. She refused to meet other children and would flee to her room when children or adults she didn't know visited her home. At school she was withdrawn, daydreaming, and at the same time tense. She did not participate in any activities, and indeed hardly seemed to notice what went on around her. Finally her parents were advised to withdraw Cathy from the regular nursery school and instead seek treatment at Children's House, a center for emotionally disabled children in Washington, D.C.

Cathy was a beautiful child, tall for her age, but underweight. She had shiny black hair cut like a page boy and big dark eyes that looked sad and frightened. When her mother brought her to the door on her first day, Cathy held on to her limply with one hand, while she clutched her lunchbox with the other. Her mother left quickly, leaving Cathy standing frozen in the doorway. She did not give any sign that she was aware of her mother's departure. I am not sure whether she even noticed her absence. She just remained standing in the exact spot her mother had led her to, staring ahead motionless and rigid.

Though I wanted very badly to reassure Cathy, something told me not to touch her. Instead I invited her quietly to come in and to choose the chair and table where she would feel most comfortable.

Cathy almost ran to a table in a corner. She sat on the chair, folded her long legs under it, and clutched the seat of her chair with her hands, still holding tightly to her lunchbox. She pulled the table as close to herself as she could and slumped down. When I asked if she would like to take her coat off, Cathy did not seem to hear me. She just sat and stared into space until it was time to go home.

For days Cathy would hurry to her table and clutch it like a life preserver. The only word she ever spoke at home or at school was "no." Whenever anyone approached her or spoke to her, that is what Cathy would say. When I went near her table, Cathy would shrink away, trying to make herself as small and inconspicuous as possible. I decided to leave her alone at first to see what she would do, but I watched her very carefully for any sign of change or any behavior at all.

For several months there were only two other children in Cathy's group, Curt and Dotty. After a while, I began to notice that Cathy's eyes often followed the activities of the other children. Then one day I noticed that Cathy became even more tense than usual whenever she saw Dotty on my lap drawing or singing with me. I watched carefully and saw this happen several times. So Cathy was beginning to become aware of her environment. Perhaps she was ready for some first interactions.

I began to sing little made-up songs with the names of the three children in them. Out of the corner of my eye I saw that Cathy seemed to be taking in every word I sang. I saw just the slightest change in her expression when I used her name in my songs, but when I talked to her directly she still shrank back.

I knew from Cathy's mother that Cathy had never been able to accept much cuddling as a baby and had not been cuddled or held at all in the last few years. Yet I suspected from her reaction to Dottie's sitting on my lap that she might wish she were in Dottie's place, but that she was not yet able to make a move on her own.

After a while I changed my songs. I made up new ones in which I did not use names, but I sang about a little girl, a beautiful little child with long legs who felt very alone, who did not know if she would like to sit on a lap, who did not know if she was loved. I sang about a lap which seemed so small for long legs. I did not sing facing Cathy, but I could see that she was listening intently now.

Then one December morning a wonderful thing happened. I was singing my songs as usual and had stopped for a while. Dottie was sitting on my lap and we were drawing together. From out of nowhere came Cathy's little, whispering voice saying "Sing songs about the little girl again. The little girl with the long legs?" I asked. "Yes, yes!" was the eager answer. I did, and Cathy first became tense, then seemed excited. Her face was flushed and her hands clutched the edge of the table. I smiled at her, and then matter of factly put Dottie on a chair next to me while I continued to draw with her. Cathy suddenly pushed her table aside, rushed over to me and sat on my lap, arms and legs rigid. It was all I could do to keep from giving her a big hug, but I knew that would be too much for her. I held her gently with one arm and continued to draw and sing. Cathy stayed for a few minutes and then got up, threw all the paper and crayons on the floor, and laughed — the first laugh I had heard since she was with us. In the next few days Cathy came to sit on my lap several times, relaxing more each time, and slowly she began to accept the cuddling she had not been able to accept as an infant.

Almost as soon as Cathy began to reach out to me, she also began to take a more active interest in the other children. Curt loved to paint and draw. Cathy would watch Curt out of the corner of her eye and paint or draw whatever he was painting or drawing. When he stopped, she stopped. When he took a book to read out loud to me, she would also find a book, open it, and move her lips as though she were reading.

I wanted to find an activity at which Cathy could excel. Curt was good at almost everything, and I didn't want to risk having Cathy's activity overshadowed by his ability. However, neither Curt nor Dottie was good at singing. Because it was with singing that I first made contact with Cathy, I decided to try out this activity as a way to get her involved with something that would be specially hers.

There were a few songs that I frequently sang for the children that Cathy seemed to like. I began singing some of these songs, but in the middle of them I would get "stuck"; I would say aloud that I liked this song so much, but I wished someone could help me remember the words. I made sure that my back was turned to Cathy. Finally Cathy reacted. I began to hear her tiny voice behind me, filling in the missing words. After some time I turned and asked her openly if she could help me out. She was terrified! She held herself tense with her face flushed, but finally she filled in the words for me. Somehow I had the sense that despite her tense posture and fear, she was just a little bit pleased with herself!

A few days later, after several episodes of having Cathy "helping out" with my songs, Curt happened to say that he thought Cathy had a nice voice. I saw a flicker of pleasure in Cathy's eyes. I was so happy with Curt that I hugged him! A little later, Cathy, with her back to us, began to sing songs on her own, still in a voice that was barely audible. I felt that it was time to approach Cathy even more directly. I began to ask her about her drawing or painting, which was nothing but random scribbles on paper. Cathy began to respond at times, but she only gave one-word answers and never volunteered information or initiated a verbal exchange. She still said "no" to most of my questions, even if I offered her something she obviously wanted.

Finally we had another breakthrough. One day Cathy was playing with a doll and seemed more tense than usual. Suddenly she hurled the doll against the wall. She stood where she had thrown the doll in a frozen, terrified posture. I picked up the doll and cuddled it in my arms. "Poor dolly," I said, "You must feel unhappy that you have to bump your head against the wall. If only you could tell me what you want maybe I would be able to help you." Cathy suddenly burst out with her first complete sentence, delivered with real feeling. "She wants a drink of water and does not know how to ask for it!" I wanted to take her in my arms, but I knew it was much too early for that. Instead, I gave the doll a little bottle with water and said to it, "Maybe your mommy, Cathy, wants a drink too." Cathy could hardly contain herself. "Yes, yes, I want a drink too! I am very, very thirsty!" I immediately put the doll down and took care of Cathy's need.

This was an important step for Cathy. She had had several periods in the past during which she had refused to drink to the point where she had had to be hospitalized for dehydration. After this incident Cathy blossomed. She learned to relate to the other children, first by mimicking them, then by following them around and finally by playing with them. She even began to show some jealousy toward them, sometimes edging another child away from me, and later trying to destroy some of their work. She also began to have temper tantrums and to verbalize her feelings, but though she became more and more aggressive, she was still terrified by the slightest sign of retaliation or counter-aggression.

Cathy became an excellent reader in a short time and began to use language appropriately, first with me, then with the other children as well. She began to draw, and within a relatively short time her drawings changed from scribbles to identifiable objects, such as houses and trees. As she began to relate more to the other children, she began to draw human figures as well, adding more and more details as time went on.

Cathy asserted herself more and more. She began to show initiative in organizing games, especially in acting out stories, took the lead in putting on puppet shows, and helped the other children with their roles. She made up most of the stories for these shows. When the other children became unruly while she was giving a show, she would patiently wait until they settled down, announcing that she could not go on while they were making so much noise.

Cathy's progress was heartening, but there was one disturbing factor about it. It did not carry over into the outside world. She seemed to function only at Children's House and only as long as I was near her. Even with other staff members she was very shy, and at home she either couldn't or wouldn't associate with children in the neighborhood.

Cathy had been tested before she entered my group. At the time her I.Q. was 85. A year and a half later she still only scored 88, despite her obvious progress. It seemed as if her functioning depended on her relationship with me. The next step, therefore, was to help Cathy to develop relationships with other people as well, so that she could use the things she had learned with me in a wider context.

Over a period of time Cathy was introduced to other staff members. At first she went to one of the psychologists for remedial teaching. She still came to my room first and I would then take her to her lessons. Her new teacher also came to visit her in my room. After a while Cathy went to her teaching group immediately without stopping by at my room first. She also began to join the other group for activities and excursions after the teaching period was over and eventually formed a very warm relationship with her new teacher. And at home she started to invite children of the neighborhood into her yard.

From here on, Cathy improved even more rapidly. She grew and gained weight. She had no more eating problems and seldom missed a day of school because of illness. When she was retested after two years of treatment and just before leaving Children's House, Cathy's I.Q. had risen to 96, well within the normal range.

Cathy was ready for public school. In her reading she was far ahead of the children her age, but she did have some difficulties with arithmetic. It was therefore decided to start her in second rather than the third grade to give her a better start in school.

After Cathy's family left Washington, she wrote to me for years. After a few difficult weeks of adjustment, she was doing well in her new school. She was leading a very active social life, rode a bicycle, took ballet lessons, and had joined the girl scouts. Many years later Cathy has married, trained and worked as a secretary, and for a time also worked at the information counter at a Convention Center.

DEVELOPING RELATIONSHIPS IN THERAPY

Establishing a relationship with a withdrawn child like Cathy is a very slow process and not all autistic children are able to progress as smoothly or go as far as Cathy did. Children come into treatment at different levels in their development and with varying degrees of impairment in their verbal, intellectual, and social functioning so that the pace of treatment has to be adapted to their individual characteristics, skills, and needs. But the basic approach used at Linwood is the same with all the children.

The process of engaging a child in a relationship begins at the intake interview. At that point the therapist not only assesses the level of the child's overall functioning, but pays special attention to any signs of awareness of the environment, of other people in the room, and of any willingness or ability to let himself be engaged in a task with another person. This first contact gives the therapist an idea of the child's social and emotional functioning and suggests the group the child might best fit into.

At Linwood, the children are treated in groups of five to seven children with two or three adults responsible for the group. This provides staff members with the opportunity to devote as much time as necessary to an individual child and eventually engage him in a close relationship, without focusing on him too intensely and exclusively. Being a member of a group allows the children to observe the same adult engaging different children in different ways, while he himself has the experience of interacting with a number of children and adults with different personalities.

Once the child is assigned to a group, he needs time to settle in. As much as possible he is included in the daily routines of the group, but except in the case of behaviors that might endanger him or the other children, his habitual activities are not interfered with. During this time the therapist's role is mostly that of an *observer*. As much as possible the therapist becomes part of the child's environment, a nonthreatening and eventually familiar object. At the same time, his observations lead to an in-depth assessment of the child's characteristics, his needs, the major manifestations of his disability, and of the level of his functioning.

This is the time to discover whether a child shows interest in a special food, object, or activity and whether he exhibits anxiety in a specific situation or shows fear of particular objects. One little girl went into hysterics whenever she saw a flashlight, and reacted equally strongly to the sight of dolls and stuffed animals. While she did not seem to notice the sound of car engines or any other noises, she would scream whenever an airplane flew overhead. Other children have food idiosyncrasies. They may not touch white milk but accept chocolate milk or may drink milk through a straw or from a carton but not out of a glass.

Children also come into treatment with a variety of compulsions. Lee had to carry his keychain with him at all times and this attachment persisted into adulthood, long after he had given up his other, more bizarre, behaviors. Terry carried one red sock around with him, Jan ignored books but flipped endlessly through catalogues of mail order houses, and Gregory was only interested in strips of paper that he flapped constantly or let flutter in the air as he ran around.

Some children do not react to spoken language but listen to humming or singing, as in the case of Cathy. Others do not seem to be aware of any of the activities going on around them but become quiet and attentive or hover at the edge of a group when music is being played. No matter how passive a child is when he comes in or how restricted his behavior, there is no child that does not eventually show some reaction or behavior, interest or preference on which therapy can begin to build.

Making oneself into an observer means making no moves toward the child unless he is in physical danger. The observer makes no emotional demands on the child, does not address him or comment on his activities, and remains passive even when the child's activities bring him in close contact with him.

Some children climb on an adult's lap as they would on a chair, or place an object within his reach. It is hard to realize that this is not an overture for cuddling or play, but that they have simply come to accept the adult as one of the objects in the room among which they move with relative indifference. During the early stages of treatment the therapist has to discipline himself to remain as unresponsive as if he actually were just another piece of furniture in the room. Taking his cue from cats who wait motionless in front of mouse holes, the therapist schools himself in patience, knowing that a premature twitch will frighten off the nervy creature hiding in his little mouse hole.

After a while the adult can start to diminish the physical distance between himself and the child, but still without reaching out to him, still remaining the safe, predictable object which can be used by the child as he would any other object. If this stage is negotiated successfully, children will often do just that and use the adult as a tool to get something they want, as a ladder to climb on, for example, or to reach something on the top of a cabinet. Many children will take an adult's arm or hand and direct it to do something they cannot do, such as opening a door, reaching a toy, turning a page, or getting some food. It is important to let the child take the initiative in these contacts and not to pursue him when he breaks them off or to offer help before it is asked for.

Even at this early stage, the guiding principle of therapy is to let the child reach out for something that is available in the environment. The child provides the cues, the therapy contributes the structure. This is the essence of "walking behind the child" and of using any existing strengths a child may display that are basic to the Linwood approach.

If it has been discovered, for example, that a child prefers a particular toy, he will not automatically be given it when he enters the room. Instead, it will be visible and available on a shelf or open closet. If the child truly wants it, he will have to devise a means of getting it, either by himself or by using the adult. As the child makes progress, the adult may name the object as he hands it to the child. Later the toy may be kept in a closed closet and the child may be required to ask for it by name.

At first the children usually do not differentiate between adults and use any available arm or hand to get what they want. As time goes on, most children will start to show a preference for one particular hand and search it out when they want help with something.

> Larry, who had been extremely compulsive about one or two objects and did not take any notice of anything outside his restricted circle of activities, be it people or things, slowly began to single out the arm or hand of one particular therapist when he needed help in getting something out of his reach. Eventually he became interested in different small objects. When he wanted to handle something that he had never used before, Larry would take the therapist's hand, guide it toward the object he wanted, put her hand on it, and then take it himself, while she was still holding on to it. If the therapist let go before he had had a chance to touch the object, he would become very anxious and the whole procedure had to start over. It took a whole year before Larry could take whatever he desired by himself, and several more months before he could take a toy without permission or reassurance that it was all right to do so.

This kind of selectivity shows that the child is beginning to become more aware of his surroundings and is able to distinguish between the objects in his environment. It also signals the emergence of feelings of preference for one object over another and of a growing attachment to a particular object. Once the child begins to make more of a distinction between inanimate objects and people, he is ready for his first tentative relationships.

Even once a child tolerates being touched or seems to seek contact by climbing or clinging, the adult must wait to respond until the child makes it very clear that he really wants interactions. A child may take an adult's arms and place them around himself, thus indicating that it is safe to hug him. But even then the hug should be light and nonrestrictive and the child should be released as soon as he wants to slip away. In fact, any holding or guiding is best done by sitting or standing behind the child. This allows for more distance within the contact, lets the child take the lead, and makes it easier for him to break away. He is also not forced into face-to-face contact, which might be too intense for him at first. Holding the child lightly helps the adult feel a child's muscular tension and reactions, so that the child can be released at the slightest signal of tensing up or resistance.

Once the therapist has become an integral and accepted part of the environment, he can start taking a somewhat more active part and become an *observer-participant*. As an observer he continues to monitor the child very carefully and to note all of his reactions, his preferences, and especially any indications that he might be ready to tolerate change. As a participant, the therapist tries to create the conditions and environment that will activate the child and draw him out of his isolation into participation in the outside world.

There is as yet no strong focus on the child or on interactions with him. Contacts are seemingly accidental or at least very casual. The therapist might play with a ball at some distance from the child, and after a while roll it in his direction without actually looking at him. If the child returns the ball, the therapist has to be careful not to show any enthusiasm, praise the child, or otherwise overwhelm him with his reactions. Instead, he seemingly ignores the fact that the child responded to his overture, and does not immediately return the ball to the child. By keeping the atmosphere unemotional and the contacts undemanding, these first interchanges remain manageable and safe for the child, and as time goes by, he will be able to tolerate more prolonged interactions. Sometimes it take a long time before a child can be approached physically.

Carl covered his head or hid under a pillow or blanket every time the therapist smiled at him directly. She persisted over several

*weeks, never giving him more than a quick smile, until the day
he smiled back before covering his head. Soon he was able to smile
without having to hide. He started to watch intently when a child
sat on the therapist's lap. She started to sing about a little boy,
sitting on the couch, and as time went on added some more personal things about him: his new blue jeans, his nice blue eyes,
etc. Day after day he moved a little closer, until he touched her
hand and finally put her hand on his head. After he had done this
several times, she responded by ruffling his hair and he did not
withdraw.*

As the child becomes more comfortable with occasional contacts, the
therapist makes toys available to him that he seems to enjoy and that might
lend themselves to activities the adult can join in. If the child plays with
blocks the therapist may at first use some of them to build a structure nearby.
If the child accepts this parallel play, the therapist will eventually take a
turn in placing one of the blocks on the structure the child is building. In
this way he follows the lead of the child, but also provides a model for
interactive play and taking turns which the child may choose to imitate.

In turn-taking, both parties are engaged in a first two-way exchange
that needs little or no language. In fact, the less the therapist talks to the
child during the early phases of treatment, the better. If speech is used at
all, it should consist of the very simplest sentences, or even of single words
directly connected with the activity or toy being shared.

Some children, who themselves do not communicate and do not seem
to "hear" spoken language, may be reached by singing to them, as in the
cases of Cathy and Carl. At first the melodies that children react to best
are fairly monotonous chants that provide a sort of background commentary to the child's own activities.

Even children who do not seem interested in anything may eventually be approached and involved in some activity. The therapist might bring
out a form board or a puzzle and, sitting next to a child, casually
demonstrate it to him. Once the child allows himself to be touched, the
therapist might put her hand around that of the child's and help him pick
up a puzzle piece, guide his hand to the correct position, and then drop
it in place. Any reaction on the part of the child, such as a voluntary tighten-
ing of his fingers around the shape or more active participation in placing
it, is ignored at first. The activity is repeated until it is clear that the child
wants to take a more active part. He is allowed to take the lead from there
on, until he has become interested enough to tackle the puzzle on his own.
The therapist holds back until a new skill, activity, or preference has taken
root before expanding on it. In this way the child is allowed to set his own

pace to adjust to a new situation and enjoy whatever benefits it offers.

It is especially important during the early stages of building a relationship never to use a child's interests against him, to take what he wants away from him or to make him work for it. Instead, if it becomes clear that a child especially likes something, the staff tries to provide it for him, both to give him pleasure and as a way of beginning to build a more complex two-way relationship.

> *Marshal was totally unresponsive when he first came to Linwood. Regardless of the circumstances, he kept up a constant wailing, which at times would escalate to nerve-wracking screaming. He cried and screamed inside and outside, when he was by himself or when he was approached. Nothing seemed to catch his interest or give him pleasure.*
>
> *One day, Marshal happened to spot a rocking chair. The slight rocking motion seemed to capture his attention and there was a noticeable break in his crying. The next day Miss Simons presented Marshal with a little rocking chair of his own, telling him that using it was to be his special privilege. The other children were told to keep away from Marshal's rocking chair and generally respected his exclusive right to it. Marshal often sat in his chair and seemed calmer there than at other times during the day. One day a staff member unthinkingly put her cardigan on Marshal's chair. Quick as a flash Marshal grabbed it and threw it on the floor, making it unmistakably clear that he considered the chair his property, and showing, for the first time, an awareness of his environment. From that time on, Marshal began to respond more, his screaming diminished, and eventually he could be involved in a wider and wider variety of activities.*

Only after a relationship is well developed does the therapist begin to demand that the child do something to earn a reward, and even then the child is at first asked to do less than it is thought he can do. To require a child to perform in any way to get what he wants, before he is ready, not only endangers the tenuous relationship already established, it also carries the risk that the child might abandon his interest, or give up something he likes rather than working for it.

Putting on too much pressure too early or increasing demands as soon as a child shows signs of interest demonstrates to him that progress has drawbacks. It is one of the guidelines of successful therapy and education *never* to *punish a child for progress*. This concept is basic to the Linwood approach to treatment, and will be discussed in various contexts throughout this book. The basic idea is not to make new demands on a child before he has had time to consolidate an earlier gain. Autistic children experience all change as painful and frightening. If they are pushed prematurely, they may well decide that the cost of progress is too high and may respond by retreating into the safety of their earlier dysfunction.

Once the therapist has become part of the child's world, it becomes possible to structure his routines and activities with certain first goals in mind, without having the child scuttle back into his shell. The therapist uses whatever skills or interests a child exhibits and tries to expand them, develop communications around them, and use them to get the child generally more involved in social interactions.

If a child shows some interest in getting into a closet, for example, getting in and out of the closet is gradually made into a game.

> *All Mary wanted to do when she first came was to hide from the world. She soon discovered a narrow closet she could squeeze into and sat there, preferably with the door shut, as long as anyone would let her. The staff was concerned for her safety and removed the latch from the door so that it could be closed but not locked. They also realized that Mary's compulsion to hide increased her isolation and defeated any benefits she might get from being in a group situation. On the other hand, it seemed as if Mary's compulsion filled a strong need for safety. To try to rob her of her refuge prematurely might only make her more afraid and compulsive.*
>
> *To get Mary in touch with the other children and limit her time in isolation without interfering too drastically with her obsessive need, her teacher invented a game that consisted of hiding in a closet. All the children in the group were encouraged to crawl in and out of the hiding hole, or play a game of closing the door and be "found." This modified form of hide-and-go-seek legitimized the hiding, while turn-taking, coming out of the safe place as well as being alone in it, and seeing other children share the closet eventually helped Mary to be more comfortable in the room and with the group.*

Obsessions and compulsions also provide good starting points for establishing first interactions.

> *Terry's obsessive interest in his red sock was used by the therapist to engage him in simple games of hide-and-seek. She hid the sock in different places and Terry, eager to recapture his prize,*

looked for it. In the course of this activity a first relationship evolved. It grew gradually, as did Terry's skills in the course of introducing more games with the sock. For instance, Terry learned how to undo different types of fasteners when the therapist hid the sock behind the doors of various cabinets with a variety of latches.

Jan's preoccupation with catalogues was used to expand his vocabulary. He was told the words for pictures he showed a special interest in. For a long time he was stuck on food processors and one of the words he frequently used was "Hamilton Beach." One day, when a favorite counselor of his was out sick, Jan sat on the steps clutching his catalogue and wailing tearfully "Hamilton Beach, Hamilton Beach."

If the therapist notices that a child listens when she is humming, she can eventually make up words to put into a simple song. The child may be able to accept this type of communication when he might shy away from spoken words addressed to him directly. Once the link has been established, the child may eventually be able to accept normal speech.

His interactions with the therapist open up doors for the child to the outside world. But every step outside the safety of their known, narrowly circumscribed refuge is difficult and frightening for autistic children. Progress is slow and they need constant support to keep moving forward. As a therapeutic relationship develops, it gives the child a first experience of social and emotional interactions that are undemanding, nonthreatening, safe, and stable. Having learned to relate to one person safely, the child will more easily be able to branch out into additional relationships, each of which can expand his world.

Carl, the little boy who had finally learned to smile, went on to develop his strongest relationship with the music teacher who came once a week to play for the children. He knew what day she came, waited for her at the door, and was entrusted with carrying the sheet music she brought along. He also went to turn the pages for her when she played. Every Wednesday he would bring a treasure from home to show her, which no one else was allowed to see.

As in Carl's case, relationships often start around an activity.

Laurence loves to throw a soft ball around and has a special interest in baseball. He developed a close relationship with his gym teacher, with whom he loves to kid around. Whenever this particular adult shows up in the yard, Laurence will chase him or tease him.

Mark gets to go out to a fast food restaurant once a week. He eagerly looks forward to this treat, but he is visibly disappointed if someone other than Miss Simons takes him. He always insists that she order something too, at the very least a cup of coffee if she does not want to have a hamburger or some ice cream.

SYMBIOTIC RELATIONSHIPS

Developing a strong relationship with an autistic child is not without its dangers, however. Child and therapist may get fused in a way that actually impedes the child's progress. To understand the mechanics of this process, which is known as symbiosis, it may be helpful to examine the emotional development of normal infants and the way they form relationships.

Every normal baby starts out life in a state of almost total physical and emotional dependency on a caretaker, usually the mother. All his needs are met by her and all his feelings are lodged in her. The baby feels and acts as if the mother were an extension of himself.

During these earliest months of life the infant's world is one of fragmented impressions, isolated events, and intense sensory experiences. Newborns are unable to make a connection between cause and effect, such as crying and being fed. Sensations and feelings flood and easily overwhelm the child, since they can neither be anticipated nor understood within a framework of past or future events.

Under normal circumstances, the baby eventually gets a first sense of structure through his daily routine. Events become predictable through countless repetition. Along with these first associations, children develop the ability to hold images in their minds for increasing periods of time, so that objects which are out of sight continue to exist in memory.

As the structure of the outside world becomes more familiar to the child, the sense of what is outside and what is inside, of self and other, also become more and more differentiated. People are no longer experienced as being part of self, but instead are seen as tools that can be manipulated and used to gratify needs. They can be summoned by gestures or sounds and engaged in interactions that are stimulating and pleasurable.

Having emerged from the experience of being one with the mother, which is the essence of symbiosis, the child eventually becomes an active partner in various two-way relationships between separate and increasingly independent individuals. In normal emotional development, a first strong, mutual relationship with the primary caretaker is considered to be the necessary base as well as the model for all future relationships. However, most babies have early contacts with "important others," such as the father, siblings, relatives, or regular baby sitters. Thus, the child does not depend exclusively on one person for emotional, social, and cognitive stimulation and his model of what human relations are like is usually a composite of all these early contacts.

Recalling the descriptions in the initial sections of this chapter, it becomes clear that once their isolation has been breached, the emotional and social development of autistic children follows much the same course as that of normal babies. The biggest difference is that with them the process does not take place spontaneously and naturally from birth on, but is delayed and distorted because of their initial difficulties with processing sensory and emotional information. On their own, they might never get past the stage of fragmented sensations. They would most likely never develop a sense of being separate individuals with means of effective control over their environment or the possibility of meaningful communications with it.

Normal babies elicit responses from their mothers practically from birth on and react to cues from her in increasingly differentiated transactions. Autistic children do not reach out to initiate contacts and are themselves largely nonreactive. The burden of nurturing and sustaining a relationship therefore rests with the adult. In some cases the child may be totally passive and may simply allow himself to be carried around and cared for as if he were a doll. An adult who accepts this charge without any attempts at helping the child to become more active and independent may unwittingly encourage the child's continued dependence, both for his physical and for his emotional needs.

At some point during their treatment many autistic children need to go through a symbiotic stage, reliving the early emotional development of normal babies. Great care has to be taken, however, that this experience does not add to their problems. Instead of "putting them back into the womb" by isolating them in a separate room with their caretaker, they should be cared for within the framework of the group. If they are held, cuddled, fed, and dressed in a room with other children, they are exposed to a variety of other stimulation through the activities that go on around them. Their caretakers, in turn, have the opportunity of interacting with other adults and with the other children in the group, of reaching out, talking with them, or even playing with them, at the same time as they meet a child's need for special closeness. In this way child and therapist do not become fused or too focused on each other. More importantly, avoiding exclusive relationships gives the child the chance to become aware of more than one person and opens up the possibility of future relationships with more than one person.

When Gary came into treatment he was almost five years old, but he looked more like two and acted almost like a newborn baby. He did not want to walk by himself, but had to be carried everywhere. When he was put down he seemed to collapse into himself and stayed where he had been deposited until he was picked up again. When he was being carried he hung limply, like a little rag doll. He let himself be cared for without protest, but he never smiled. Despite the fact that one person cared for him almost exclusively and by necessity carried him around with her much of the day, there did not seem to be any real awareness of the therapist as a separate person. What existed was at best a symbiotic relationship.

The only thing that seemed to evoke a spark of pleasure from Gary was lollipops. It might have been tempting to use his interest in lollipops as a way of making him more aware of his therapist and of beginning to build a more real relationship. But the therapist was very conscious of the danger of locking Gary into an exclusive dependence on her. While still carrying Gary around and attending to his other needs, she made a point of having some other staff member give Gary his lollipop. At the time he did not seem to mind or register whose hand he got the lollipop from, but long experience with autistic children suggests that they remember things that happen to them long before they show any overt signs of awareness. The therapist wanted to make sure that as early as possible, Gary would have pleasant associations with adults other than herself.

The same principle is applied to older children who already have a good relationship with one staff member and who show a marked preference for him or her. Whenever possible, the favored staffer will create the opportunity for another adult to hand the child a special treat. If he asks her for a cookie, for example, she might say, "lets see whether Diane has one," and take the child over to the other counselor who will reward him. Or a child might ask for a favorite toy or game, and the therapist might find that she does not have the desired toy in her room and take the child to another room to ask for it. Or she might indicate that she does not have time at that particular moment to play a game with the child but suggest that another staffer might be free to do so.

In every case the goal is to avoid an exclusive involvement with one person and to provide the "outlines of doors" that might lead to future relationships. It is especially important for autistic children, with their disinclination to form any relationships, to be exposed early to a variety of positive contacts so that they will experience a variety of human responses. For one thing, every new relationship provides one more path out of the autistic aloneness in which the children are initially imprisoned. For another, it will enable them to cope better with the diversity of social situations and demands that they will encounter outside the shelter of the treatment situation.

Also, every relationship tends to be somewhat different and therefore helps develop a different facet of the personality. One person may be somewhat more motherly and protective. She may be the one who helps the child put on his shoes or teaches him to button his coat. She may be the one he goes to when he needs to be cuddled. Another person may be more brisk and bracing and engage the child in a game of catch or encourage him to try out a new athletic skill. Yet another may have a particular skill that attracts a child, such as playing the piano or the guitar.

It is important to do everything possible to draw the children out and engage them in relationships, but it is equally important not to create an emotional dependence that would make it impossible for them to move on their own, or to function outside of Linwood. Pathologically prolonged symbiotic relationships, even with normal children, are most often the result of the caretaker's inability to let go or to adjust to changes in the relationship produced by the child's development.

Any therapist, but especially those working with autistic children, must know and monitor his own emotional needs and responses continuously to make sure that everything that happens within the therapeutic relationship is for the benefit of the child, rather than filling some emotional need of the adult. Since autistic children do not reach out and may not respond for long periods of time, the therapist gets very little initial return and emotional gratification for his efforts. To compensate, he may over-invest himself in the child and identify with him and his progress to the point where the whole responsibility for the relationship and the child's progress lies with the adult. Yet most children have some skills, however limited, that can slowly be developed and encouraged, even while experiencing the security of a close, caring relationship. Here too, it is important to let the child take the lead and let him indicate his needs, rather than anticipating and gratifying them. The following anecdote illustrates this point.

> *Ryan who was 13 at the time and already attending school outside of Linwood, spent a weekend at Miss Simon's house because his parents were on a trip and he could not go home as usual. When he had gotten into bed, Miss Simons went in to say goodnight to him. As she was preparing to leave the room, he motioned for her to approach the bed, then he pointed to his sheet*

and blanket, indicating by his gestures that he wanted to be tucked in. Miss Simons complied and was about to leave again, when he pointed to his right cheek, making it clear that he was asking for a goodnight kiss. When she kissed him lightly on one cheek, he presented the other one for a kiss too, then snuggled under the covers and quickly went to sleep. Up to that time he had never kissed anyone or allowed himself to be kissed.

Despite the fact that Miss Simons had a good relationship with Ryan she would never have attempted to initiate these kinds of close interactions on her own. Ryan was allowed to set the tone of the relationship and to indicate what his needs were and what degree of closeness he was ready for. We have described this process in the earliest stages of building relationships with autistic children. The same principles hold true once children have made considerable progress.

Not all children express their readiness for relationships or closer interactions as clearly or as readily as Ryan did in the incident described above. Often, only close observation of a child over a period of time will allow the staff to interpret something he does or doesn't do as an indication that he is opening up and is ready or even eager to relate.

When Dan came to Linwood at the age of ten he was described as "invisible." He was so passive and withdrawn that he had been diagnosed as severely retarded at various times, though a few professionals had also described the child in terms of infantile autism.

In the course of his residence at Linwood, Dan emerged from his extreme aloneness, though he continued to shy away from any close contacts and exhibited all sorts of extreme compulsions and at times a sort of maniac-like behavior as a defense against interacting with people. Within the first two years of his stay, Dan learned to read fluently and even picked up some knowledge of French. At thirteen he exhibited at least normal sixth grade knowledge, though his social difficulties made placement in a public school impossible.

One of the things the staff was working on with Dan was his handwriting. It was so sloppy that it was almost impossible to read. Indeed, it seemed reasonable to assume that Dan did not want to communicate even in writing and was "hiding" behind his bad handwriting.

Dan had a special interest in popular music. To motivate him to improve his handwriting, he was given a transistor radio. Every time he had practiced his handwriting, he was allowed to go off

on his own to listen to his radio. After his handwriting had im-
proved enough, he was told that from now on he could use the
radio any time he wanted during his leisure time. It was quickly
noticed that he never did, and when asked about this, he withdrew
or said "I don't know." When pressed at a later time, he responded
with, "I don't want to talk about it."

When given an opportunity to detach himself from the group
to use the radio, Dan relapsed into stereotypic rocking and twirling
which he had not done for a long time. His therapist interpreted
this behavior as a clue that Dan did not want to be apart from
the group anymore and instead was ready to emerge from his
aloneness. After some prodding, he was finally able to verbalize
this himself. There followed a brief period of violent temper tan-
trums, an indication of Dan's anxiety about the changes taking
place in his life. From then on, Dan's progress was spectacular.
At fourteen and a half Dan was a happy adolescent, capable of
verbalizing feelings, and relating to most adults and some peers.
Eventually he went on to regular high school, where he earned
A's and B's and from there to a junior college and eventually to
a library job.

TREATMENT AT TWO LEVELS

Most autistic children do not go through a phase where they develop
a full-blown symbiotic relationship with a therapist. But many, if not all,
of them exhibit infantile needs at one point or another while they are in
treatment. Because of their early emotional cut off, the children never had
many of the sensual and emotional experiences, such as sucking, or of being
cuddled, that normal babies enjoy while they are being cared for. As they
come alive emotionally, the children, even older ones, give strong indications that they need to live through experiences they missed out on at the
appropriate age. Therapy has to provide the structure to allow the children
to gratify their needs without infantilizing them.

The key to the balance between helping a child to keep and develop
skills he already has while allowing him to fill gaps in his early emotional
development is to *treat him at two levels*. In every situation and with every
child the therapist has to look for ways a child's infantile needs can be
gratified without pushing him back completely to an inappropriate
developmental level and losing the gains he may have made in some other
areas.

Johnny, at seven, had adult speech, but had developed a single
strong relationship with one therapist. One day, just before it was

time to go home, Johnny climbed on the therapist's lap and started to wail, not with real tears, but like a very young baby. He then mumbled, "It's a girl."

The therapist remembered that Johnny had very recently gotten a baby sister. She held him in her arms and, looking down on him, said, "This is a beautiful little boy." At that she felt him relax a little. While the therapist softly hummed to him and rocked him a little bit, he cuddled up to her even more closely, quietly sucking his thumb. Since the time was drawing near when Johnny would have to get on the bus to go home, the therapist was faced with the dilemma of wanting to indulge Johnny's need to be a little baby but having him leave Linwood functioning at his proper age level.

She looked around the room and softly sang about the things she saw that needed to be put away. In her song she wondered how she was going to be able to put a big table back in place by herself and wished out loud that she had a small but strong six- or seven-year-old to help her carry it. At this, Johnny jumped up and said eagerly, "I can help you." He helped move the table, then left without further ado, behaving like a seven-year-old.

A similar approach to treating a child at two levels is taken with children who exhibit a need to experience the pleasure of vigorous sucking or drinking from a bottle.

Neil, an eight-year-old, had made good progress but every once in a while he would dreamily suck his thumb and at times also make sucking motions with his lips resembling that of a young baby sucking at the breast or the bottle. Thinking that he might have missed sucking as a baby the staff made sure that all the ingredients were at hand so Neil could fill this particular gap.

At snack time they added a pitcher of milk, some doll's bottles, and a baby bottle to the usual juice and the regular cups. Neil was first offered a doll's bottle, but he was not satisfied with that and reached for the baby bottle, looking around for a nipple to put on it. The therapist suggested that they pour some juice into the bottle together, but Neil asked for milk instead, which he helped pour. He then insisted on a real nipple and was helped to screw it on.

Neil happily settled into the therapist's arms and began to suck on his bottle. After a short time he laughed out loud as if at a good joke, unscrewed the top, poured the rest of the milk into a cup

*and drank it that way. He did this for several days, always start-
ing out with the bottle and ending up by drinking from the cup,
but always cuddled on the therapist's lap.*

*After a few days he poured the milk into the bottle first, but
then immediately decanted it into the cup, drinking from it on the
adult's lap. Eventually he moved to a chair of his own next to the
therapist, and shortly thereafter he gave up the bottle ritual
altogether.*

By letting the child take the lead in this way, the skills he exhibits are
supported, while his infantile needs are acknowledged and gratified. If the
therapist were to simply guess at them, she might take the child further
back than he needed to go. By offering him a filled baby bottle immediately,
for example, the message to the child might be that he is viewed as a baby
that is incapable of acting for himself in any way. The child might accept
this interpretation, but he might also be uncomfortable with it and become
anxious or resentful. Instead, he is encouraged to make his own choices.
This way he feels accepted, supported, and in charge, despite the fact that
he might temporarily behave like a helpless baby.

What applies to younger children also holds true for older ones.

*Patrick was already in the schoolroom (the placement for the
highest functioning children) and was almost ready for the transition to public school when the staff noticed that he took every
opportunity to sneak into the room of the youngest children, where
he furtively handled the stuffed animals. The problem now
presented itself of how to contrive a situation that would let Patrick
play like a small child and indulge his obvious need for cuddling
toy animals, without losing his status as a schoolroom boy.*

*The solution was to tell Patrick that a helper was needed to
tidy the room of the youngest children in the afternoon and he was
offered the job. When the children left the room, Patrick had it
to himself for a while. Ostensibly tidying up, he had a legitimate
reason to play with the stuffed animals to his heart's content. On
the one hand he was given a responsibility commensurate with
his age, on the other hand he had the chance to become a little
boy again for a while. When his interest in stuffed animals seemed
to fade and an opportunity naturally presented itself, Patrick's
schedule was rearranged, and he was given some other job more
appropriate to his overall level of development.*

Treating children at two levels, letting them reach out for what they
need, and "sharing" them whenever possible prevents them from becom-

ing immobilized through a pathological dependency. Sharing children makes it easier to avoid a compulsively intense relationship that might become an intolerable burden for the adult whose life the child invades with his insistent demands.

A child's need to be with a particular staff member at a particular time can also become a weapon to control the environment. A balance has to be found between his need and that of the staff and the other children. One solution is for the staff to decide on a rotation that best fits their schedule. The child may claim one staffer at a certain, predetermined time, another one at another time. In this way he gets the attention he craves from his favorite people without being allowed to interfere with the staff's work with other children and without using his attachment as an attention getting mechanism.

Sharing children brings additional benefits. Among other things it gives the whole staff an investment in every child and thus prevents jealousy among staffers that could be detrimental to a child's progress. When a child takes a step forward, when he utters his first word, eats a new food, allows himself to be hugged or stops screaming or hurting himself, the teacher working with him at the time is bound to feel gratified, especially since such signs of visible progress are usually few and far between. But having shared the care and education of the child in some way or other along the road, everybody knows that this progress is the result of a long, hard team effort. No one needs to feel that he has failed because a child did not take great strides under his tutelage. This removes the temptation of imposing unrealistic treatment goals on the children, of pushing them too fast and thereby punishing them for progress.

NEGATIVISM AND RELATIONSHIPS

As long as a child is encapsulated in his autistic aloneness, he moves through the environment as if it were inhabited by shadowy wraiths without substance or reality. It is only when he begins to develop a first awareness of the world around him that he has to concern himself with other people, their actions, their emotions, and their impact on him.

While they may seem totally oblivious of their surroundings, most autistic children actually have a very keen sense not only of what is going on, but of the emotions and intentions of the people around them. One young woman who had been described as interacting with people like an automaton when she was little, recalled the intake examination at Linwood, when she was less than five years old. She did not remember the people involved, but she did describe her sense of being tested. She said that she didn't know what was going on, but that it was very clear to her that she was not just being played with, that it mattered somehow what she did, how she reacted, and how she performed.

Awareness of others is obviously a necessary first step toward establishing relationships, but autistic children, who experience change as painful, tend to avoid anything that might alter the known, safe structure of their routine. Their first conscious acknowledgement of the existence of others is therefore often signaled by an active retreat from any involvement with them. A child might move away from anyone who tries to interest him in a toy, or he may drop a toy he is holding if somebody else touches it. He may stop an activity an adult imitates or attempts to join, or he may refuse to continue doing something if he is praised for it. He might also use objects he is handed inappropriately, or fail a task, such as completing a puzzle, even though he is clearly capable of doing it.

Resistance, while difficult to deal with, is actually seen as a good prognostic indicator. For one thing it shows that the child is aware of what is going on around him and is intelligent enough to figure out what is wanted of him. Avoiding the one correct solution among many involves making a conscious decision and choice. Negative behavior can thus be interpreted as the expression of an independent will that springs from a budding sense of self on which therapy can capitalize. How this is done will be examined in detail in a separate chapter later in the book.

A child may exhibit negative behaviors from the moment he enters therapy, or they may surface only once he begins to develop relationships with adults. Sometimes this is simply the result of social ineptness. The child has not yet learned acceptable ways of interacting with others or of getting their attention in positive ways. He may pull people he is especially interested in by the hair, push, poke or kick them and generally make their lives miserable by liking them "not wisely, but too well."

> *Nat, who is an adult now, still remembers his favorite counselor, Pauline, and how she ran away from Linwood because of his persistent pursuit of her. Whenever he had the opportunity, Nat would chase Pauline and pull her hair hard. At first, it was simply his clumsy way of showing her how much he liked her, but Pauline made the mistake of showing Nat that hair pulling bothered her, and the more she evaded him, the more he began to hound her. Though she was an excellent therapist, she had gotten off to a wrong start with Nat and eventually other staff had to step in to shield her from his unwelcome attention.*

The best way to deal with this and with other negative ways of getting attention is to demonstrate more acceptable ways of interacting, while ignoring negative advances as much as possible. For instance, many children try to get a sitting adult's attention by pulling his hair. Their grip is usually very strong and it takes two people to pry them loose. Calling for assistance in a case like this results in two adults concentrating on the child. This makes hair-pulling, or other, similar types of behavior, a super-effective attention-getting device.

A better way of dealing with such a situation is to seemingly ignore it without letting the child get away with it. The person whose hair is being pulled simply holds the child's hands firmly in place by pressing down on them. This stops further pulling without a big fuss. The therapist otherwise ignores the child, continuing whatever activity she was originally engaged in with some other child. She is free to talk to other people in the room and in a general way might include the hair puller in the conversation without, however, alluding in any way to the fact that there is anything special in his situation.

After a while the child will get tired of being immobilized and his grip on the adult's hair will begin to relax. As soon as the therapist senses that the child has released the hold on her hair, she can easily lift his hands off her head. He can then be included in whatever activity is going on at the time or the therapist can find something constructive to do with him that will assure him of her positive attention.

One way to ignore negative behavior is by distracting the child and involving him in a constructive activity.

> Eric was upset, thrashing around, spitting on the floor and at other children. He also accidentally got some spit on his new jacket, of which he was particularly proud. The therapist happened to have a wet cloth in her hand and she started to clean his jacket with it, talking about what a pity it was that there should be spots on it, but otherwise not alluding to the spitting at all.
>
> Eric became interested and began pointing out further spots for her to tackle. The therapist continued to distract him by focusing on the jacket, saying things like, "Oh, here is another spot on the back of your sleeve." Meanwhile she was casting around for another activity to involve Eric in.
>
> Some children were drawing and the therapist suggested drawing Eric's jacket. By this time, Eric seemed to have forgotten his earlier upset and was not spitting anymore. The therapist drew the outlines of a jacket. Eric watched with great interest, pointing out further details, like the hood and pockets, which the therapist added to the drawing.
>
> When the picture was finished, Eric spontaneously picked up

a crayon, saying, "It has to have eyes." He drew in eyes, a nose, mouth, teeth and hair, as well as arms with hands and legs with shoes on them.

The therapist suggested that Eric draw the jacket by himself, which he did, even adding strings to the hood. Then he again drew a person inside. As he drew the fingers he counted, "one, two, six, five." The therapist helped him count correctly. She also helped him to add the correct design to the jacket. He wanted the pants striped, but didn't know how to go about getting the right effect. The therapist did one leg for him. By that time other children had gotten interested in the drawing, and Torsten, the boy Eric had spat on earlier, offered to do the other leg. At this point the therapist withdrew from the activity, and Eric was fine for the rest of the morning.

While the therapist was occupied with Eric, Clem threw himself on the floor, laughing and fooling around in a way that made it clear that he too was trying to get her attention. Looking around, the therapist saw one of Clem's pictures displayed on the wall. While continuing her activity with Eric, she wondered out loud "who drew that nice picture?" Clem stopped his silliness, stood up, and started to tell her what the picture was all about. She asked him whether he thought he could make another picture as nice and offered him a chair at the table close to her. He began to draw, wanting her attention on his activity. She told him that she preferred the drawing to be a surprise and that she would not look at it until he was finished. Working with Eric, she occasionally glanced at Clem, giving him an encouraging wink. That was all he needed, and he did not interrupt her work with Eric anymore.

Whenever a child reacts negatively or has an upset, his negative behavior is not only ignored while it is going on, it is also not alluded to once it is over. While a child is never rewarded for temper tantrums, naughtiness, or aggressive acts by having undue attention focused on him, his need for attention, his anger, or his attempts at testing limits are noted and accepted by the staff. Instead of punishing him for his behavior, every attempt is made to satisfy his needs in positive ways, to keep him busy, to interest him in activities from which he profits and learns, and to strengthen relationship bonds.

At times a negative child's behavior taxes even the most creative and patient staff person. In these cases, sharing a child provides temporary relief and keeps the child from experiencing rejections from adults who might otherwise get pushed beyond the limits of their strength.

There are a variety of reasons why children may become more negative or aggressive once they have begun to establish relationships. One of the causes of inappropriate behavior is the fact that in the early stages of development, the emotions of autistic children are undifferentiated. They often react in the same way when they are frustrated, angry, or frightened as when they are happy. Undifferentiated anxiety is often signaled by silliness or laughter. Self-aggressive children may bite or hit themselves when they become emotional, while other children may bite or scratch an adult with whom they are interacting, even, and sometimes especially, when the experience is a positive one or they are in a really good mood.

Four-year-old Michael does not distinguish between people yet, or relate to them as people. He uses them as he does chairs, tables, the slide, or the jungle gym—to climb on. Running and climbing are his favorite activities, and he has to be closely watched, because he will launch himself off anything regardless of its height.

Whenever someone gives him a hand up, he worms his way toward their face and bites them on the neck or the ear. People quickly learn to hold him at arm's length while allowing him the pleasure of scrambling all over them.

Negative behaviors may also be an expression of the ambivalence a child may feel about opening himself up to relationships in the first place. Autistic children at first lean away from progress. Engaging in a relationship carries all sorts of potential risks. The pressure to perform may intensify slightly once a child has begun to react and respond in a relationship. Having to deal with human beings rather than with objects also involves a certain amount of uncertainty. More importantly, relationships engender emotions that may be incomprehensible and unsettling to the child and may even be frightening.

This ambivalence and confusion often expresses itself in negative ways of interacting. Dorian used to yank the hair of people he especially liked, while Laurence teases them or bangs on tables and starts to brag or to talk loudly when he is with a person he likes.

A close relationship may also free a child to express negative feelings for the first time in his life. Many initially passive or compliant children begin to express emotions as they get more in touch with themselves and the outside world, and most often the first emotion expressed is anger.

Children may scream endlessly, hit, kick, or scratch, throw toys or furniture, spit, or pull hair, or punch and kick holes into walls and doors. Often these children turn their anger on the staff member with whom they have developed the best rapport. Though this seems paradoxical at first glance, it is simply an extreme case of a normal human phenomenon.

Everyone, whether child or adult, tends to mind his manners in public and relax in private. A child who is commended for his beautiful table manners at somebody else's house often eats like a little pig at home. Meek and obedient at school, another child may go through a phase of constantly talking back to his parents. A man who is invariably considerate and polite to his staff, may at times be thoughtless and grumpy with his family. The fact is, that everyone lets his guard down at times with people he likes best because he feels safest with them.

The same holds true for autistic children. They tend to be negative, temperamental, or aggressive with the staff member they feel closest to because they trust him. Anger can be a frightening and destructive force and the child needs repeated reassurance that the adult not only accepts his anger without withdrawing his affection and support, but that he will be able to protect everyone, including the child himself, from getting hurt. This makes the child feel that it is safe to be angry and to show it, which in time frees him to experience and express other emotions as well.

In the meantime, the trusted and favored adult may well become the recipient of all the child's aggressive behavior, regardless of who the child is angry at or what he is upset about.

After three years of treatment, Larry, who was originally totally passive and withdrawn, began to become actively aggressive, and most of his dissatisfaction was communicated to his favorite counselor in a very tangible way. Whenever he was upset he scratched her. He would scratch when someone didn't immediately understand what he wanted, or handed him the wrong food or toy. He scratched when other children interfered with his play. At first he would just wring his hands, turn in circles, shake his head furiously or fling himself against hard surfaces. But as he progressed, he would more frequently fling himself on the counselor and cover her with scratches, as if holding her responsible for the wrong done him by other children or by another staff member.

He was so quick that it was impossible to avoid all the scratches, especially on exposed areas like the hands. One day the counselor could not face the prospect any more of having her hands scratched and put on gloves to protect herself. This did not faze Larry for long. During his next upset he launched himself toward her and before she was aware of his intentions, lifted up the leg of her blue jeans and gave her some deep scratches on the leg.

Most of these types of negative behaviors tend to diminish as the child learns to distinguish emotions and to handle them and as he becomes more adept at conventional social interactions. Once he is able to tolerate closeness, he can more easily respond with hugs or other positive expressions of attachment, and he will also feel less ambivalent about relationships and have less of a need to pull away from them. The development of some means of communication eventually allows him to attract attention by gesturing or talking rather than by hitting out.

It is also important to remember that a period of naughtiness is part of normal development and is a healthy sign of an emerging sense of self. During the phase of the "Terrible Twos," normal toddlers begin experimenting with their rapidly developing skills that allow them increasing self-determination. They alternately cling to their mothers and take off to explore their surroundings with nerve-wracking inventiveness, learning about themselves and the environment in the process. This is a necessary phase for the child, though it may be an exhausting one for the parents.

In autistic children too, naughtiness is an expression of healthy development and a sign of progress. A child has to have some awareness of his surroundings and some interest in them to start "getting into things" and he has to have some awareness of self as an independent agent who can make things happen, to "act out." True naughtiness, a deliberate act of disobedience, of testing limits, or of experimenting with the set order of things, is therefore a positive sign.

Depending on their special areas of interest or skill, the children may repeatedly ruin the plumbing by stuffing anything that will fit down the toilet. They may rip anything that is not screwed down tightly off the walls, including fixtures, pictures, and posters. They may "paint" the walls with anything handy, including food, spit or feces, or they may go on a rampage of shredding any paper, magazines, paper cups, or books they can get a hold of.

> *Walter steals keys and hides them. He also snatches at any piece of chalk within his reach and puts it in his mouth. Arthur takes off his socks and shoes in the yard and throws them over the fence whenever he can evade supervision, always into the areas with the densest underbrush.*

While some of these acts may spring from a simple desire to experiment, most of them are deliberate and intended to provoke. Children misbehaving in this fashion often make sure they are seen while they commit minor and major infractions of the rules. Sometimes they watch the adults out of the corners of their eyes to assess the effects of their naughtiness and many of them clearly enjoy the resulting commotion.

Both the normal two-year-olds and the naughty autistic children need to be handled in such a way that their natural curiosity, their need to experiment, and their budding independence are respected and encouraged without, however, letting them wreak havoc with the environment, interfere intolerably with others, or endanger themselves. At Linwood, a child is usually allowed to enjoy his "naughtiness" for a while, so that he can savor his independence and can test himself, the situation, and the adults with whom he is dealing. After he has had his chance, the adults usually indicate to him in some way that they are on to him, and then structure the situation to limit the most extreme manifestations of the naughtiness, indicate what might be acceptable, or divert the child's energies into different channels.

Sometimes it is enough to ignore behavior that is only mildly disruptive for it to go away by itself. Often an unexpected reaction from an adult will disconcert or distract a child.

> *Hal was testing the limits by urinating everywhere except in the bathroom. He had been toilet trained for some time, but he discovered that urinating elsewhere got people riled up and earned him extra attention. One day at lunch, when all the food had been served, Hal stood up and prepared to "bless" the food. Instead of trying to deflect his aim, scolding him, or removing him from the table which would have been too late, the counselor calmly said, "Under the table, not on it."*
>
> *Stumped, the child hesitated for a moment, then sat down without going through with the act and ate his lunch without further disruption.*

When it becomes clear that a child uses some naughty behavior as a weapon to get undue attention and to get everyone jumping, the staff will play along with him for a while to satisfy his need to be in control. Eventually they will clearly indicate the limits to which they are willing to go. And at some point the children who are further along in treatment may also be given some responsibility for their own behavior.

> *One little girl kept the night staff busy by soiling herself. Every time she was cleaned up, she would mete out another little portion. Several times in a row she was patiently given a bath and changed. Instead of reprimanding her, the therapist pretty much ignored her while casually mentioning to the night aide that it was very lucky that they had so many clean pajamas and sheets for*

the little girl. The fact that her behavior did not seem to upset the staff, that they did not seem to be worried about running out of pajamas and appeared prepared to change her indefinitely, seemed to give the child pause. The next instance of soiling came after a considerably longer interval. Again she was cleaned up without comment and without any show of displeasure. When she was tucked into bed again, the counselor fetched the remaining stack of pajamas and sheets and said pleasantly, "Ellen, here is a whole lot of pajamas and sheets. You know now what to do. I am going to bed now, because it is getting very late and I am tired. I'll see you in the morning. Sleep well." She walked out of the room, firmly closing the door. There was no protest from Ellen. It was also the last time she soiled that night, or any other night.

The way problem behavior is handled determines not only how constructive this phase can be, but also how emotionally secure a child will feel within his relationships. This holds true for normal children as well. The emotional support a child gets from his parents includes not only the way they deal with him when he is praised and encouraged, but also when he is disciplined. At such moments a child may feel that he has lost the love of his parents, but when the discord is over, he discovers that nothing has changed and that he is accepted and loved as much as ever. In this way he experiences the fact that a temporary loss of love does not threaten the basic relationship and that disapproval does not mean rejection.

Unconditional love that denies a child nothing, or love that is tempered by fear of upsetting the child if demands are made and enforced, robs him of guidance and leaves him feeling insecure. A child who has done something naughty and who asks "Do you still love me?" is often told, "We love you no matter what you do." Since the child sees how upset the parents are about his behavior, such an answer may be more confusing than reassuring. It might be easier for him to understand that "Right now I don't feel very loving toward you but don't worry, in a little while I will love you again." This is a more honest and therefore more effective answer than the one also often given by parents or teachers, "I love you, but I don't like your behavior."

A child and his behavior are not separate entities, and dividing them up in this fashion may make the child feel that his actions have a life of their own for which he should not be held responsible.

During her third year one very intelligent little girl went through a phase where she lied a lot. Whenever she came under suspicion of having done something forbidden, she vehemently denied any responsibility, even if she was faced with clear evidence of her guilt. This little girl thought that she had to be perfect. She was so afraid of a possible loss of esteem that she could never admit to anything, even when she was not threatened with punishment. What she was really trying to say when she fibbed was not "I didn't do it," but "I didn't mean to do it." Once her parents understood her fear of losing their approval and love if she slipped in any way, the lying stopped.

At Linwood, children have the experience of being accepted and loved in spite of anything they might do. As Simon expressed it, "At Linwood, you can do what you have to do, and then they help you so you don't have to do it anymore." This does not mean that there are no expectations which the children are asked to live up to. There are definite standards of behavior that are demonstrated to the children in the course of the daily schedule and activities. The adults model them for the more advanced children who in turn act as behavioral and performance models for the younger children. Within his potential, every child will eventually have limits imposed on unacceptable behaviors.

In this way the children experience the fact that limit-setting can be part of a positive, loving relationship even though discipline may at times be experienced as punishment. Over time a child usually develops relationships with several staff members. This makes it easier to avoid locking a child into a negative situation. If he has an upset with one staff member, for which he gets into trouble, he has a chance to redeem himself and earn a privilege with another staffer.

> *Jason had a craving for coffee. Since he liked it so much and it is ordinarily never served at Linwood, Jason would get coffee from different people as a reward. His regular counselor would share some coffee with him if he had gotten through a day without an upset. He would also get coffee from Miss Simons with whom he worked individually on his speech.*
>
> *On good days, Jason could look forward to two cups of coffee. But every so often he misbehaved in his room and lost out on his reward there. This was no reason, however, for everyone to be angry at him. Despite the fact that he was being punished by his counselor, Jason still got his coffee from Miss Simons.*

The same holds true for all children.

> *Mark had punched a hole in the wall during a temper tantrum and was told that he would not get an extra snack that day.*

On the same day that he was punished by the loss of this treat, the older boys had one of their regular group meetings during which they traditionally share a snack. Because he had contributed to the group discussion, Mark received a sweet there, even though his destructiveness had led to his losing the treat in the evening.

It is sometimes difficult for people to understand how or why this approach works. They fear that children might interpret it as weakness and either take advantage of it or be confused by it. But despite what strict disciplinarians might think of as spoiling or over-indulgence, there is an underlying consistency to the treatment approach at Linwood. The children are held accountable for their behavior but the consequences of their actions are closely related to specific situations. Misbehavior or infractions of the rules do not earn a child universal disapproval that follows him around from person to person throughout the day. While he may have blotted his copy book with one person, he may redeem himself with another.

Every therapist operates somewhat differently, depending on his or her personality. Because of this, the child not only has many chances to start over and learns to adjust to a variety of interactional styles. His relationships with individual members of the staff are different and personal.

The flavor of the relationships with different staffers is also influenced by their function at Linwood. Often the regular counselor with whom the child may have his closest association also has to be the strictest and most demanding, since he or she has the responsibility of working with the child on specific skills. His classroom counselors may be compared to a child's parents whose responsibilities toward their children also include teaching them rules and manners and disciplining them.

Luckily, most children have grandparents, relatives or neighbors-who may have extra time for the child and who can afford to indulge him. In the same way, a child at Linwood may receive extra attention when he is sent on an errand to the office. Or a staffer who doesn't have a daily involvement with the child may take on the role of a grandmother who is allowed to spoil him a little bit. Conversely, when a classroom teacher is in the process of establishing a relationship with a child, she may not want to endanger it by disciplining him too frequently. Instead, he may be sent up to the director's office for a time out or reprimand and then be greeted again sympathetically by his teacher after his return downstairs.

Often a special relationship starts around something concrete. A certain adult may take a child who has a special interest in baseball to a ball game. Another staffer may instruct him in the use of tools or may cook or bake with him. Yet another one may take the child camping or play music with him.

The experiences the children have at Linwood are models for future relationships. As a child starts opening up he is eventually able to relate to other people, such as the other children in his group or in schools he attends outside of Linwood. Most important are the relationships he establishes with his siblings and parents. These will remain central to his life, while Linwood is only a station, though a very important one, on his road elsewhere.

RELATIONSHIPS WITH PARENTS

Most of the children don't have relationships with anyone when they come to Linwood. A few cling to their mothers and a few react to their admission to Linwood with temporary agitation. But in most cases this seems to be a reaction to change in general rather than being due to the kind of separation anxiety one might observe in normal young children. In cases of extreme clinginess, child and mother may be bound in a symbiotic relationship. In these cases it is often the mother who has trouble letting go of the child rather than the other way around.

Some children seem to recognize their parents when they drive up to Linwood for a conference or to fetch them, but as often as not they seem as interested in the familiar car as in the person driving it and run to it without acknowledging their parents. Sometimes children are very insistent about going home, like one little girl whose main spontaneous utterance is "Friday." But as often as not the wish to go home is not so much a sign of genuine attachment as the need to pick up a familiar routine. The same little girl who longs for Friday keeps saying "Linwood" throughout her weekends at home and puts up no resistance to the return trip. Some children actually get upset when they have to stay home an extra day because of a holiday or illness.

Nat, who lives in an apartment for autistic adults, calls home almost every day asking about the most minute details of his family's daily life. When he is home for a weekend visit, on the other hand, he is constantly on the phone to his apartment mates, seeming to miss his interaction with them. In fact, his need to keep informed is probably more a compulsion to keep his routines intact. In both settings he misses familiar activities and people, and the change from one setting to the other creates anxiety as well as pleasure.

Andreas does not talk. During the week he is in residence in an institution. He spends one or two weekends a month at home. He seems to have a good relationship with his family. When he is in a relaxed mood, he likes to sit very close to his mother and to cuddle up to her. But the most important part of coming home has to do with food. In the car, Andreas' father talks to him about the special meal awaiting him at home. As soon as he gets home he goes to the stove to check on his favorite soup. Then he opens the refrigerator, where a large platter of spaghetti is all ready. He motions for his mother to put it in the oven and then settles down contentedly to his meal. The familiar food and the invariable routine provide the necessary stability and ease the transition from one situation to another.

In a few cases there is a genuine, observable attachment to the parents while the children are at Linwood. These children react with distress when their parents leave or are on vacation. They look forward to going home and prefer being home to being at Linwood. They may even pretend to feel sick, when it is time to return after the weekend, just like children the world over who develop stomach aches on Monday mornings when school starts again. Mostly, these are children who have already made considerable progress. The majority of children, however, do not initially relate to their parents or other family members and only begin to do so once they have opened up at Linwood.

It may be hard to understand and accept that children can relate to strangers while the most intimate and natural bond between parent and child fails to develop. Even Leo Kanner initially suspected that this was due to the parents who, for some reason, were unable to generate the emotional warmth children need to thrive. Kanner soon corrected his perceptions, however, and the image of the "refrigerator parents" is no longer accepted.

In part, this shift stems from observations of a greater number of parents of autistic children. In part, it is due to the fact that more recent research has changed our perceptions of early childhood development in general. We have not only become aware of the abilities of newborn babies to see, hear, and imitate, but also of the active part a baby plays from birth on in the process of relationship formation. Normal babies not only react to a caretaker's ministrations and stimulation, they actively initiate contacts and trigger interactions. Mother-child relationships are based on two-way interaction, and disturbances in the relationship can come from various sources: from a breakdown in communications, an inability to read each other's cues correctly, as in the case of some deaf or blind children, or from an absence of reaching out by either partner.

It may be the child who originally reaches out. When there is nobody consistently responding, as in the case of some institutionalized babies, autistic symptoms may develop. With early placement in a favorable setting, children who suffer from what might be called "superimposed autism," have a good chance of recovery.

In the case of true autism, the child's ability to reach out, and to react appropriately to the mother's cues is severely impaired. When parents initiate interactions with their child they either get no echo or bizarre responses. Trying harder and harder to reach a child who does not react as expected, the parents may actually add to the confusion in the child's mind and make it even more impossible for him to process the sensory and emotional cues he is bombarded with.

Even the most accepting parents have some expectations and hopes for their children. Comparisons with siblings or peers are almost inevitable, as are thoughts of the future. Parents often put too much pressure on their children. Looking desperately for signs of progress and hope, they may latch onto any new skill and immediately raise their expectations of the child to unrealistic levels. Resisting the pressure, the child may regress and close himself off even further, frustrating any efforts the parents make to keep in touch with him.

At Linwood, the child enters an atmosphere that is benevolently neutral in every way. He meets with no standard expectations. He is accepted as he is. At first only the most routine demands are made of him and treatment is paced according to his needs and abilities. Yet, there is a firm structure to support him. The opportunities to engage in relationships are there. The child is never pushed into them but observant therapists are ready to pick up on any clues indicating a readiness for first interactions, and then slowly and patiently expand them until they lead to relationships.

Once the child has had the experience that relationships are safe, and possibly even pleasurable, he can begin to develop a repertoire of emotions and of social skills that will allow him to interact with a variety of people, including his parents and siblings. The course of reconnecting parents and children does not always run smoothly, however, and parents and children may have to be helped over a variety of hurdles.

Some parents, tired and discouraged by their long and fruitless attempts at engaging their children in a relationship, may simply have given up hope or may have run out of strength. They may be so afraid of getting hurt again, that they would rather not risk themselves in a relationship with their child.

Even where the parents are willing and eager and the child is able to interact, difficulties may arise. One of the major ones is the fact that many children go through a phase of naughtiness as they come alive emotionally. We have discussed this phenomenon, which is actually a positive sign of growing awareness, a need to assert themselves or to experiment. As we have seen, the early signs of an emerging relationship may well be increased aggressiveness toward a particularly favored person. Instead of being especially cuddly and lovable, children may actually start to provoke staff or parents and test their limits. Teasing too, may be a way of making contact and it is not always what parents hope for or can immediately recognize and accept as a sign of progress. The more intelligent, physically active, and well coordinated a child is, the more ingenious and therefore trying his naughtiness may be. It is one thing to outsmart and control a lively toddler, another to keep one step ahead of a naughty ten-year-old, who socially and emotionally may just have reached the "Terrible Twos."

A few children who are relatively easy to handle at Linwood may turn into little monsters at home, often because parents are afraid to be firm with them. They may be afraid to undo the progress the child has made by putting demands on him and push him back into some earlier distressing behaviors such as screaming or self-aggression. Or they may fear that disciplining the child might spoil the tenuous bonds they have established with him.

In these cases it is important to help parents understand the children's naughtiness in the context of their overall development, while giving them support and practical advice to get them through this phase and help them limit the more unacceptable manifestations of the children's behavior at home.

> One mother complained that her child who loved to ride in cars had taken to rocking back and forth in his seat to the point where it distracted her from driving. Her commands to him to stop were either ignored or provoked even more violent rocking. The solution was simple. Every time the child started to rock, the mother was to drive to the side of the road, stop the car and tell the child that she could not drive unless he sat still. After two or three times of waiting him out, the excessive rocking stopped.

Conversely, some children who act out at Linwood are more passive at home. The fact that there are fewer restraints in a therapeutic setting than in a familial one may account for some of this difference. At Linwood, the whole routine, as well as the environment, is structured to allow the children maximum freedom of movement and expression. Neither the opinions of neighbors nor the needs of other family members have to be taken into account. At home, a child escaping naked into the yard, urinating in public places, or screaming during a temper tantrum may bring the police to the door or at best provoke hostile stares. At Linwood, the staff is freer to wait a child out and to ignore behaviors that are socially unacceptable than parents who have other duties as well. Children can also more easily be kept away from dangerous situations and supervised at times and in places that are potential trouble spots, such as bathrooms.

The fact that autistic children are usually oblivious to danger makes many activities that show initiative and should be encouraged, potentially dangerous. One boy likes to cook, for example. Since he only sleeps for short periods during the night, he has to be locked into his room to prevent him from getting up in the middle of the night to fix himself a hot snack. The danger from the hot stove, from boiling water or soup is too great, and the parents cannot always trust themselves to wake up to supervise his activities.

To the extent that parents have the understanding and support of neighbors, live in surroundings that allow the child a fair amount of freedom and are able to child-proof their home, they will be able to relax and the child's behavior at home may become more like that at Linwood. But just as a child has different relationships with different staff people, so his relationship with family members will have a unique flavor. A child may relate to a parent through shared interests of activities.

> *Nathaniel and his father built a powerful telescope as well as a harpsichord together. Ryan's father, originally interested in painting, was inspired by his son's interest in computers and is presently rewriting a computer manual in more comprehensible terms and simpler language. He is helping his son to learn word processing which the parents hope will lead to a more interesting job for him in the future.*
>
> *In one family with two autistic siblings, the lower functioning one has an especially good relationship with his older, more independent brother who is the only one who knows how to discipline and manage him when he has tantrums. In another family it is the younger, normal brother who takes on much of the care of his autistic sibling. In another there is a special attachment to a grown sister. And there is often a special closeness between mother and child, sometimes to the point where the mother has to be helped to let the child become more independent as he grows older.*

Tragically, occasionally no attachment to one or the other parent develops even though the child may relate closely to other people. But on the whole, the children usually develop attachments to their families to the degree to which they become capable of relating. Several aspects of the Linwood treatment approach help to facilitate the transition from therapeutic relationships to more lasting ones at home and in the outside world. One factor is the schedule children follow while they are in treatment. Depending on their needs and level of development, children may attend Linwood during the day only, stay for an extended day program, or be in residence. But even the residential children spend their weekends at home, assuring regular contact with their families. Also, children and parents are given help, support, and advice to ensure that a child's progress is not unwittingly undone at home, and last, but possibly most importantly, the staff at Linwood is aware of the importance of multiple relationships for these children and knows how to share the children from the beginning.

In the previous chapters we have demonstrated the importance of observations for the timing and execution of therapeutic maneuvers and the central role of relationships as mediators between the child and his environment. In the following chapter we will explore how the information obtained from observing the child and the opportunities to draw him out of his isolation by engaging him in relationships are used to motivate and teach him, limit undesirable behaviors, and help him develop to the limits of his potential.

FOUR
✦✦✦

Shaping Behavior

INTRODUCTION

Educating any child means teaching him to behave in certain ways. Several basic conditions have to be met to make learning possible. For one thing, a child has to be *ready to learn*. In most cases, this means that he is at a developmental level at which he is both physically and mentally equipped to learn a given task.

For example, children who are too physically immature to control their sphincters cannot be toilet trained and children who have not yet developed fine muscle coordination, cannot learn to cut with scissors. A child has to have reached a certain level of intellectual and emotional maturity to be able to deal with abstractions and be able to define concepts like "honesty" or "compassion."

Readiness for learning depends in part on genetically determined *maturation*. It is only when the whole organism, including the brain, the skeleton, and the muscles is developed sufficiently to make a function like speech or walking possible, that practice and stimulation have any significant impact on the speed with which a new skill is learned.

"Readiness," however, is to a large extent a state of mind. People who are uncomfortable, anxious, tired, resentful, or bored learn less well than those who are relaxed, self assured, happy, and interested in a subject or task. This is where the second great force in education comes in: *motivation*. Motivation plays a decisive part in what things are learned, how they are learned, and at what pace they are learned.

Even if a child is normal and maturationally ready and the environment favors and encourages learning, the acquisition of new skills or behaviors often means giving up something that was comfortable or pleasurable. This requires an effort, or even a sacrifice, that may make learning painful and, in such a case, a child may well actively resist change. He may not be ready to exchange the pleasure he gets from sucking on a nipple for the frustrations associated with learning to drink from a cup.

To motivate a person to learn, the environment has to be structured in a way that makes learning both possible and enjoyable. Where either element is missing, learning will not take place, or will be slow or incomplete. Institutionalized babies, for example, who are confined to their cribs most of the day and rarely see or hear other children or adults, start to vocalize much later than babies who are cared for in a normal family setting. Lacking strong emotional ties to their caretakers, and therefore the emotional support and stimulation normal infants experience, these babies show little interest in crawling, pulling themselves upright, or learning to walk, which are all activities that seem an inborn and natural part of any child's development.

The process of learning is hard enough under normal circumstances. In the case of autistic children there are several additional hurdles in the path of progress that do not exist for most normal children. Autistic children strongly resist any kind of change. Their disinterest in adult approval also makes it much harder to motivate them. In addition, therapy with these children often means undoing habits and behaviors which are already established and which are either nonfunctional or harmful. Educational therapy with autistic children, therefore, consists not only of motivating them to learn, but also of limiting undesirable behaviors while eliciting more appropriate and useful ones. This shaping of behavior calls for specific techniques that will be examined in the following sections.

We are indebted to the behaviorist school of human development for an analysis of learning that stresses the role and importance of motivation. Behaviorists are interested in observable behavior and in those factors in the environment that elicit or encourage it. By observing spontaneously occurring behaviors and by noting the conditions under which they change, increase, or disappear, researchers working first with animals were able to demonstrate that specific behaviors could be reliably evoked. By giving rewards, such as food, every time the behavior occurred, the frequency of a specific activity could be maintained or increased. When no rewards were forthcoming over a period of time the learned behavior diminished and eventually disappeared. A behavior could also be influenced by punishment, such as mild electric shocks. This set up a negative association, so that activities linked to painful consequences were temporarily suppressed. However, by far the most reliable way of extinguishing a behavior was to consistently ignore it.

What was first studied in animals was later translated into techniques for working with humans and the shaping of behavior, or behavioral conditioning, as it is called, has become incorporated in many modern teaching and therapy approaches. In the treatment of alcoholism, for instance, Antabuse is sometimes used. When taken together with alcohol this chemical substance produces violent nausea, which by association is supposed to give the patient a lasting disgust or fear of alcohol.

Parents and teachers have known about the motivating powers of rewards and punishment since time immemorial and have used them to influence children's behaviors long before scientists demonstrated the effectiveness of behavioral conditioning. To some extent, all learning depends on conditioning, since all behavior has either positive or negative consequences which encourage or inhibit further actions.

Some activities are rewarding in and of themselves, such as listening to music. Others may lead to gratification once basic skills are mastered, such as reading. The more a child reads, the easier and more enjoyable the activity becomes. This increased pleasure acts as a strong motivator to keep reading and to perfect the skill so as to be able to read more interesting stories. On the other hand, painful experiences, such as repeatedly falling off a horse while learning to ride, may make a person more cautious or fearful and inclined to give up his attempts altogether.

In the instances described above, the pleasurable or painful consequences a person encounters are an integral part of the situation. Additional motivation may come from outside sources, from people who monitor or comment upon the way an individual performs in a given situation. Verbal praise, encouragement, awards, or a pat on the back from someone he cares for may spur an individual on and encourage him to sustain or even increase his efforts, while disinterest, disapproval, or punishment tend to discourage further attempts in the same direction.

Behavioral conditioning depends in good part on finding spontaneously occurring behaviors that can be shaped, changed, or expanded as well as discovering rewards that are meaningful and therefore motivating for an individual child. This is very hard to do with autistic children whose initial repertoire of behaviors is usually extremely limited and who do not operate within a relationship system that would make them responsive to social rewards.

The following case study shows how therapy uses whatever interests a child exhibits, no matter how bizarre or limited they may be, and how it capitalizes on these interests to motivate the child to expand his activities.

Henry had been diagnosed as brain-damaged when he came to Linwood at age five. After about one year he had some speech and had developed some awareness of people and a first relationship with Miss Simons. But Henry's only real interest was keys.

He went after everybody, including visitors to Linwood in order to get their keys from them. If he was prevented from rifling their handbags he would become frantic. Instead of running its course, Henry's compulsion with keys increased to the point where his mother could not take him on any outings anymore. Everywhere they went, he would accost strangers, grab their purses and try to get their keys. At that point it was decided that Henry needed help with limiting his compulsion so that his energies could be diverted into more productive directions.

Henry was told by the staff and by Miss Simons that the time had come for him to do some other things and play with other toys besides keys. Twice a day he would be allowed to go to Miss Simons' office to play with keys, the rest of the day he would have to do without them. Henry accepted these restrictions without visible protest.

When he arrived for his first session upstairs, his face lit up, and he quickly appropriated the four keys on their key ring lying on the desk. Miss Simons let him handle them for a while, casting around for ways of getting him interested in activities that were centered around the keys. Taking a piece of paper and a large crayon, she picked up Henry's hand holding the keys and positioned it so that the largest key was resting flat on the paper. She then drew a circle, by following the outline of the top, saying, "This key is round and round."

She gave the crayon to Henry, taking the keys out of his hand but holding them very close to it. Without hesitation Henry drew a big circle, and as soon as it was completed, the keys were returned to him. Miss Simons pointed out to him that the tops of the other keys were different from the round one. One had a square top with "one, two, three, four sides." Holding on to the keys and jingling them, Henry repeated, "one, two, three, four." He also copied a design, four dots connected by lines to form a square.

The next key was more difficult because it did not have a regular geometrical shape. Miss Simons confessed herself stymied as to what this should be called, and Henry suggested "bumpy." Since she said that she didn't know how to draw "bumpy," he took a stab at it himself without having a model to copy from. All this time the keys were kept close at hand, and in between drawings Henry would hold them or play with them.

The activities around identifying shapes, drawing them, and counting continued and expanded over the next sessions. New shapes were added and then it seemed to be time to move on to something new. Miss Simons showed Henry that the keys were different in color too, one being gold-toned, the other three silver-colored. He seemed to have trouble seeing the distinction, so the next activity was to learn to distinguish and identify colors.

At first Miss Simons made up a game, pretending that the real keys had been lost and that they had to draw some more. As the drawn keys were all the same shape, they had to be distinguished in other ways. They were given different colors and names, "green," "red," etc. When Henry was able to name the crayons used to draw the keys with, they switched to cards made out of colored cardboard that had keys drawn on them, and they played with those until Henry knew all of his colors.

At this point counting was reintroduced as the main focus. There was one gold key and three silver ones. They could be counted separately, by color, or together. Each number could be written down in order, 1, 2, 3, 4, or numbers could be written to indicate different groupings, 1 (gold), 3 (silver), for example. Within a few weeks Henry was able to do all the arithmetic between 1 and 4, and he was taught how to write down the operations he was performing; a plus sign for adding, a minus sign for taking away some keys from the bunch. Miss Simons made up flash cards with the facts from one to four, and later added a couple of keys to the original bunch to expand the range of Henry's figuring.

After a further period of time, Miss Simons pointed out to Henry that other people might not know what the figures they were working with stood for and that it was possible to show them by writing down the word for "key." This introduced Henry to the concept of writing. At about the same time, he found a drawer full of tiny keys with diamond shaped heads. Miss Simons was afraid that this treasure-trove might reawaken Henry's obsession with keys which had begun to fade. She immediately used the keys to make all sorts of intricate designs by putting the points of the tops together in different ways. Henry not only copied every design correctly, he also discovered any errors or changes she introduced into the designs.

Henry's evident ability to distinguish subtle differences alerted Miss Simons to the fact that he had a well-developed spatial ability and therefore the potential to make distinctions between letters. Step by step Henry's interest in shapes that had developed through the activities connected with keys, was used to get him involved in all sorts of projects, such as making kites. He was also given

*blocks with intricate designs he could copy. From there the next
steps led to copying letters, and then on to mastery of the alphabet.*

*As soon as Henry had started to work with Miss Simons, his
key compulsion diminished, not just at Linwood, but at home as
well. Soon it was confined to the office and the more Henry's activities, skills, and interests expanded, the more it weakened there
too. After Henry had had a chance to enjoy the drawer full of small
keys for a while, Miss Simons told him that it was time for him
to start playing with other things and that from then on any keys
around would only be used by the people they belonged to who
needed to use them for a specific purpose. Henry seemed unfazed
by this restriction and from that time on never exhibited any kind
of compulsiveness around keys anymore. At the same time Henry's
sessions with Miss Simons were terminated. It had been possible
to include him in regular activities with his group even while he
was working with her. Later he developed other relationships, did
some arithmetic, and learned to read and write at the third grade
level.*

THE USE OF MOTIVATION IN THERAPY

Henry's case is one of many that illustrate the fact that the most effective motivators are those that have an immediate relevance to a child in
a given situation. This holds true for normal as well as for autistic children.
If a child's own needs provide the stimulus that activates him, if it is his
own actions that lead to desired goals, or if rewards are inherent in a given,
real-life situation, the reinforcement is immediate, meaningful, and natural.

A child who hates to be alone will be motivated to get his homework
out of the way so that he can then spend the rest of the afternoon with his
friends. A shy child, on the other hand, might find the prospect of hanging out at the street corner more frightening than attractive. He might work
for the privilege of listening to records or watching TV when he is done.

A child who wants to make the little league team, will be motivated
to practice hitting and pitching without much encouragement. He may be
less eager to practice the piano, especially if it is something he does only
because his mother insists on music lessons. Or a child may persist in learning to dress himself or to tie his shoelaces, because these skills make him
more independent and their usefulness is demonstrated to him wherever
he goes. At the same time he might continue to eat with his hands, rather
than using the correct utensils, because it is faster and easier. It may not
be until it is pointed out to him that he cannot accompany the family to
a restaurant before he has learned to handle a spoon and fork, that he might
be motivated enough to learn that particular skill.

Especially with young children, behavior and reward have to be closely linked in time for the reward to be effective. This is true for normal children who need to get an immediate positive response to every piece of work they complete to sustain their effort. It is even more important for autistic children who have little or no concept of time. "Soon" or "in a little while" or even "this afternoon" are meaningless to a severely impaired child for whom only the moment exists. Every opportunity that presents itself to encourage, strengthen, or expand spontaneously occurring behaviors has to be used with these children. This means that one has to be alert to any indication of burgeoning interest, any sign of growing awareness, or changes in behavior that can be reinforced or used as motivators for further learning. Working with children in this way requires a great deal of flexibility. The right moment may not always be the convenient moment. A child's progress is often erratic, rarely predictable, and often does not fit existing schedules or stated goals, as the following incident illustrates.

Bob had been at Linwood for several years. He was still nonverbal and because of his size and age, and because he had made very little overall progress, was soon to leave for another placement. The only thing he did consistently and with gusto was eat.

Bob was included in an experiment by an outside research team in which the children were introduced to the concept of tokens, in preparation for using tokens as motivators in teaching machines. In an attempt to use Bob's interest in food to teach him to follow simple instructions, he was taken aside before lunch each day and required to do a simple task, like pushing two blocks together. As a reward for doing this, he was then given the token that admitted him to the dining room.

After a while, Bob began to enjoy the extra attention he was given and began to dawdle over his task. It was decided to ignore his attempts to get extra attention and, rather than coax and encourage him, to let him take his time. Though children are not deprived of food under ordinary circumstances, it was felt in this particular instance that facing the possible loss of a meal might be the only thing that would motivate Bob to pay attention and do some work. And even if he missed a meal, he could always get an extra snack later on to make up for it.

But Bernard had other ideas. Bernard had only started to talk recently and had never shown any particular awareness of other children or expressed concern for others. On the contrary, he acted as if the world was his alone and he trampled anything under foot that stood in his way. But when Bob was late for lunch for the third day, Bernard was clearly upset. He wanted Bob to have his food. He obviously knew what was keeping him and declared firmly, "Me go help Bob."

The staff was faced with a dilemma. If they let Bernard carry out his plan, the experiment with Bob would be ruined. On the other hand they could not afford to stymie Bernard's first expressed feelings for another human being. The struggle was brief. Bob's interest in food was not going to go away and could always be used another day to motivate him, but Bernard's concern was new and had to be encouraged. So he was allowed to leave the table and go to Bob's rescue.

Bernard marched into the room and told his friend, "Bob, me help you." The therapist showed Bernard what task was required of Bob, who quickly pushed the blocks together under his direction. Bernard then handed him the token, took him by the hand and led him to the dining room, assuring him that "Me help you tomorrow, Bob."

The following day went smoothly, Bernard asking the therapist what task Bob had to complete, and Bob following Bernard's directions. But on the third day, Bob started to tease Bernard as he had the therapist on the preceding days. Instead of attending to his task, he ran around the table and did not respond when Bernard called him.

"Put blocks together, Bob, me very hungry," his friend urged, and when Bob did not respond, he left the room. That did the trick. Bob quickly finished the task and followed Bernard into the dining room. At least at this particular time, Bernard had proved to be a more effective reinforcer than either the token or the food, while the satisfaction he got from helping Bob opened Bernard up to a new awareness of others and to his place and role in the group.

Another, even more dramatic, incident happened with a boy who had very little speech and was seemingly emeshed and isolated in a web of compulsions with little awareness of, or responsiveness to, his environment.

It was summer and people were talking about vacation plans. Miss Simons was due to leave on vacation in a couple of days. All of a sudden Kevin stumbled painfully into speech, "Mountains . . . . hundred miles . . . . . ." It was obvious that he had something definite in mind that might possibly have been triggered by talk about vacations reviving earlier memories of hearing about distant mountains. In any case, Miss Simons felt that the boy was on the verge of an important breakthrough and that whatever idea was working in him had to be reinforced and possibly used to get him more in touch with the real world. She told Kevin that she would take him on a vacation to see the mountains a hundred miles away. They would need to pack a suitcase for their trip.

Taking him to the dormitory, she had him name all the things he would need for an overnight stay, "Toothbrush, soap, pajamas," and had him help her pack them. Then they drove off toward the Blue Ridge Mountains in Western Maryland for the boy's first glimpse of mountains. When they stopped for lunch, and later for the night, Kevin was told the choices on the menu and had to order what he wanted from the waitress. All of these things were "firsts" for Kevin, but he dealt with them well and seemed to take in everything that was happening. Upon his return situations were contrived at Linwood that motivated him to be more active, and he began to use words more often and more appropriately.

It takes close observations and an intimate knowledge of each individual to learn what is most gratifying and motivating for him. Even with normal children what motivates them is not only highly individual, but not always easily predictable. One little boy who still wet his bed when he was five, was asked what might help him stay dry at night. To the surprise of his parents, he confessed to an urgent desire for proper pajamas. It turned out that up to that time he had been made to sleep in the outgrown nightgowns of his older sisters. The night he first wore the coveted boys' pajamas was the first night he controlled his bladder.

Autistic children can usually not communicate their needs in this fashion and often do not even seem to have identifiable wishes. Their range of behaviors is narrow, and it often takes a period of trial and error to discover something that is meaningful enough so that it can be used as an inducement for eliciting new behaviors. At times a child's reactions in a situation may give an immediate pointer a therapist can pick up on.

One little boy was so hyperactive during an intake examination that it was hard to catch his attention long enough to demonstrate a task or to keep him focused or motivated to perform in any way. He did not react to attempts to attract his attention by talking or calling to him, did not respond to his name and escaped from his chair to flit around the room as soon as the therapist released her hold on him.

In the course of the examination the therapist blew some soap bubbles. For the first time the boy showed definite interest. He followed the bubbles with his eyes, reached for them, and smiled. By blowing bubbles near the table, the therapist got the boy to come close to her. She then took his hand, helped him pick a shape from the form board, guided his hand over the correct hole, and let the piece drop into place. Quickly she blew a stream of bubbles, then again helped the child pick up a puzzle piece, but waited with blowing more bubbles until he had dropped it himself. When he left the table, she stopped the bubbles, keeping the soapy ring poised, however, to indicate her readiness to continue as soon as the boy had attended to a further task. He quickly caught on and went through several simple tasks in anticipation of more bubbles.

Another child frequently played with a set of cups that stacked inside each other. This favorite toy was used to motivate the child to work on a puzzle, in much the same way the bubbles had been used with the little boy. Initially the puzzles were of the simplest sort. All the child was required to do was to push a piece into the hole. She would then be immediately rewarded by being allowed to play with the cups. As she became more skilled and interested in the use of the puzzle, more was expected of her before she could use the other toy. Over time, the puzzles she was set to work on became more complicated but at the same time, her interest in them picked up and she needed less and less inducement to work on them.

In therapy, as well as in education, it is usually necessary to set intermediate goals and to reward small steps to keep a person motivated to learn, change, or adjust to something new. With autistic children especially, tasks have to be realistic, that is, geared to their skill levels, or even slightly below, so that they can experience success at every step. The steps they are asked to take also have to be very small. At first the mere hint of a desired behavior that approximates what the therapist is aiming for gets an immediate reward. This holds true even if the approximation is unintentional. By rewarding it, it will nevertheless be reinforced and is likely to become more frequent and deliberate. A little girl who had endless and seemingly unprovoked crying spells may serve as an example.

It was discovered that Karen liked sweetened tea. During one of her temper tantrums she was in the room where one of the teachers was drinking tea. Though Karen was screaming and thrashing about she managed to convey her desire for some tea.

Every time she interrupted her crying for even the briefest moment she was given a sip of tea. At first the only pauses occurred when she drew breath. Later she was able to interrupt her crying long enough to indicate her wish for more tea and finally she had quiet spells that lasted long enough to allow her to hold her own cup and drink from it normally.

As a child starts to change, every small step has to be well consolidated before further steps are attempted or increased demands are made of him. This holds true in every situation, but it is never more important than in cases where a child's compulsiveness or his strong dislike of change stand in the way of something he needs.

When children first come into therapy they often eat such a limited diet that it threatens their health. They either eat too little, or they accept only one or two things, like Rice Krispies or donuts. Children are introduced to new foods very slowly. At first, only the most minute quantity of a new food is placed in front of them.

A boy who originally only accepted crackers and marshmallows was presented with a quarter of a peeled pea on the tip of a spoon. His plate was pushed somewhat to the back of the table and the spoon positioned between the plate and the child. At the beginning, the therapist held the spoon. Later the boy was expected to pick it up himself.

At first, touching the pea with his lips or tongue was enough to allow the boy to continue with his regular meal. Later he had to taste the miniscule morsel, and though he gagged on it at first, he eventually learned to swallow it. The amount he was offered was not increased for some time, until picking up the spoon and swallowing the quartered pea became a routine part of the meal. At that time an additional tiny piece of pea was introduced during the meal, and only after a period of weeks was the boy given a bit of pea and mashed potatoes on a regular plate which had to be cleared before the rest of the food was served. Once the barrier had been broken and one unfamiliar food accepted, the introduction of further items took less time and met with less resistance. The reward was eventually reduced to one donut after a more or less normal, balanced meal.

Timing is a very important part of getting a child to comply with demands. If he is asked to do something before he is ready for change, even strong motivators may not work. A child who is pushed too early or too fast, may give up a favorite activity, a toy, or even food rather than do what is asked of him. And even if he goes along to a point, he may suddenly balk, refuse, or regress. It is important to be flexible about requirements and ease up on them rather than get into a power struggle and possibly undo the progress up to that point.

If a child's initial resistance persists, the experiment may have been tried too early. The child is told that "You are really not ready to try any new foods, we will have to wait a few weeks." Then the staff makes sure that the child eats his regular foods normally for a while and looks for possible indications that he is ready to have a minimum of pressure applied, before the procedure is tried again and something new is introduced to him.

CHOICE OF EFFECTIVE MOTIVATORS

Experience has shown that a number of motivators that work well with other types of children are ineffective with autistic children. For one thing, they are largely unresponsive to praise, adult approval, hugs, or smiles that please and motivate normal children. This is especially true at the beginning of therapy, before the children have established proper relationships; but even later, social and emotional motivators may not only be ineffective, but sometimes even counterproductive with children for whom all contacts with the outside world are unrewarding or even frightening.

Autistic children are usually impervious to subtle and not so subtle signs of social disapproval, since they are largely disinterested in their environment. They may disrobe in public, indulge their physical needs, or blurt out candid observations without any regard for the reaction of others, in the fashion of very young children.

In some cases, especially negativistic children who are already more in touch with what goes on around them may set out to provoke adults whose discomfort with their behavior they sense, so that disapproval may end up reinforcing the undesirable behavior rather than suppressing it.

Tokens, in the form of colored disks or pieces of paper that can be used similarly to money and can be exchanged for various treats, are often used to train and motivate emotionally or intellectually impaired children. When they were introduced experimentally at Linwood, they proved to have definite disadvantages. Autistic children are very literal in their thinking. We will discuss this trait in more detail in a later chapter. For these children the concept of tokens may well have been too abstract and the delay between getting a token and being able to exchange it for a more meaningful treat made the reward frustrating rather than motivating.

In some cases the tokens also became the focus of a compulsion. Instead of spending them, some children hoarded their tokens and therefore derived little benefit from earning them. In other cases the children became fixated on tokens of a certain color and got upset when a teaching machine dispensed the "wrong" token.

Candies, cookies, and other food items often used instead of tokens, are also of questionable value as motivators for most autistic children. For one thing, these children often don't like to eat in the first place and will go without food rather than perform for it. For another, there is only so much food a child can eat before he becomes sated. If he is totally oriented toward a "candy economy," he will simply stop working when he has had enough to eat. To work most effectively, animals or children have to be deprived of food to "perform" for it.

At Linwood children are never allowed to go hungry. Sometimes extra helpings of an especially coveted dessert or an extra snack are used as motivators to achieve a desired result, such as using a spoon to eat with rather than hands. Or a child may be temporarily restrained from continuing his meal until he has stopped misbehaving. Depending on his level of development, a child may also be required to sit at the table before his food is served to him and, occasionally, an addiction to certain foods may be used to motivate a child to try something new.

The fact that food is not routinely used as a reinforcer does not mean that its highly motivating aspects are ignored. But like every other motivator, food is only used in its proper context. It is the total meal situation that provides the opportunities to teach and reinforce a great variety of social skills, limit compulsions, expand food preferences, and build relationships. Other situations offer different opportunities to work with the children and contain motivators that are logical and integral parts of those situations or activities. Apart from such "natural" motivators, compulsions may be used very effectively to motivate a child, especially in the early stages of therapy.

There are two ways of using compulsions as motivators and we have seen examples of both of them. One way, for which Henry and the keys provides a perfect illustration, is to *use the compulsion itself* as a base for further activities. Since one is working with something of intrinsic interest to the child, and new activities and skills are at first closely, then more generally, associated with the compulsion, the tasks themselves are motivating, and it is relatively easy to keep the child involved and moving.

The second approach is to elicit new behaviors, teach new skills, or get the child interested in a different activity by *using a compulsion as a reward*. Task and reward do not necessarily have anything in common and are linked only in as far as one is the consequence of the other. A passing interest in soap bubbles, a delight in roughhousing, an obsessive attachment to a toy, a strong preference for a specific type of food, anything that captures and holds a child's interest, may be used in this way, and the stronger the compulsion, the higher its value as a reinforcer.

The new behavior is introduced slowly, and at first the child is rewarded frequently by being allowed to gratify his compulsion. The intervals between rewards are gradually lengthened while the task the child is asked to do becomes a little harder, a little longer, or a little different. By and by a new skill is perfected which becomes an integral and hopefully pleasurable part of the child's activities.

With some very compulsive children, newly acquired skills often temporarily become compulsions in their own right and they have to be weaned from them in the manner described above. Interests in some activity, toy, or food can eventually serve as motivators. The children are always given the opportunity of enjoying these additions to their repertoire without strings attached and it isn't until they have become a firmly established part of their routine that they are used to help shape further behaviors. Children are never made to feel that they have become vulnerable by opening themselves up to new experiences which is another way of saying that children are not punished for progress.

> *Jack was taught how to string beads to capitalize on his interest in strings. He soon became even more obsessed with the string of beads than he had been with the original bits of string. He shook it, chewed on it, dangled it in front of his eyes, and wanted to carry it around at all times. His compulsion was indulged without restrictions for a while. When it became clear that his interest in the beads persisted, Jack was asked to give them up for short periods of time while other activities were introduced that built on his stringing skills, such as sorting beads by size or color onto upright rods. Jack was rewarded for his work with the beads until gradually play with the beads was restricted to periods of free play between work sessions.*

Though a child may be strongly motivated to engage in an activity, such as playing on the rocking horse, riding a bike, or getting undressed he may lack the prerequisite skills to do so by himself. He may rely totally on an adult to help him onto the rocking horse, to hold the bicycle up, to unzip his fasteners, or to take off his coat. Instead of doing everything for the child, his interest may be used to motivate him to take a more active part in the proceedings and over a period of time became totally independent of help.

A child who eagerly strains to be put on the rocking horse may have his one foot placed in the stirrup and his hands held. If he wants to get on properly, he will have to lift his other leg over by himself. Over time he will have to hold on by himself and eventually get on alone if he wants to rock. In the same manner, the adult may pause while the child still has one arm in a sleeve and let the child's eagerness to get out of his coat motivate him to pull the coat off completely by himself. Later he will receive less and less help, until he is able to unzip, unbutton, and take off the coat on his own.

INDIVIDUAL PRIVILEGES AND REWARDS AS MOTIVATORS

Children can often be activated more or less immediately by using something they are interested in, like blowing bubbles, during the intake examination. However, intervention aimed at working toward long-lasting changes and the acquisition of new skills are usually only successful once a child has made some progress in establishing relationships. We have discussed the importance of relationships for the therapeutic process in an earlier chapter. Among other things, the range of rewards a child responds to usually increases with the establishment of relationships. Certain rewards become more clearly associated with specific situations or people, and there are increasing opportunities to demonstrate the link between performance and reward. Once there are relationships, it is also easier to convey expectations. The more clearly a child understands what is expected of him in a given situation or by a given adult, the more effectively rewards can be used for motivating him and for reinforcing specific behaviors.

As the child begins to open up and to become more active, more aware of expectations and of the consequences of his own actions, he begins to learn that he has the ability to influence outcomes. He realizes that what he does makes a difference, and this makes him more conscious of himself as a person who can ultimately be asked to take on some responsibility for himself and for his behavior.

The more individualized rewards are, the more they support this process. If children are treated uniformly by essentially interchangeable personnel who dispense impersonal and therefore largely meaningless rewards in a routine fashion ("good boy"), they will neither get the chance to develop differentiated relationships nor gain a sense of their own uniqueness.

At the beginning, all of a child's rewards and privileges stem directly from his observed preferences. The staff tries hard to discover something that has special meaning for a child and to make it available to him. He is not asked to do anything in return. The privileges are simply meant to give him pleasure and to confirm his uniqueness.

> *Eddie had always reacted well to music and had shown an interest in it. As he progressed in therapy, it was discovered that*

he had a definite musical talent and he was given piano lessons. To protect the piano from abuse it was kept locked, but Eddie had free access to the key any time he wanted to practice or play the piano. Eddie eventually left Linwood, entered a regular high school and later enrolled in a music academy. When asked what had most helped him at Linwood to overcome his problems, Eddie talked about the pleasure he had gotten from playing the piano and about the feeling he had of being special because he was the only one trusted with the key to the piano. The sense of being somebody special helped him accept himself and made it easier to face his problems and to overcome them.

Other children may not have such a definite talent, but for most of them something special can be discovered that can be theirs alone.

Denise showed interest in the house cat. She is the only one allowed to feed it. Mark is obsessed with dates, he gets to check off the office calendar every morning. Victor needs to know what each day holds, otherwise he gets very anxious. He gets to check up on the daily menu as soon as it is posted and is also admitted to the kitchen to ask about snacks.

Some children with a sweet tooth get extra candy, others with specific food preferences get double helpings of them even though other children may have to share. Since every child gets what he especially wants or needs, children rarely complain about the preferential treatment an individual receives. In fact, they usually accept individual privileges as a matter of course, and may even protect a child's right to a specific toy or an extra portion of a snack.

Similarly, one child may get in trouble for behaving in a way that is ignored or even welcomed in another one. When a child starts throwing food around for the first time, for example, and this is the first time he is actively doing something naughty, his behavior will be accepted as a sign that he is becoming aware of the environment, is beginning to experiment, or test the limits. Another child doing the same thing, might be sent from the table. He may already have had his chance to test limits, be further along in treatment and is therefore better able to control himself.

Much the same principles of choosing treats according to individual preferences and of making demands that are geared to a child's abilities, apply to the education of normal children. Parents will offer chocolate milk to one child, lemonade to another because they know their children's taste. They will watch with smiling indulgence as their toddler attempts to drink from a cup and gets soaked in the process. But they will react impatiently if their older child carelessly spills his drink all over himself.

With autistic children, expectations have to be geared to mental age and developmental level rather than to chronological age. As the children progress in treatment, expectations are raised. The children keep individual privileges with no strings attached, but some of their rewards have to be earned.

> If Tom has completed his assigned tasks in the schoolroom he is allowed to go outside and play in the sandbox, since that is the place where he is happiest, while Charles is given access to a set of blocks which he likes to arrange endlessly in intricate designs. If Victor has had a good day he is allowed to help carry in the snack tray, something no other child in his group is particularly interested in, and Frank will ask for pencil and paper to spell out lists of words whenever he is given a choice of toys during free play.

Some of the privileges the children have are connected to their level of development. Once they are able to conduct themselves properly in public, they may be included in a group of children that go on a weekly outing to a shopping mall where they can spend the money they have earned with small daily chores at Linwood. Children who are already going to school outside Linwood or have part-time jobs, may be taken to a fast food place or a restaurant once a week, where they learn to order food for themselves and can practice their table manners. Older and more advanced children may also get to go to a ball game or go camping in a small group. They may be given certain daily responsibilities, such as setting up the dining room for lunch and dinner. At mealtime these youngsters sit at a specially designated table together, where they get to serve themselves rather than having their food brought to them by counselors.

Privileges that reflect their own wants and needs confirm the children in their individuality and makes the granting or withholding of a privilege especially effective. The privileges that come with progress demonstrate that progress to the child very clearly and also set up goals other children can strive toward. Being included in the group that gets to go to the mall not only shows a child how much he is able to do, but also makes him conscious of the behavioral standards necessary not to lose this privilege.

PUNISHMENT, IGNORING, AND NATURAL CONSEQUENCES

The most successful stimuli are positive ones, with animals as well as people. Punishment may be useful and even necessary at times, but it also has serious drawbacks. For one thing, the shock value of punishment tends to decrease over time and negative sanctions have to be escalated to remain effective. For another, the anticipation of pain produces fear, which paralyzes. A threat of punishment may therefore be temporarily effective in keeping a child from doing something forbidden, but does not work well to get him to perform better. Shouting at clumsy children or slapping them to get them to hurry up or improve their performance, usually has the opposite effect of making them even clumsier and slower. Threats of retribution intimidate, rather than activate, children and punishment may also produce anger and resentment toward the person administering the punishment and resistance toward the task that has to be performed or toward learning in general. Physical punishment, especially, is not only nonconstructive, it is particularly inappropriate and ineffective with autistic children who are often impervious to pain. A child who has been slapped regularly at home or in an institution may be so conditioned that he automatically offers his hands or arms for slapping when somebody yells, or when he knows that he has misbehaved. This does not alter his particular behavior, however, nor does it teach him about acceptable behavior in general.

In some cases, with normal as well as with autistic children, punishing a behavior may even serve to perpetuate, rather than suppress it. In school, children who discover that they can attract attention by being disruptive may accept the negative consequences of their naughtiness rather than be quiet and therefore ignored. Certain compulsive behaviors, and especially screaming or hurting themselves when they are upset, sometimes result in autistic children exerting a great deal of control over their environment. Since interfering with these behaviors tends to exacerbate them to an intolerable degree, family members or teachers often go far out of their way to appease the child. As long as their behaviors attract attention and are either punished or indulged, they tend to persist or even increase. If, on the other hand, they are consistently ignored, the seeming lack of interest usually extinguishes them fairly quickly. An example is given below. The various techniques for limiting and extinguishing or changing specific types of undesirable behaviors will be described in detail in the next chapter.

> *When Andy came to Linwood he used to beat his chest with his hands until he was bruised and repeated everything that was said to him over and over again, especially if it was an instruction, a reprimand, or a request. He reacted in the same way if other children were addressed in his presence. Though he talked a lot by echoing what he heard in a normal tone of voice, his voice took on a particular guttural quality on the occasions when he*

went into his breast beating routine which was especially noticeable during meal times. Every time something was needed like more milk, meat, or dessert, Andy would call for it in his peculiar voice and hit himself. He also imitated other children's requests, and if he asked for something and was told to wait a minute, he would repeat, "Wait a minute—wait a minute."

Rather than drawing attention to this behavior by asking him to stop it, it was at first ignored. When the therapist felt that Andy was ready, she arranged things so that he received a minimum of stimulation and reinforcement for his behavior. For one thing, she talked as little as possible to the other children at the table, so that there was very little speech to imitate. For another, she addressed Andy only in a whisper and as rarely as possible. She also withheld things, like more milk when he beat his chest or talked with the unnatural, guttural tone. Within a few supper hours, the frequency of Andy's chest beating that had persisted for several years, declined dramatically, and he not only asked for food in his normal voice, but at one point even said, "I want milk," instead of his normal, "Andy wants milk."

If punishment is used, it has to be constructive to be effective in the long run. This goes for all children, but it is especially true in the case of autistic children. Punishment should do more than set up negative associations. It should teach the child about the connection between cause and effect and about his own ability to influence outcomes.

Being faced with the negative effects of his own action is an important counterpart to being motivated by the pleasure a child gets from favorite activities or special privileges. As we have seen, intrinsic motivators are the most powerful ones. In the same vein, deterrents that are directly linked to the child's own behavior arc more easily understood and are therefore more effective than some punishment, like scolding, that only expresses the adult's disapproval, something that has no immediate logical connection with the misbehavior.

This holds true for normal children as well. If a child is sent from the room without being allowed to finish his meal because he misbehaved at the table, the punishment fits the crime and makes more sense to the child than when he is sent to bed without dinner for using bad language. Autistic children to whom the rules of the outside world are hazy and confusing, who are generally uninterested in adult approval, and who have trouble establishing connections between events, have to learn about acceptable standards of behavior in well-defined, well-structured situations. They also need to develop a sense of self. Experiencing the consequences of their own actions is one way in which they learn about the impact they can have on their environment and about the control they can have over their own lives.

Right from the beginning, the Linwood treatment approach stresses the natural consequences of a child's behavior. Early on little may be said, but eventually a certain routine will establish links in the child's mind between his actions and what happens to him. Snacks, for instance, are always dispensed at a table and can only be eaten there. By quietly returning a child to his chair, or by removing food from his hands when he leaves the table, the expectations of a certain kind of behavior around snack time are demonstrated to the child. He is free to leave the table at any time, but if he wants to snack, he has to conform to certain minimal standards of behavior. Similarly, shoes and coats have to be worn to go outside in winter. Children who take off their shoes, or won't put their coats on, may have to stay in or may be returned indoors. Depending on how badly they want to play outside, they will eventually tolerate clothing.

Not every child may understand the consequences of his actions equally well or be able to control certain types of behaviors. Depending on his level of development, one child may understand what is meant when he is told that he is obviously not ready yet for some activity because he is unable to control himself, but another may not. But if children consistently experience the consequences of their actions, they will eventually be able to understand the connection.

If they take down their pants and attempt to urinate in the playground, they are taken inside to the bathroom and told that that is the correct place for that particular activity. If they start throwing food around, it will be removed. If they behave aggressively toward another child, that child will get extra attention and sympathy, while the aggressor will find himself temporarily ignored.

Children at Linwood are faced with the natural consequences of their actions even before these can be properly explained to them. If a child wrecks his room at night a cot may be set up for him in the hall where it is easier to keep an eye on him. After a night or two he will be allowed back to his own bed, but will be put in the hall again if he is still destructive. As time goes by, most children realize that they will have to demonstrate that they can control themselves to be trusted with a private room. If their privacy or their own bed is important to them, this will motivate them to limit their destructiveness. Depending on the degree of their impairment, the strength of their destructive compulsion, and the level of their understanding this process may take a longer or shorter time, and some children have to be helped further, perhaps by having windows protected or furniture nailed down. They may also be taken on outings to provide them with specific educational opportunities and experiences, before they fully understand the rules of social behaviors. For the lower level children support and controls are provided from without. Extra staff ensures one-on-one supervision in such situations.

But generally children are not taken on trips outside of Linwood until it is judged that they are able to control some of their inappropriate behavior. Sometimes an attempt is made too early or a child tests the limits and will have to be reminded of what may be acceptable at Linwood and what is expected in public. The following examples show how such situations can be dealt with constructively.

> *A child might be judged to be ready for a trip culminating in an ice cream treat, but have an upset on the way. He will be returned to Linwood and told that a mistake had been made, that it was actually too early for him to go. Beyond losing out on the trip he is not penalized, however, and the promised treat is brought back for him. This makes it easier for the child to accept the limits and prevents anger from building up. At the same time, the expectations are not lowered.*
>
> *On a next outing, the child may misbehave more purposefully, because he counts on getting the refreshments regardless of his behavior. For the first few times he might be allowed to get away with this testing of the limits, be returned to Linwood, but have a treat brought to him. But after a further unsuccessful attempt, no refreshment will be forthcoming. The therapist will reiterate the type of behavior expected of children who are taken along and are given ice cream, and the child will be told that since he was unable to make it through several times, the therapists will decide when he is ready. After a period of several weeks during which he watches the others leave on their outing without him, the child will again be included in the group, and by that time he is usually able to behave appropriately.*

The more advanced a child is and the more it becomes possible to communicate with him, the more effective this kind of approach becomes. If a child has a special problem with destructiveness, he may be told that the school cannot afford a usual treat for him because they have to replace something he broke. If he keeps running away, he may be told that he obviously cannot be trusted outside and will have to be excluded from any outings or trips. And the more purposefully a child acts and the more he can be expected to control himself, the more strictly the rules will be enforced and the child faced with the consequences of his actions.

Brian loved ice cream and was eager to join the older boys on their weekly outing to the ice cream parlor. Though he had made a lot of progress, he still had some habits that made it difficult to take him along. Among other things, his toileting habits were erratic, and he frequently soiled in the car when he was being driven somewhere.

It was finally decided that Brian might be ready to comport himself properly and he was taken along. Before leaving, the expectations were made very clear to him: He was to use the toilet before the group left. There was to be no soiling in the car. He readily agreed and behaved well on the way out, but as soon as he had had his refreshment and just before arriving back at the house, he soiled himself. He was told that it was obviously too early to take him on outings. He did not get to go for the next weeks and also did not have refreshments brought back to him.

Another boy was driven back all the way from an overnight camping trip when he broke the rules that had been specified for participation in the outing. He probably counted on being able to get away with some infraction, since the camp was several hours' drive away from Linwood. The prompt reaction obviously surprised him and he was less inclined to test the limits on future occasions.

The most advanced children are motivated and regulated almost exclusively by being confronted by the short and long-term consequences of their own actions. They may set their own rewards as in the case of Norman, who wrote out his own schedule of daily rewards and a culminating weekly treat which consisted of Miss Simons feeding him an ice cream sundae. And they lose rewards, treats, or privileges if they behave inappropriately.

We have already mentioned that no child is ever threatened with the loss of anything essential such as food. In addition, treats that occur only rarely, perhaps once a week, such as swimming or a trip to a shopping mall, are usually not made conditional on a child's long-term behavior. Only the most advanced children who are nearly ready to leave Linwood and who can be expected to control their behavior consistently, work toward more infrequent or spaced-out rewards. But even they will not have to earn one-of-a-kind treats, such as seasonal celebrations or special outings.

So far we have focused on ways of drawing children out and of activating them to change and learn. We have also shown that there are effective deterrents that can be used to change behaviors that interfere with the children's social adjustment. And we have demonstrated the importance of finding the most effective motivators to encourage change.

In the following chapter we will describe in detail how behaviors commonly exhibited by autistic children can be changed and limited. At the same time it should become clear that the basic approach used for shaping the behavior of autistic children is applicable to education in general. Though autistic children initially develop and behave markedly differently from normal children, their course of development parallels that of normal babies in many ways once they begin to open up. Even some of their most striking characteristics, such as their need for sameness, are only extreme manifestations of a phase most normal infants go through. One of the differences is that normal children usually progress quickly and naturally through the stages of development while autistic children tend to remain "stuck" unless they are given help.

What specific techniques are used to work with particular behavior depends on the individual child, on his level of impairment, his characteristics, and his needs and his strengths. The basic approach in each case is to set limits to the undesirable behavior while developing existing elements in the child's repertoire to make it more varied, more acceptable, and more functional.

FIVE
✦✦✦

Limit Setting

INTRODUCTION

One of the main goals in the education of all children is to encourage them to grow more and more independent, while at the same time become acceptable and productive members of society. To be able to do this, a child has to be helped to discard old habits while developing new skills. He must learn to substitute more long term goals for immediate gratification. He must be given increasing control over his own life while being taught to accept additional responsibilities for himself and others.

Education is thus a constant juggling act between letting go and holding on, between encouraging independence and setting limits on a child's activities and behaviors.

Setting limits and enforcing them takes a great deal of skill, patience, and persistence as well as the conviction that what one is asking is reasonable and in the best interest of the child. If a child understands the reasons behind limits imposed on him, it usually makes it easier for him to comply with them. On the other hand, unreasonable or capricious demands, limits that are difficult to check on, or rules that are enforced inconsistently, weaken the adult's credibility and confuse the child.

If no one is there, for example, to see whether a child comes home at a prescribed time, if he gets punished one day for being late while lateness is ignored on another day, he will have a hard time learning to be on time and will tend to ignore or test other limits as well.

Limit setting has to be done intelligently, creatively, and realistically. It has to take into account what an individual child is able to do, rather than imposing standard expectations on all children. Adding a privilege or a reward to a demand is always more effective than threatening punishment in case of noncompliance. This is true at every age level. One high school boy's grades improved dramatically when he was promised that he could drive his mother's car to school one day per week for every *A* he got on his report card.

Having a child live with the natural consequences of his actions is another effective way of limiting undesirable behavior. A child who is careless of his possessions and keeps losing newly bought clothes, sports equipment, or toys will learn more quickly to remember to account for his possessions when he has to make do with hand-me-downs or cannot play with his team for a while, than when he is scolded but knows that the lost things will be replaced by his parents. In setting limits a sense of humor is a great help and so is flexibility: a willingness to see another's point of view and to seek alternatives, rather than getting into confrontations and end up in an exhausting and potentially destructive power struggle.

Children often go through phases, for example, during which they strongly resist going to bed. They may be afraid of the dark, be afraid of bad dreams, or may try to take increasing charge over their own lives. In any case, they usually find endless excuses to delay going to sleep. Parents who are willing to give a little, usually manage to shorten these periods considerably. Instead of bodily dragging a reluctant child to bed or threatening to lock him into his room, they try to create an atmosphere in which bedtime becomes an especially attractive part of the day. It may be a time for reading a story to the child, if that is what he especially enjoys, or the whole family may share a favorite activity like listening to records or singing together. If the child fusses too long over getting ready for bed, these activities may have to be curtailed—another way of teaching a child to accept responsibility for his own behavior by impressing him with the consequences of his own actions.

Sometimes it is necessary to find a compromise or to temporarily suspend a rule. Nap times or regular rest periods may be suspended for a visit or an outing. A child who is expected to stay in his own bed at night may need the parents' closeness when he has had a bad nightmare or when he is sick. As long as it is understood that this is done for a good reason and under special, clearly defined circumstances the rule is unlikely to be challenged on other occasions.

Finally, adults should be able to admit when they have made a mistake. Some rules, limits, or demands may have been imposed hastily. They might be unfair, impossible to keep up, too restrictive, or outdated. A child may have outgrown his need for a midday nap, a school-age child may work better after a couple of hours of relaxing, playing, or running around than being asked to do his homework when he comes home from school, an older child may be ready for a more relaxed curfew. Listening to a child's arguments with an open mind and yielding gracefully does not impair the adult's authority. Instead it gives the child the feeling of being treated with consideration and fairness. If he is given a reasonable say over his own life, he will also more readily accept the responsibilities that go along with this. This goes for all children, normal as well as impaired ones. Examples of flexible limit setting with autistic children will be examined in detail in the section on avoiding power struggles.

All children need limits, especially during times when their sense of self is weak or confused because they are in transition from one stage of life to another or from one level of development to another. One such major transitional phase occurs between two and three when children alternately struggle to get away from the mother and cling to her, answer every demand with "no," yet often do not seem to know what it is they want. Another unsettled stage is adolescence where teenagers, teetering on the edge of early adulthood, are torn between their need to test themselves and establish their independence, and their fear of leaving the support and security of their families. Autistic children who enter treatment experience a similar confusion. Their sense of self is almost nonexistent or at best fluid, and because they are reluctant to leave the safety of their isolation, they stubbornly and anxiously cling to routines or compulsive behaviors.

Like crabs who are in the process of discarding their old shells and who hide under stones from predators, all of these children who go through major changes and upheavals are vulnerable, prey to many anxieties, fearful to expose themselves, quick to dig in, and hard to budge. They need to be reassured that the passage from one stage to the next is safe. One way of doing this is to provide a firm framework of rules, expectations, and limits that provides support and guidelines on the road into the unknown.

Particularly for the autistic child, limits create structure and a feeling of security. They assure him that there is somebody in charge who will protect him from the consequences of his own impulsive actions as well as against the intrusions or attacks of others. While limits may at times be experienced as punishment, they nevertheless often come as a great relief to a child who is struggling with the overwhelming task of controlling himself and his environment. Without this support his ability to function in new and more productive ways remains severely limited.

> Lee, the child described at the beginning of this book, spontaneously described the difference Miss Simons' approach to him had made. He told her one day that there are three kinds of people. "There are people who are KIND and FIRM (with a strong accent on both words). That is you. You are kind and you are not afraid of being firm. That makes me feel secure. Then there are people who are KIND and fi.i.r.r.m ("Firm" was said in a whisper-

ing, somewhat trembling voice). Those are people like your friends I like so much. They are always kind, but they are afraid to be firm with me. That makes me feel sorry for them. Then there are the people in institutions. They are FIRM (said loudly and sternly) and only kind when parents come to visit. That makes me feel lonely."

As with all interventions used with autistic children, limit setting is a slow process, which has to be accomplished in minute steps and only after periods of careful observations. In the following sections, we will examine various situations or conditions for which limit setting is necessary and describe specific techniques useful with autistic children but also applicable to normal children.

SETTING LIMITS TO DANGEROUS BEHAVIORS

When a child first enters Linwood, his behavior is usually not interfered with since he needs time to adjust and the staff needs time to observe and assess his functioning. The only limits that are imposed from the beginning are those that are necessary to ensure the safety of the children.

One of the characteristics of autistic children is their inability to recognize danger. Unsupervised, they often get themselves into potentially harmful situations. Like sleepwalkers they may be found standing on high window ledges or on rooftops. They may climb on tables, cabinets, or other equipment, and launch themselves into space or dash into the street in front of oncoming traffic with total disregard for the consequences. They tend to burn themselves because they do not understand warnings about hot pipes or flames, or they injure themselves by punching or kicking at windows or walls.

Obviously the first step in limiting any of these dangerous behaviors is to make the environment as safe as possible and to never leave the children unsupervised. This not only takes unswerving vigilance, but planning ahead for every eventuality as well as quick reactions and inventiveness. Autistic children who often seem totally oblivious to their surroundings and do not react to what is said within their hearing, nevertheless often prove to be better informed about the "lay of the land" than even the adult supervisor. And they are not only incredibly observant, they also go after the things they want with single-minded determination. Furthermore, children who at times seem passive to the point of immobility, can move as fast as quicksilver when they have a specific goal in mind. They take advantage of the slightest distraction to escape or to get what they are after and they are endlessly inventive when it comes to ways of circumventing supervision.

One budding pyromaniac produced matches out of nowhere and then used flour he stole from the kitchen to extinguish the many little fires he set at every opportunity. Another boy managed to disassemble the metal plates, bolts, and hinges that held the front door in place without anybody noticing anything, until he brought the whole thing crashing down with one swift push. Since he was known to have a predilection for taking things apart, he was always carefully watched, and anything resembling a tool was taken from him. Yet he had somehow managed to smuggle in a tiny piece of metal between his toes which he used as a screwdriver while sitting, day after day, apparently unmoving, with his back against the door.

Yet another boy palmed nails, stuck them into one hole of electrical floor outlets, then dropped another nail into the second hole, thus short-circuiting the outlet without getting hurt.

Often autistic children are indiscriminate in what they eat. Some of the things that they put into their mouths are simply inedible, but sometimes they have a taste for substances that are dangerous and manage to get them despite the most careful supervision. One little girl craved tar. She ran away one day when a road, separated from Linwood by a wooded hill, was being tarred and was found happily gorging on the fresh tar which she alone had smelled. More dangerous, though rare, are glass eaters.

One little Linwood patient had to go to the hospital because of severe seizures. He was partially paralyzed, isolated in a crib with high sides and further hampered by an IV. The nightstand was pushed out of his reach, and he was only given paper cups to drink from because of his known tendency to chew glass. Nevertheless, particles of glass were discovered in his mouth one day. Unobtrusive observations revealed that he was able to wriggle himself far enough down in his crib to be able to reach through the slats of the crib with his leg, to grab the thermometer on the nightstand between two toes and to maneuver it back into the crib.

With all of these potentially dangerous behaviors the most important thing is to make the environment as safe as possible, to supervise the children closely, and to involve them in alternative activities whenever possible. As they become more responsive and better able to understand rules and limits, the natural consequences of their behavior are demonstrated to them. If they open doors in a moving car, for instance, they have to forego outings. If they run out into traffic, they may not walk by themselves or may not even be taken on walks or excursions at all for a while.

Even children who are not very far along in treatment can be taught to limit such dangerous behaviors as eating nonedible materials. Many children go through a period of chewing on crayons. If they do this only occasionally or only eat small amounts, the best thing to do is to ignore it. If it is necessary to interfere, the child is given a small piece of crayon to draw with. The therapist stays with him and as soon as he starts putting the crayon in his mouth, shows him some food, like a small piece of cracker, and says to him, "Crackers we eat, crayons we draw with." While the child is given the piece of cracker, his hand may be guided to draw with the crayon. If he puts the crayon in his mouth anyway, before it can be prevented, the therapist will say, "You ate it," and change activities.

If the child wants to draw, this will eventually motivate him to keep from putting the crayon in his mouth. The compulsion to eat the crayon may be stronger than the wish to draw, however. In that case the child may need a little additional help. He will be given a very small piece of crayon and will only be allowed to make one line with it. After that the crayon is immediately taken away and the child praised for the drawing. This serves to prevent the child from being tempted and at the same time focuses on the desired activity, the drawing.

If, after several attempts to stop him in this manner, the child persists in trying to eat crayons, it is best to discontinue the activity before it turns into a power struggle. After keeping all crayons out of sight for a while, a new attempt can be made. At that time, of course, there is no reference made to the previous habit.

LIMITING SELF AGGRESSIVE BEHAVIORS

There are other behaviors that put children at risk that may be even harder to control than those that are caused by their inability to foresee or recognize danger. Many autistic children are severely self-aggressive when they first come to Linwood. They scratch or bite themselves raw, they hit or slap themselves, bang their heads rhythmically against any hard surface they can find, or pull out their own hair until they have large bald spots. In some severe cases children have even endangered their own eyesight by poking or digging into their eyes as if to gouge them out. Other children bite the inside of their lips bloody or almost chew through their cheeks.

Whether self injury in autistic children is the expression of anger or frustration turned inward, is a sign of some other strong emotions such as anxiety over change, or whether it is an obsessive habit that got out of control, is often impossible to determine. In some cases it may be the result of self-stimulation carried to excess, such as rocking, combined with head banging, or it may have become an attention-getting device. Regardless of the possible causes it is often apparent that there is a certain urgency in stopping or limiting at least the more extreme manifestations of self-aggression as quickly as possible.

Any kind of punishment in these cases is not only useless, but could easily aggravate the problem. To hit a child for hitting himself—or others—sends a very contradictory and confusing message to him, quite apart from fueling feelings of helplessness and anger. Isolating a self-abusing child who is already imprisoned by his inability to communicate only locks him more tightly into his inner isolation.

On the other hand, it is understandable that adults may be hard-put not to overreact to self-aggression. It is extremely painful to have to watch a child hurt himself, and the very real possibility of major, lasting injuries in particularly severe and persistent cases may call for protective measures or temporary restraints.

As a rule, however, focusing on the self aggression by either interfering with it too directly or by openly and emotionally reacting to it is neither helpful nor effective and may even produce additional problems, such as turning self abuse into a weapon. Children who come to sense their parents' dismay or the staff's concern over self-destructive behaviors may eventually come to use this to control their environment instead of developing other, more positive ways of communicating their wishes or feelings. If a child stops his self-aggression as soon as he is alone, it is more than likely that he is using it mainly as an effective attention-getting device. Very often this kind of self-abuse stops if it is consistently ignored. On the other hand, cajoling or attempts to reason with the child as well as scolding or punishment may prove to actually reinforce the behavior, since a child may want attention at any price, even if it is negative.

Ignoring the behavior does not, of course, mean ignoring the child. It is important to give a child as much positive attention as possible when he is not hurting himself to keep him busy and occupied and not to wait to involve him in an activity until some negative behavior calls for distraction. In the same way, normal children who are quiet and well behaved should get as much or more attention from parents and teachers than children who are disruptive. This is the most effective way of making it clear that it is neither necessary nor useful to misbehave to be noticed. In extreme cases it may be necessary to protect the child from himself. Andreas periodically had great open sores on the sides of his head from hitting himself. During times when he seemed especially tense or agitated he was given a helmet to wear. Other children have had their hands wrapped to prevent them from scratching themselves bloody.

If the self-aggressive behavior occurs without observable triggers and the child is difficult to distract, he can at least be offered support and alternatives to help him through an episode and to lessen the physical damage to himself. Children who chew on the insides of their cheeks, for example, can be given a substitute, such as straws to bite on.

> *Mark came to Linwood at age six with arms that were raw from his biting on them and with hands that seemed deformed because of the scars and ridged calluses which his gnawing on them had left. It proved impossible to keep him distracted and occupied enough to stop this assault on himself. His biting was accepted as something he had to do but he was also told that the staff wanted to help him. This was accomplished by wrapping wet towels around his arms, so that he had the satisfaction of biting into something soft, while his injuries had a chance to heal. During the course of his stay at Linwood, Mark learned alternate and less harmful ways of expressing his emotions. At first he would come for help when he felt an overwhelming urge to bite himself and indicate his need for towels by running to a therapist with outstretched arms. Today he is mostly able to control the impulse by himself and instead may scream or cry when he is in distress. During one recent upset he twisted all the buttons off his sweater, but was then able to calmly sew them back on when the episode was over.*

Sometimes a mild reminder, such as touching a child's hand or arm, may be sufficient to stop the self abuse. In rare cases a child may have to be restrained more forcefully from injuring himself. But this is always done in a way that still leaves him as much freedom to move as possible. While the therapist holds or restrains the child lightly from behind, the self aggression as such is ignored and the therapist directs his attention as much as possible away from the child. He may talk with another child in the room, roll a ball to him with one hand or with his foot, or sing a song mentioning the names or activities of the other children in the group.

In extreme cases of especially violent or active children, or with children who do not tolerate being touched or held closely, a sheet, folded lengthwise several times and wrapped around their middle proves an effective restraint. It can be twisted in the back so as to give the adult a firm grip on the child, but leaves the child relatively free to move his arms and legs.

> *A restraint like this was necessary for little Alfred who kept climbing onto tables and other high places in an attempt to jump*

off head first. When he was not too upset or self-aggressive, he would run for the sheet and hand it to the therapist which showed that he really wanted to be stopped. He stood on the table, trembling all over and waiting. Then he jumped, safe in the knowledge that he would not be allowed to injure himself. The need for this kind of restraint is rare, however. Over a thirty year period, it was only used with about four children.

Sometimes there is an observable rhythm to a small child's self-abuse which the therapist can pick up if he lightly holds the child from behind. Jeanne Simons has often been able to use this rhythm to temporarily stop self-aggressive behavior. Moving or walking with the child, she at first adjusts to the child's rhythm, and may even accentuate it by humming softly and monotonously to the beat of their combined movements. She is very much aware of the child's every move, but at the same time her attention is ostensibly directed toward other children in the group so that the focus on the child and on his self-aggression never becomes too intense.

After a while Miss Simons may try to change the rhythm very slightly. If the child adjusts to the change, she may alter her pace or the beat of her humming even more, accelerating or slowing it down. If the child responds, the change is often effective to stop the self aggression for that particular period or that particular day.

As long as the child is largely unaware of his environment, the therapist is simply an object to the child and it is important not to try and intrude on his activity as a person but simply become an object that moves with him. Once a relationship exists, a child may actually seek out a therapist and take his hands if he wants his self aggression stopped for a while.

It is imperative, of course, that the whole environment be made as unstressful as possible. Careful observation often reveals objects, sounds, or activities a child is especially fearful of. He may react with increased self abuse to specific demands, to the disruption of a regular routine or to other children who are particularly active or noisy. The reader will remember the case of Lee who became frantically anxious when he was shown his room in Miss Simons' house. She eventually realized that he was afraid of getting locked in and was able to defuse his anxiety and stop the self abuse by creating a dutch door that preserved her privacy but assured the boy of free access.

It is not always possible to shield children from stresses. Victor gets very agitated when skies are overcast, for example. Mark is especially afraid of small children. Both boys are frequently in situations that trigger anxiety and both of them have had to learn slowly to tolerate what cannot be helped. A gradual program of desensitization is most useful in these cases, frequent talks about the weather with Victor, daily encounters with other children for Mark in which he was at first protected from any direct contact until he learned that he would not get hurt when other children were around. Though he still keeps a wary eye on them and tends to give them a wide berth, he is now able to enter a room where smaller children run and play and does not exhibit severe anxiety any more even in such relatively unfamiliar places as stores.

The best way to prevent or limit self aggression is to keep the child active by engaging him in a game or with a toy. Again, observation will suggest the kind of activity most likely to interest and distract him. Sometimes staff or parents notice that a child is less self-abusive while he is outside, or that he stops screaming when he is allowed to sit in a certain corner of the room or when he can hold on to a specific object. It is, of course, tempting to send the child outside or hand him some food or a particular toy every time he becomes upset or self abusive. The problem is that a child usually catches on to the fact that his actions have certain predictable results, and the relief may be short-lived. What was pleasurable may quickly turn into an obsessive need in its own right, and increased self abuse may result if it is not forthcoming. Or the child may begin to use his self abusive behavior more self consciously as a weapon to control the environment.

In one institution children are put into an isolation room whenever they become violent or self-aggressive. When they calm down, they are released and are given a sweet or a cookie. Instead of limiting the undesirable behavior, this sequence may actually set up the association in the child's mind that acting out is eventually rewarded and that they can generate sweets at will.

At Linwood a child is indulged with his favorite activities only to the extent to which they fit naturally into the regular flow of the daily schedule. They are seen as helpful tools to break the stranglehold of negative or self-abusive behaviors. But a child is not sent outside regularly to stop his screaming. He is expected to come in for snack time or other planned activities. If it is time to go to the dining room, he will be asked to leave his toys behind or put them away, even if these demands result in a temporary increase in self abuse or screaming. If it is ignored and other activities are focused on, the negative behavior tends to diminish and eventually disappear. Sometimes a child has to be gradually weaned from some pleasurable or obsessive behavior so as not to put too much pressure on him and increase or maintain his self abuse.

Philip gets agitated when he has to sit still for any length of time. Lately he has developed a need to take his pants down and

to smooth his hands over his abdomen, buttocks, and legs. He is
not allowed to do this in the dining room, but he is free to get up
from his chair when he needs to and to go through his routine in
the corridor. He is then able to return and resume eating normally.

SETTING LIMITS TO AGGRESSION TOWARD OTHERS

Stopping self aggression is important, but it is not enough. The child next has to be helped to develop to the point where he relates enough so he can start to turn his anger outward when appropriate. Without treatment, autistic children are often nonaggressive and may even have to be taught to openly express anger or to defend themselves against aggressive acts by others.

When children do begin to exhibit aggressive behavior it is usually first toward the staff, and often the person the child is most attached to tends to come in for an inordinate share of the abuse. We have already discussed the possible reason for this phenomenon in the chapter on relationships. Though this is usually seen as a positive development, it is obviously important to control the situation and to relieve a staff member before he loses his patience or his tolerance. Autistic children are often especially atuned to the emotional state of the adults with whom they have a relationship or with whom they interact. Any feelings of impatience or anger, however well concealed, will usually be sensed by the child and tend to be experienced as rejection. It is therefore better for the staff to take turns working with especially aggressive children and it is healthier if a therapist asks for help before he is pushed beyond his point of endurance.

A child's need to express his anger or other emotions must be respected without putting the environment at undue risk. Children who throw sand, for example, may be allowed to have the sandbox to themselves at certain times of the day. Throwing toys may be limited to certain areas of a room or the hallway, or hard objects a child routinely attempts to throw, such as plates or cups, may be replaced with soft ones made out of paper or plastic. A child who attempts to stab another one with the point of a pencil will be given thick crayons to draw and write with. If he tries to hit a child by aiming a block or another hard object at him, he will be given balls made out of crumpled up paper instead.

Sometimes a child in the throes of a temper tantrum hits out indiscriminately. If a staff member happens to get in the way of such an attack any resulting hurt must be handled as discreetly as possible. Children are often frightened by their own uncontrolled emotions and reactive anger or the knowledge that they have hurt somebody will frighten them even more and tend to drive emotions underground. Reactivity also tends to focus attention on the aggressive behavior and prolong it. It takes a great deal of self control, patience, and understanding to accept and tolerate a child's aggressiveness, to continue working with him calmly and cheerfully, and to look past his behavior to his healthy potential.

As the child makes some progress, he will be expected to bear some share of the responsibility of not hurting others even when he is angry. A child who kicks a staffer when he is angry or upset may have his shoes removed and is told by the therapist, "If you kick me with your shoes on, it will hurt a lot and I might not be able to stay patient, but if you kick me with your feet, it will hurt me, but I will stay patient." This serves the additional purpose of reassuring the child that his anger is not only legitimate, but that expressing it within the limits set will not cause him any problems or disrupt his relationship with the adult.

Children are also taught to express aggressiveness in more controlled and acceptable ways. Older children may be taught to have a go at each other with boxing gloves when they are angry at each other. At first staffers may hold on to each child's belt to make sure the bout does not get out of hand. Later the boys may be taught proper boxing etiquette as well as concepts of fair play that govern a sport like boxing. Or they may be given sponge baseball bats to swat at each other in order to let off steam.

Once a child has begun to communicate, he will be reminded that he can express his needs, frustrations, demands, or anger verbally. Actual incidents are reenacted and possible responses are rehearsed with the children. "If Johnny tries to take your toy, you can pull it away from him. If Tommy comes too close to you, you can tell him 'go away.' If Jan pushes you, you can push him back and you can say 'no.'" With older children group sessions in which the events of the day are discussed also lend themselves to such reenactments and to the rehearsal of expressing anger appropriately. Some examples of such session will be found in a later chapter dealing with emotions.

All along attempts are made to channel a child's aggressive energy into more acceptable and constructive activities. Instead of throwing blocks around indiscriminately he may be encouraged to build something out of blocks and then knock the building down by throwing a ball at it. This may, in time, lead to a proper game of bowling, which in turn introduces counting of the knocked-down pins and even adding to arrive at a final score.

Though children are encouraged to direct their anger outward, care has to be taken that aggressiveness does not gain a child automatic attention. If a child attacks another child, attention is first given to the attacked child to make it clear to the aggressor that this is no way for him to get extra attention. The child who hits, pushes, bites, or scratches another child is gently restrained from continuing but is otherwise ignored, while the other child is consoled or encouraged to defend himself. After a short time of focusing on the victim, the aggressor is then involved in some activity that keeps him out of the range of the other children and more constructively occupied, without referring to the altercation.

Only children who are further along in treatment and can be expected to control themselves may be reminded of what is and what isn't acceptable or may be involved in a later discussion of the incident. It also has to be remembered that an aggressive child may have been provoked. Sometimes a child who seems to be the victim of an attack has actually been the instigator of the trouble by teasing the other child, grabbing his toys, getting too close to him, or by otherwise purposely or inadvertently upsetting him. In every case the child who has been provoked is protected and is shown acceptable ways of reacting while the child who upset him is either temporarily ignored, restrained, or kept busy in the least stressful way for him.

As in the case of self-abuse, the most effective method of shortening, limiting, and eventually extinguishing aggressive acts is to ignore them. This is not always easy, however, and children are very astute at testing how genuine the staff's seeming disinterest in aggressive behaviors really is.

> *Larry was a severely withdrawn and compulsive little boy. After several years of treatment he began to develop a close relationship with Miss Simons. At first he became cuddly, then aggressive, and eventually he started to throw objects around. At first he did this only when he was upset, but later he seemed to do it for the pure pleasure of it, and it became a daily activity. As long as the objects he threw were small, the staff tried not to pay obvious attention to this activity. But Larry sensed the underlying alertness and did not seem pleased with the lack of attention he commanded. So gradually he began to choose larger and larger objects to throw, making very sure that the staff saw him doing it.*
>
> *Once, he was getting ready to throw a big truck and two staff members tried simultaneously to prevent him from doing so. He laughed out loud. Though it was wonderful to see him come alive in this way, the staff also had to make sure to protect the other children. They tried to distract him instead of limiting him, but Larry had found a sure-fire way of getting everybody's attention any time he felt like it, and was not about to let go of his advantage. It was obviously time to set some limits.*
>
> *One morning Larry came in preceded by his lunch box, which he threw so hard that all the glass jars of food it contained broke. The box burst open and the staff had to hold off barefoot children*

while they cleaned up the mess. Larry watched with obvious en-joyment. The therapist told him that it was too early in the day to throw things and that he would have to spend some time in the play cabin if he did not quiet down a little. He looked at her at-tentively but the next moment another big crash and gales of laughter proved that he had not taken her too seriously. When he was sat down in the cabin he first looked at her in a puzzled way, then he started to cry—the first real tears he had ever been seen to shed. It was hard to insist on his staying in the cabin, but Miss Simons felt that having to experience the consequences of his ac-tions would be more helpful to the child in the long run than be-ing let off the hook too early.

On another occasion this proved to be true. Larry had just barely missed the head of a child with a big truck he had thrown and had been sent to his seat in the play cabin. He cried so pathetically that Miss Simons relented and gave him permission to come out. There was nothing pathetic about the little boy who came bursting out of the cabin, however. He charged at the bookshelf and, before it could be prevented, brought it crashing down. The he ran back to the cabin and sat down on his seat again, laughing so hard that he had to hold onto his stomach. He did not come out of the cabin again until he was given permission, and for the rest of the morning he played peacefully. By and by his throwing lessened as did his need for so much attention. He started to form good relationships with other staff members and only insisted on being with Miss Simons when he was in great distress or engaged in a new activity.

When it is necessary to restrict a child's activities, to remove him from a situation, or to have him face the consequences of his actions, he is bound to experience this as unpleasant interference with his needs or even as punishment. But if it is done right, limit setting can be healing. To be con-structive, no confrontation should ever conclude on a negative note. The child should always end up with a positive experience.

If he has thrown the pieces of a puzzle around in frustration and has been made to pick them up again, he will not be left with his feelings of failure or anger. Instead the therapist may start the puzzle for him once he has calmed down, and help him to complete it before it is put away for good. If he has been removed from the room because he was hitting out at people, he will be brought back as soon as possible and engaged in some positive interaction with them. Sometimes a teacher will have to send an aggressive child out of the room and hand him over to another staff member for a while. This may well be a person with a particularly good relationship with the child who may be able to help him control himself, or it may be somebody who carries special authority, such as the director, from whom a scolding is especially impressive. After a while the child is returned to his own room where he may be consoled and reintegrated into the group's activities.

In no case is there any further mention of the misbehavior, nor is it referred to at a later time. A child who has to be sent from the dining room for throwing food around will not be greeted the next day by a remark such as, "Well, do you think you can behave yourself today?" Every situation is seen as unique and every day carries with it the opportunity for a fresh start. There are goals and standards toward which the children are pointed, but it is up to them how long it takes them to get there.

One boy, who lost out on a trip to the soda fountain, anxiously asked whether he had lost his chance. He obviously thought about "chance" as a limited commodity, something tangible which, once lost, was gone forever. He was reassured that "at Linwood we never run out of chances." To the autistic child with his literalness and concrete thinking, this answer must conjure up the image of an inexhaustible cornucopia of chances. Being a bright and articulate child, this particular boy's response, after he had pondered the answer for a while, was "That's right, we never run out of chances, but the time between chances may differ."

The assurance of unlimited chances is the most important corollary to limit setting. On their road toward health, these children have to contend with many limits and suffer numerous setbacks and frustrations. If all their upsets, regressions, and small failures are treated as a natural part of learning and they are not permanently penalized for them, they do not need to lose courage even if progress is slow and uneven. There is always another chance around the next bend of the road.

SETTING LIMITS TO DESTRUCTIVE BEHAVIOR

Every so often an autistic child becomes destructive. At home such children may smash, rip, or break everything that isn't nailed down and their homes often resemble prison cells, with all small or breakable objects moved out of range or locked up. At Linwood too, such children may punch or kick holes in walls or doors, break windows, throw around tables or chairs, tear their clothes, or rip off fixtures. Generally such aggressiveness is seen as an expression of strong feelings a child cannot deal with in other ways. At first the child may not yet be in touch with his own anger or may be too timid to express it openly. Some children may only be able to feel anger vicariously. They get pleasure out of watching other children act out emotions which they themselves are unable to express.

Nathaniel at four was an unsmiling child who sat by himself in front of the window most of the day, talking to himself. He did not show any interest in what was going on around him though it was possible, as time went by, to have him sit nearer other people.

Even though he was afraid of children in general, he became fascinated with three-year-old Allen, an active, mischievous little boy, who took great pleasure in breaking toys and furniture. Allen's specialty was throwing blocks at the windows. He would jump up and down with pleasure when his aim was right and the window broke. One day when Allen was quietly playing with blocks, Nathaniel took two large blocks and slowly walked toward him. He put the blocks down, gently shoving them toward Allen. "Break window," he whispered. Allen promptly threw the blocks and one of them broke the window. Nathaniel covered his ears, but it was the first time that there was the beginning of a smile on his face. He stayed for a while near Allen and even got more blocks for him but the therapist decided that one broken window was enough. She sat down with Nathaniel next to Allen and helped him build a tower which she then encouraged Nathaniel to knock down. In this way she capitalized on the budding involvement of Nathaniel with Allen and laid the groundwork for Nathaniel's destructive urges to come out more directly and acceptably.

In some cases a child's destructiveness may simply be the result of an excessive interest in taking things apart. It is basically the same kind of curiosity that leads normal children into prying off the tops of containers, poking fingers into openings, taking apart toys, emptying drawers and closets, and generally getting into every possible kind of mischief. With some autistic children the need to take things apart may become an obsession and may focus on particular objects.

When a new heating system was put in at Linwood, Teddy followed the work with great interest. He knew exactly where the network of pipes ran under the floors and at every opportunity he pried them up and broke them.

Teddy seemed to have a passion for anything connected with plumbing and an overpowering need to take things apart or to break them open. He systematically attacked faucets, wrecked toilets, and broke any other installation he could reach. He was fast, ingenious, and determined and could not be left unsupervised for even the shortest period of time without wrecking something.

During one Christmas break Teddy was unable to go home because his parents lived too far away to make a trip practicable. So Miss Simons took him to live with her at her cottage for a few days. It was an exhausting time since Teddy, sensing new fields of endeavor, had to be watched at all times to keep him from wreaking havoc. During the day it was easier to keep an eye on him but the nights posed a special difficulty, since Teddy, like many autistic children, had long wakeful periods. Whenever he judged Miss Simons to be asleep, he would head for the bathroom and his favorite activity.

Miss Simons quickly solved the problem of night-time supervision by attaching a strong thread to the bed in Teddy's room. Invisible against the floor board, it led from his room to hers and ended in a little bell, which jangled anytime Teddy moved in his bed. He must have been greatly puzzled to encounter Miss Simons in the corridor whenever he tried to leave his room at night and to be gently escorted back to bed without ever reaching the desired goal.

The same child went around ripping out any plants, bushes, and small trees he could reach and thus singlehandedly defeated any attempts at landscaping at Linwood. As it proved impossible to keep him under constant supervision, keep him otherwise occupied, or deflect him from his purpose, a compromise had to be found. The solution to the problem was as creative as it was simple. Teddy was given his own tree in the yard with which he could do whatever he wanted, on the condition that he left all other plants alone.

He immediately asked for a hatchet, but was told that all he could use were stones and his hands. Slowly, methodically, and doggedly Teddy went about destroying the tree. Branch by branch he sawed away with sharp stones he found in the yard. He ripped at the tree with his teeth and clawed at it with his nails, and over the course of a year reduced the twelve foot ash to a trunk and the tip of the crown. At that point he was given a hatchet and under supervision was allowed to cut the whole tree down. By the time he was through with the trees, Teddy's destructiveness had diminished to the point where it was no longer a problem.

Teddy's case is a perfect example of some of the ways in which children with uncontrollable destructive behavior are dealt with at Linwood. First of all, it is necessary to protect the environment, to supervise the children, and to keep them occupied as much as possible in order to contain the impact of their destructiveness. This often takes a great deal of forethought and ingenuity, such as the thread tied to Teddy's door to check on his movements at night.

But while the children's destructive urges have to be reasonably limited, their need to express them is accepted and they are given every opportunity to do so without hurting either themselves or others. Rather than calling a child bad for destroying things and punishing him for it, the environment is structured in ways to make it possible for him to indulge his needs safely and without doing too much damage.

> *Tom, who was initially uninterested in food and had a difficult time remaining in the dining room, occupied himself by gouging at the table top around his plate with his fork and spoon. He was seated on a bench against the wall to prevent him from wriggling out and was given plastic cutlery to lessen the effect of his scratching. As he began to eat better, he confined his scratching to his empty plate. Eventually he could be moved to a chair and trusted with regular implements.*

With some children it is initially necessary to screw down the furniture in their bedrooms so that they cannot topple it over, or to move closets in front of the window to keep them from breaking it at night. Sometimes it is possible to offer the child a compromise that shows him that while his behavior is accepted, others have rights and needs too, and their pleasure and safety have to be taken into account also.

Linwood sacrificed one tree to Teddy's destructive urge. With another child it might be one object he may be allowed to throw or one toy he can take apart or chew on. Children who enjoy ripping up books are given magazines from which they can tear pages, or they may be allowed to rip paper cups or plates used at snack time. As in other instances, negative behavior is ignored as much as possible until a child is ready to give it up, have some limits set, or turn his behavior into more constructive activities. Expectations are raised slowly but eventually the children are expected to take some responsibility for their own behavior. As soon as possible, children are involved in their own care as well as in the care of their rooms. They are invited to help with tidying up and are given small jobs like wiping tables or sweeping floors for which they get a small payment. They are thus rewarded for keeping things whole, clean, and comfortable rather than being punished for messing up.

If a child is at the point where he badly wants something and is looking forward to it, like an outing, this may be used to help him control his destructiveness, as in the case of Terry.

Terry had a habit of ripping his clothes whenever he was bothered. Most days he would go through several shirts, tearing them or ripping off their buttons. One Friday, when his group was scheduled for their weekly afternoon trip to the ice cream parlor which Terry greatly enjoyed, he began to rip shirts again. The therapist told him that the only way to go on an outing was properly dressed in a clean, whole shirt. She showed him the small pile of untorn shirts he had left for that week and said, "Aren't you lucky to have shirts left to go out in tonight." When Terry ripped another shirt he was told, "You have two shirts left to go out in tonight." Weighing his pleasure in the trip against his destructive urge, Terry was able to control himself and produce an acceptable shirt for the outing. By and by his supply of shirts was limited so that he had to control himself more and more to get his reward, until the clothes ripping stopped altogether.

Once the children are older and more fully aware of their own actions, more is expected of them, and they may lose some special reward or miss out on some activity if they slip back into destructive or aggressive behaviors that they have generally outgrown. A child may be told that the school cannot afford a usual treat for him because they have to pay for replacing something he broke.

The best defense against uncontrolled destructiveness is to keep the children busy and occupied, and much of the classroom routine is designed to divert uncontrolled urges into more constructive activities, such as constructing things out of Tinker Toys or interlocking blocks which may take some strength to take apart again. When asked as an adult what helped him to stop ripping up things, David said, "They gave me other things to do." But in spite of careful supervision, substitutions, and limit setting, damages from destructive children can never be totally avoided. Their quickness and ingenuity defies most reasonable precautions. Holes and cracks appear mysteriously all over Linwood all the time, and a handyman is kept busy full time repairing panels, fixtures, walls, doors, and furniture.

At first glance it might make sense to have all the children live with the consequences of their behavior, as is done with normal children. If a child living with his family intentionally breaks a toy, the parents don't usually replace it. If he negligently loses or ruins a piece of clothing, he may have to do without it, and when he makes a mess, he is expected to clean it up. If autistic children are treated differently, if the damage they do is repaired and broken equipment is replaced promptly, will they ever become aware of the effect of their destructiveness? And if they don't, how can they be expected to learn to control themselves or to accept limits?

The answer, again, lies in Linwood's philosophy of providing a structure that is supportive, and guidelines the children can follow when they are ready to. Children learn, in good part, by example. Parents, teachers and the way the environment is arranged, demonstrate the standards, the values, and the behaviors by which children can orient themselves. An autistic child may be a long way from being able or willing to conform to these standards, but unless they are there for him to see, and unless they are kept up, regardless of his own behavior, the child will lack the necessary models and will not understand why certain things are asked of him. Children are unlikely to learn about or accept the importance of cleanliness or tidiness if they are left to go around in torn or dirty clothing. It will be hard to instill respect for things in them if the toys they handle are broken. If holes in the walls are left unrepaired, it is a signal that walls with holes are normal and acceptable. The same goes for broken windows, littered rooms, dirty sheets, or messy tables. Therefore, every effort is made at Linwood to keep the children and their surroundings neat and clean.

The house, the dormitory, and the yard are tidy and cheerful. Rooms and furniture are brightly painted and in good repair. The equipment is plentiful and anything that is broken or torn is thrown out, repaired, or replaced. Though the walls are of necessity relatively bare, and toys and materials are generally locked up until they are used under supervision, the whole costly effort is aimed at having the children live in surroundings that are as normal, orderly, comfortable, and attractive as possible. At the same time the environment is designed to accommodate the children, not the other way around, and their needs clearly take priority over any attempts at presenting an institutional showplace.

LIMIT SETTING WITH NEGATIVE CHILDREN

Once autistic children start emerging from their isolation, they often go through a very negativistic phase. We have briefly discussed this phenomenon in the context of developing relationships with such children. The behavior pattern that characterizes this stage is primarily aimed at guarding the child from outside intrusion.

It is as if the children were aware of the fact that the more they reveal their feelings or thoughts, abilities, interests, or needs, the easier it is to influence their behavior, to interact with them, and to draw them out of their protective shell whether they feel ready for it or not. The picture that comes to mind is that of a snail, slowly and cautiously extending one feeler to test the environment. If there is any movement nearby, or if anyone touches the feeler, it is immediately withdrawn, and the snail remains motionless inside the shell for a long time before venturing out again.

Autistic children are just as reluctant to expose themselves. It takes very little to frighten off these shy, but stubborn little people. Speaking to them directly about an activity they are engaged in might frighten them. Showing them that they have been observed when they reach for something for the first time, utter a new sound or a first word, might make them freeze. So could a word of praise, acknowledging some new behavior. Tense and uncomfortable on the threshold of a new world, the children are constantly poised for flight. One wrong, premature move, and the new interest, the new skill, the new sound, may disappear from view for a long time.

Some children go to extraordinary lengths to protect their private world and only the most painstaking and prolonged observation will eventually uncover some hidden need or ability.

Fred, at four, did not communicate in any way. He not only was mute, but he seemed unaware of anything that went on around him, did not react when he was addressed, and most of the time sat passively, staring ahead. Observing him over a period of months, it struck the therapist that his posture seemed to change ever so slightly during the weekly music session, when a music teacher came in to play the piano for the children and to sing with them. Something in Fred's posture and the tilt of his head seemed to indicate an alertness that was missing at other times, even though he neither moved nor participated in the singing.

One day the pianist played a little tune that seemed to bring the briefest flicker of pleasure to Fred's face. The therapist privately asked the music teacher to repeat the tune, but to play it with one wrong note. She did so and, as the wrong note spoiled the tune, Fred flinched. The therapist's suspicion that he had been listening to the music all along, was confirmed by his reaction. Again she asked the teacher to produce a faulty theme, and again Fred grimaced at the appropriate moment. When she made a third mistake, Fred could stand it no longer. He got up, marched over to the piano, pushed the pianist off the bench, climbed up himself and faultlessly played through the last tune she had played. Then, with a satisfied expression of "so there!" on his face, he returned to his former position.

In the face of such stealth and self control, therapists have to develop a great deal of finesse and patience. They have to observe the children at all times without making them feel watched. They have to be sensitive to the slightest change in them, but be very careful not to reveal too soon or too abruptly what they have learned. Only when they are reasonably sure that a child feels comfortable in a new situation or is ready to practice a new skill, should it be acknowledged in the most casual manner and carefully used to bring about some further change. This was the case with Cathy, who was eventually asked to help out with the words to a tune as a way to get her to talk and to relate.

The same goes for an observed preference. The therapist has to be very confident that a child is unlikely to give up the gratification before using it as a motivator for some other desired behavior. Children who feel that they have betrayed themselves or worse, have been betrayed by an adult whom they have admitted past their defenses and disguises, may "cut off their nose to spite their face." They may give up a favorite food, object, or activity rather than having it used to influence them or to force them to interact. At first the therapist simply tries to provide anything he sees that the child likes. To require him to do something for what he wants would not only risk his abandoning that interest, but might also endanger the building up of a relationship with the child. Even when the relationship is well developed, the child is always asked to do less than he can probably do, since autistic children resist every step out of their own safe world. Unlike normal children, who are anxious to please their parents with new skills, autistic children lean away from progress. They have to be gradually shown the advantages of moving forward, but if they are pushed too hard, they are more than likely to retreat into their shells again.

Rather than resisting passively by not allowing themselves to react, or by trying to hide their behavior from observation, some children may be more actively negativistic. This is usually a sign of budding self awareness and as such is a positive development. Because their sense of self is still weak, however, any conflict between their own needs and the demands of others can only be resolved by either giving in completely or by resisting completely. The stubbornness of the toddler and the negativism of the autistic child both stem from the same need to assert themselves and to defend themselves against being overpowered.

Even though it indicates some progress, a child's persistently negative attitudes may be hard to deal with on a daily basis. It can disrupt the daily routine as well as special activities and the behavior has to be dealt with if it becomes too disruptive to others, or if it keeps the child from functioning at his proper level.

Therefore it is necessary to deal with negative behaviors in ways that will make them less disruptive and, in time, may allow the child to give them up altogether. As in everything that demands change, progress is measured in minute steps and every sign of cooperation and compliance is promptly rewarded. It is also important to time any kind of intervention properly, especially if a child is asked to do something new or something he is not interested in such as cleaning up.

The best time to start working on something the child resists is before an event the child is looking forward to, such as going outside, going to lunch, going swimming, etc. A sufficiently large amount of time has to be set aside for the task, be it cleaning up some toys, putting on socks and shoes, or taking off a coat. Neither therapist nor child must feel rushed or harried. While the focus has to be very clearly on the task to be accomplished, the child is not nagged about it but is simply reminded of the time he still has to get ready for the activity to follow. It is important not to be deflected from the main task by a child's opposition to it. When children are first asked to do something, they may react with temper tantrums, scream, throw things, kick, or hit out. It is easy to be sidetracked by this kind of behavior, to react to it and try to stop, limit, or punish it to the point where the original demand is totally forgotten. Thus the child manages to defeat any attempt at getting him to perform a certain task, and the interaction escalates into a battle in which the child calls the shots. Even if his temper tantrum is eventually controlled, he has escaped doing what he didn't want to do in the first place.

By calmly ignoring any behaviors that have nothing to do with the task at hand, and by reminding the child from time to time of the approaching activity or treat, the therapist circumvents the child's attempts at escaping the task, while keeping the focus on the positive and rewarding consequences of compliance. Most children, but autistic children especially, tend to react to the negative part of a statement and block out anything that comes after it. Demands that stress the positive, are therefore much more effective than those that point out the negative.

"You can go out as soon as you have cleaned up," focuses the child's attention on the desired result, while, "If you don't clean up, you'll miss going out," or, "No, you can't go out until you have cleaned up," contain a threat that either discourages the child or gets up his dander. Better still is a totally neutral and factual statement, such as "You still have fifteen minutes to put away the blocks before lunch." Here, neither promise nor threat are emphasized. The therapist does not show a preference for one course of action over another, so that the child has nothing to react and revolt against. The adult simply states a fact and lets the child draw his own conclusions.

When it does become necessary to specifically prohibit something, the positive part of the statement must always come first, such as "You can do that at Linwood, but not here at the drugstore," rather than, "If you behave here in this way you will have to go back to Linwood."

Obviously, behaviors cannot be changed all at once. At first token compliance is taken for the act itself. If a child moves toward, or touches a toy he is supposed to put away the therapist quickly picks it up and puts it away for him, indicating that he has noted the child's willingness to help. Later, the therapist may put away any toy the child pushes toward him or the toy box, and eventually child and adult may take turns putting things away with the child doing more and more of the job, until he does the whole task by himself. A child who is told that he has to go outside before he can play with a favorite toy or before he can go to lunch will, at first, be rewarded even if he took the demand literally and just stepped outside before coming in again. After all, he wasn't asked to stay outside. Later, the demands can be qualified and the periods of staying out of doors lengthened.

In another situation a child might be expected to comply in a limited way with a demand, but be allowed to indulge himself at other times. A child who refuses to sit down at the table to eat, or who eats everything with his hands, may be told that a particular food, such as a favorite dessert, can only be eaten sitting down or with a spoon: "For dessert we all sit down," or "For ice cream we all use a spoon." Very slowly, further limits to standing up are introduced until the child is sitting down properly for his whole meal.

A few children who have already developed relationships react over-sensitively to all limit setting. They become anxious whenever they are told to do something, as if the directives were severe criticisms or personal attacks. For these children it is easier if limits are set for the whole group. "We all have to put the bikes away now and go inside."

They may also be able to tolerate demands better if they are ostensibly addressed to another child. "You know, Andy, that at this table we have to use spoons to eat," rather than being told directly, "Stop using your hands, Harry."

In some cases, undesirable behavior can be eliminated by turning it into a game and then limiting and altering it little by little in ways that not only make it more tolerable, but introduce new concepts and teach new skills as well.

Gil was four when he entered Linwood. He was always in motion, his hands flapping in front of his face. Much of the time he screamed. Sometimes he sat for long periods picking up leaves or grass, throwing them in the air and letting them float down. Indoors he tore paper into little pieces and threw them in the air. After two years of treatment he had developed some speech connected with food, and had a good relationship with his therapist. But he also developed a habit of spitting. How he could produce all that spit, nobody knew, but wherever he was, the floor, tables, and toys were wet. When he was annoyed, he also used the children and the staff as targets. This went on for several months, and since the activity increased, rather than decreased, it became impossible to ignore it any longer. It was hard to find something he wanted badly enough to motivate him to limit his spitting. The thing he liked best of all was a special kind of donut that he often got at the end of his supper. On account of his spitting, Gil had half a table to himself. One day he asked for his donut. The therapist got it, but stopped a few feet from Gil's chair. As usual the floor around him was slippery with spit. She looked at the floor, then stepped back and told him that she was tired of stepping in that spit. Gil immediately took some napkins and made an attempt to clean the floor around his chair. He got his donut, but he was told that from now on he could only spit around his plate and not on the floor. It worked, but the spitting around the plate continued and a way had to be found to help him stop it.

One day after supper when the other children had left the dining room, Gil was told that he would play a little game with the therapist before he got his donut. The therapist had cut out a large circle of cardboard which she placed at one end of the long dining room table. "I can spit better than you can, Gil," she said, and accurately spit right smack into the center of the circle, a skill she had practiced before engaging Gil in this competition. "Now it is your turn." Gil made an attempt, and the two took turns. When Gil wanted to spit twice in a row he was told, "No, it is my turn," and he not only accepted this rule, but took obvious pleasure in the game. The contest was continued until the cardboard circle was thoroughly wet. Then the therapist took out some crayons and started to color the circle. She let Gil have some crayons as well and he worked along with her. He was clearly fascinated by the result. The finished piece of "abstract art" was hung up. Then the therapist introduced Gil to watercolors, and together they painted another abstract with water, paint, and brushes. Gil got an extra donut for his efforts and was told, "Now that you can paint, you don't have to spit anymore." Spitting in the dining room stopped completely. Occasionally he still did some spitting outside or when he was especially angry at a child or staff member. But Gil continued to paint, learned his colors, started to cut out shapes, and eventually to count, activities he had not been interested in before.

In dealing with strongly negativistic children it is a good rule never to openly offer them anything. Even if they wanted it, they would refuse it. Instead, the approach is to make things available unobtrusively, for example, by letting a child see a favorite toy on the shelf in an unlocked cabinet. Instead of pointing it out or pressing it on him, the choice and the initiative is the child's. If he wants the toy, he has to take it himself. Eventually it might be made a little harder for him to get the object. The cabinet might remain locked, and the child might have to ask for it by name, ask for the cabinet to be opened, or ask for the key to open it himself. In every case the child has to reach out for what he wants, instead of being forced into refusing an offer.

Some children may initially be so negative that they even refuse to eat food that is prepared for them. They may avoid the dining room altogether, or stop eating if they feel watched. The only way such children can be induced to eat is by pretending that nobody cares whether they do or do not. The child is allowed to stay behind in the room or hall when the other children go to the dining room. He is never left alone but the adult who stays with him seemingly pays no attention to him or to the food that is left in the room for him.

Once the child feels unpressured and unobserved, he will usually eat something. This is not acknowledged in any way but eventually the food may be placed closer to the open door of the dining room and eventually it might be mentioned casually within his hearing that there is a chair reserved for him there and food made available for him there. At first he may be allowed to wander in and out at will. Once it is clear that he is able to accept some first limits, and a food is being served which he particularly likes, it is casually noted that this particular treat can only be eaten while sitting at the table. It is often easier for a child to comply with requests that are addressed to a whole group in a general way, rather than being singled out. If the staff announces something like "There is a second helping of dessert, and for this we all sit down," the child can choose to follow the example of the other children or to forego the extra treat. In any case he has not missed out on anything essential.

A very negative child may refuse to join in group activities and voluntarily isolate himself in a corner or in another room when there is something like a sing-along, or a group game. Children are never pressed into participating. On the other hand, they are never left completely alone, ignored, or excluded from the group. If a child is in another room, the door is always left open and a chair placed near it for him. The child is tacitly invited to join, and casually included in the activity if he does so, but he is never called or asked until it becomes very clear that he is ready and willing to be drawn in. Sometimes a formerly negative child makes very rapid progress and then suddenly and inexplicably slips back into old negative or more immature behavior patterns. The same thing also happens with normal children. A child who has been toilet trained may start wetting his bed again after an illness or after the birth of a sibling, or he may return to an old blanket or teddy bear for comfort. All sorts of outside pressures, new demands, or stressful or traumatic incidents, may cause such regression but it usually disappears again by itself when the cause of stress has been removed or when the child has had time to adjust to the new situation.

With inept handling, the regression itself can become a factor of stress. If a child is ridiculed or punished for "acting like a baby," shame, unhappiness, or anger may push him even further back and set up a vicious circle from which it is difficult to extricate him.

The most helpful thing, both with normal and with autistic children, is to either ignore the regression altogether, to deal with it unemotionally and as something of little importance, or to offer support and reassurance if the child seems unhappy or concerned about his lapses. If no outward cause can be found for regression in an autistic child, it may be assumed that the child may simply need some extra time to consolidate his gains.

LIMIT SETTING TO "NAUGHTY" BEHAVIOR

Every member of society is constrained by certain limits, and everyone rebels against them at one time or another. Even adults enjoy beating the system once in a while. They drive above the speed limit or fiddle with their income tax returns. If they get away with it, they derive an inordinate amount of pleasure from these minor victories and may even boast of them to their friends. Yet the same adults often treat children who break their rules as if they were little criminals. Instead of appreciating the ingenuity children display in testing the limits, they feel threatened by what they see as a challenge to their authority. Children, like adults, enjoy outwitting the system. Autistic children are no exception. They too can be "delinquent angels" and come up with endless ways of testing the patience of parents and staff. It takes a well-developed sense of humor and real understanding of child development in general and autistic processes in particular to stay calm and pleasant in the face of strong provocations and even to enjoy the fact that a child is beginning to come alive and to define himself in new ways. When autistic children are naughty on purpose and get pleasure out of it, this is often a sign that they have made a great deal of progress and they should be allowed to enjoy themselves for a while before their behavior is limited.

At Linwood the attitude toward such children is generally one of watchful delight. Their behavior is more or less ignored at first to give them a chance to become more confident and to experiment further. After a while they are shown that the staff is onto their tricks but is prepared to indulge them within limits. Only when they have had their fun are limits gradually imposed or reimposed.

There are a multitude of anecdotes about most of the more advanced children and all of them are told with a chuckle: how Harold gave himself a Mr. T haircut; how Marvin imitated what he saw on TV, put eggs in a suitcase and threw it downstairs, gleefully delighted in the resulting mess. Another anecdote concerns the little boy who urinated standing in the open window of the top floor at Linwood, because "my pee wanted air."

True naughtiness is tricky to control and eliminate. The only way is to stay relaxed and nonreactive. Autistic children are keen observers. Since they don't think about themselves and how they impress others or whether they are liked or not, many autistic children can concentrate on the outside world more acutely. While they themselves are adept at hiding thoughts or feelings behind an expressionless mask, they are very good at reading faces and gauging the state of mind of others. They know exactly when an adult's attention is distracted for some reason and take advantage of any lapse of concentration to test a limit or to get what they want. They also sense when adults are upset about something and enjoy provoking them to get a rise out of them. Children who are spitters, for instance, are more likely to spit at people who show that they don't like it and tend to select another target if they get no reaction from someone.

Pretense is useless. Children always see through it and escalate their naughty behavior until they have pushed the adult past his breaking point. On the other hand, they "hear" anybody who is honest with them about what the limits of his tolerance are and who tells them plainly how far he will go to accommodate them. When Lee was first living with Miss Simons his table manners were atrocious. In fact the way he ate was so messy that it spoiled everybody else's appetite to watch him. After a while Miss Simons told Lee that he was free to eat any way he wanted and that she would sit with him while he ate but that she could not enjoy her own food sitting at the table with somebody who ate this messily. She would therefore eat by herself after he had finished. As their relationship grew and Lee took pleasure in her company, he was able and willing to improve his behavior to the point of becoming an acceptable dinner companion.

At times it is the very reactivity of the adult that turns something a child does into a potential battlefield. Many children go through a phase of playing with their feces, for example. This has to be discouraged, of course, if only out of sanitary considerations. The key to stopping this, or any other undesirable behavior, is not to alert the child to the fact that his activity bothers the adults. Sensing their dismay, he may otherwise persist in doing something in order to upset them that he happened upon by accident and experimented with quite innocently. In this, as in other situations, success comes quickest if the adult is able to calmly demonstrate the necessary limits or rules.

A child who plays with his feces does not think of it as something dirty or forbidden. On the contrary, small children are often proud of their product and experience an adult's disgusted reaction to it as a rejection of themselves. It is obviously necessary to demonstrate to them the difference between their bowel movement and their toys. As long as no particular emotion is attached to the B.M., it is possible to convince the child that it is an object among other objects and like them has its place and its function. Blocks or play dough belong in the playroom. They have their proper containers and can be played with in certain ways. Just a blocks are stacked, rather than thrown, and play dough is molded, rather than eaten, the B.M. has its proper place, the bathroom, where it is handled in a certain way.

If a B.M. is produced in the wrong place, the child can be involved in helping to take it where it belongs and to handle it in the proper way, by flushing it down the toilet. Ceremoniously wrapping it in a pretty paper napkin and carrying it to the bathroom will demonstrate to the child that it is a legitimate object that is respected, and will help him to understand and accept this particular rule. There will also be less temptation to disobey if the adult is no more reactive in this situation than during other interactions.

How to handle play with feces may be an extreme example of ways in which adults can create or defuse a situation with negative potential. There are many others and every parent or teacher can come up with examples of their own. Who doesn't remember an occasion when children were perversely naughty just when it was especially important to their parents that they behave well? Who doesn't recall a child's open rudeness to a visitor who clearly preferred children who were neither heard nor seen? Why do children resist going to sleep on the one evening on which parents have plans for going out? A child does not have to be autistic to react to the moods of adults, but autistic children are almost uncannily sensitive and enjoy exploiting emotional reactivity wherever they come across it.

Knowing how to avoid sensitizing an issue is part of the art of dealing with children. Another is to set limits in ways that make it easy for the child to accept them and develop in new ways rather than having to expend his energy on resisting them.

AVOIDING A POWER STRUGGLE

Before demands are made, the therapist has to be as sure as he can be that a child is ready for some limits and that the gratifications that are offered are sufficiently compelling to overcome the resistance to change. But despite every precaution children will sometimes refuse to comply with a request or persist in being openly defiant. At that point the least productive thing is to get into a power struggle with the child.

Anybody who has ever been in a contest of wills with an autistic child knows that there is no way of winning it, unless one is willing to escalate punishment to an unacceptably harsh and ultimately destructive level. A variety of mistakes can lead to such a situation.

A demand may have been made too early, or when the child was in a bad mood. A demand might have been made without sufficient motivation or without a strong enough relationship to back it up. Children will often accept limits from one person, but balk at them when they come from someone else. Finally, a demand might have been made in a way that activated a child's negativism. Whatever the reasons, once one is in a power struggle with an autistic child, one has done the wrong thing and the best solution is to admit it to oneself and to him and to step out of the situation as gracefully as possible.

At times it takes quick thinking to back out of a situation that threatens to develop into a power struggle, and once in a while the adult simply has to acknowledge that he has been outsmarted.

> Clyde, with whom Miss Simons had already developed a good relationship, went through a period of frequent temper tantrums during which he screamed, kicked, and threw his shoes around. On one particular occasion, Miss Simons took his shoes off to reduce the impact when he kicked her. Clyde himself then ripped off his socks and threw them, continuing to scream and carry on.
>
> After a while he seemed to calm down and demanded to go outside. "Yes, you can, but put your shoes on," Miss Simons directed him. "Sims put shoes on," the boy said firmly, and it looked as if he was ready to argue the point all day. Some quick thinking was in order. "Wait a moment," he was told. "That's right, I took your shoes off, but you took your socks off," and Miss Simons handed them to him. Without demur Clyde put on his socks and then Miss Simons put on his shoes and he quietly went outside to play.

In this encounter both parties won. Clyde, because he felt that he had some control over his own situation, the therapist because the child reacted to the appeal to his rational and healthy side. Instead of ending up in a useless, wearisome confrontation, the relationship remained undamaged and may have been strengthened by the respect shown the child.

A similar mechanism comes into play whenever a child has a violent temper tantrum. At first he is usually so much out of control that it is impossible to make any demands on him, and the only thing is to protect everybody from getting hurt. Once he calms down a little, an appeal to his rationality may become possible. The message is always, "There is no need to scream, you can show me, or tell me what you want." The tantrum is ignored as much as possible and never gets rewarded, so that the idea eventually gets through to the child that this is a nonconstructive activity.

Elizabeth was a very disturbed child who was always getting into trouble. One evening at supper Elizabeth threw a violent temper tantrum because she could not have all the dessert she wanted. The children had cake and ice cream and a limit of two desserts per child had been set. After everybody had had their share, there was still some cake left over and Elizabeth wanted it. She was told that she had had her two helpings and that the cake would be left for the next day.

Before anybody knew what was happening, Elizabeth started throwing things, including her chair. She left the room when told to do so, but as soon as the therapist went to talk to her she flew into a terrific rage. She threw herself around, ripped her dress, flew at the therapist and scratched, slapped, and bit her. By tying a folded sheet around Elizabeth's middle, the therapist managed to hold her in a way that the child could not bite her, but which still left her the freedom of jumping up and down. She told Elizabeth that she had to hold her this way because she did not like to be bitten but that this allowed her to stay with her.

For the next hour the therapist held Elizabeth by her sheet. For much of that time she was screaming, raging, trying to kick and bite. When she did this, the therapist tightened her grip on the sheet. When she relaxed, the sheet was loosened. Once, when she was trying to kick out, she lost her slipper. She became even more angry and demanded it back. She was told that she could pick it up later. Angrily she threw off her second slipper and then screamed even louder because now she didn't have any slippers.

During this struggle the therapist talked very little. Some of the things she did say were to make sure that Elizabeth was physically comfortable and that the sheet was not too tight. This was to communicate to the child that she was being held to protect her not to punish her. The therapist did not mention the dessert incident at all but instead focused Elizabeth's attention on what was going on in the present situation, such as the problem with the slippers.

A tantrum is an outburst of irrational, uncontrollable emotions. By talking to the girl about the details of the immediate situation, it was hoped to get her to respond on a more rational level, closer to her usual, more mature functioning, and to defuse the rage. Finally Elizabeth began to calm down. The therapist asked another staff member for a hair brush so that she could smooth out Elizabeth's hair once she was feeling better. Elizabeth demanded that the sheet be removed and was told that it would come off as soon as she was calmer. She quickly quieted down completely.

When she was rational again, Elizabeth was asked to explain why she had become so upset. She said that everyone had been promised two desserts, but that she had had only one serving of ice cream and cake. She regarded the two things as one dessert and had felt deprived of the promised second portion. The therapist acknowledged the possibility of a genuine misunderstanding but pointed out to her that next time something happened she could talk about it and would not have to get so upset. She was told that grown-ups could not read children's minds and that it was important to speak up. Elizabeth seemed to understand this and the episode was settled.

Elizabeth was not an autistic child, and the process described above is fairly unusual. It is a last resort to be used only when a child's tantrums become potentially destructive to himself or others. For other kinds of tantrums, particularly those that start when a child does not get his way, ignoring it is the best strategy. The therapist focuses on whatever he wants the child to accomplish, ignoring anything, including temper tantrums, that does not have anything directly to do with the activity in question. The following example is described in an earlier article by Jeanne Simons and Charles Ferster.[14]

Kathy, who had a substantial relationship with Miss Simons and liked to be with her, got upset when Miss Simons took away the two cups that she was banging on the table during lunch. In a fit of pique Kathy threw her plate with half an uneaten sandwich on the floor. She was asked to pick up the sandwich, but instead threw a temper tantrum and tried to grab other food on the table.

During the next half hour Miss Simons calmly prevented any activity other than picking up the sandwich, including finishing lunch, any kind of play or personal interactions. Throughout intermittent crying, foot stamping and thrashing about, Miss Simons kept the sandwich within Kathy's reach, reminded her frequently of the need to pick it up with remarks like, "You can have your milk when you have picked up the sandwich." Finally Kathy picked the plate off the floor and tendered it a little way toward Miss

Simons. This compromise was acceptable and Kathy was allowed to finish lunch. However, if Kathy were to repeat her actions, she would be required to make a somewhat bigger effort before being rewarded.

Some tantrums can be defused simply by putting the child out of the room or by leaving the room oneself. In some cases, a remark such as "We don't have time for that now, we might miss lunch," can get the child back to a rational consideration about the consequences of his behavior. As soon as a child is thinking rationally, he is unlikely to continue a tantrum. A good example of defusing a tantrum by appealing to the child's rational self is the confrontation lived through with Dale.

One day all of the children in Dale's class were enjoying arts and crafts. Dale did not join in, but bothered the other children by rolling clay balls over the table. When the counselor interfered with this, Dale threw a violent temper tantrum, trying to bite her, pinching her arms, and hacking at her feet with the heels of his shoes.

The counselor took him out into the hall but it was impossible for one person to contain him. Another staff member helped to put Dale onto a bed where one person held onto his hands, another to his feet while he was wriggling to get free. After a while the therapist said to Dale, "I don't think you know who Houdini was, but he did really neat things with his feet. He could get out of any restraint. I don't think you are that good." Dale became interested and the counselor told him more about Houdini. He watched as his feet were wrapped in a sheet and tried to get loose, but didn't manage it.

He still tried to bite and the therapist said thoughtfully "I wish we had a nice muzzle." Again Dale was interested. "What's a muzzle?", he asked. Since it was hard to explain, the therapist drew one for him. By this time the tantrum was gone. Dale was too interested in what was going on. He was allowed to color the muzzle, while the therapist explained that this was a device that was used to keep a dog from biting people. Dale asked her to draw a dog, and by the time he had colored that too, his temper was completely under control, and five minutes later he rejoined his group in a game.

Flexibility in enforcing limits also avoids power struggles. Even well-considered, logical, and fair rules do not fit every situation. Sometimes it is more important to recognize the need for an exception, than to follow through regardless and end up in a confrontation or miss out on an opportunity for real growth. The following example illustrates this point.

In the dining room at Linwood children who are at different levels of development sit at separate tables. Different standards of behavior apply to these tables and children are moved from one to another depending on their ability and willingness to conform to them. If a child starts behaving inappropriately at his table, he is usually told that he might need some more time before he is ready to sit with that particular group, and he is moved back to a table where less is expected of him. He usually gets the message fairly quickly and is then allowed to rejoin his former group.

In some cases, however, behavior that is theoretically inappropriate for an older or more advanced child and would result in his being moved down, is actually a sign of progress. To penalize it, or to suppress it too quickly, might be harmful. The child has to be allowed to indulge in it without undue pressure. At the same time, the general rules at a given table have to be upheld for the sake of all the other children. Meeting the needs of the individual without losing credibility with the group is a challenge that needs ingenuity and quick thinking, as in the case of one youngster who had recently joined the table of the older children.

> *Donnie functioned well in the group, had the privilege of going out to the drug store and had begun to talk more after being very quiet at first. He had never particularly acted out. Then one day at dinner he started to blow bubbles in his milk, spattering it all over his face and even onto the table.*
>
> *Another child would have been asked to come and sit with the smaller children for a while, but for this child the experimentation and the small naughtiness was a sign of progress. It was important to allow him to continue without taking away from the status he had already achieved. At the same time the rules in the dining room had to be upheld for the sake of not confusing the other children. The solution was to offer Donnie a compromise.*
>
> *He was told that milk was for drinking not for bubbling, but that if he needed to blow bubbles he could have some water and that he could turn his chair around and bubble at the next table reserved for less advanced children. Instead of water, he asked for tea, and it was agreed that he could play with tea at the table behind him whenever he felt like it. He did not take up the offer that day but finished his meal without playing.*
>
> *When he blew bubbles in his milk the next day he was reminded of the agreement. He quickly finished his milk then asked for tea, turned his chair around and bubbled to his heart's content*

at the other table. Donnie indulged in his privilege several times
a week for about a month, then the behavior stopped by itself. Had
another child tried to pick up on Donnie's behavior, he would have
been stopped and told, "You are not Donnie. This is Donnie's
privilege." But in fact none of the other children laughed at him,
took any particular notice of his behavior or tried to imitate it.

By avoiding a possible power struggle with Donnie and by offering
him an ingenious compromise, the staff allowed Donnie to gratify his needs
without backsliding in other ways. In the case of "Spitting Gil," the cir-
cumvention of a confrontation eventually led to the acquisition of new skills
and more social interactions with other children. Clyde was shown that
he had some control over what happened to him, as was Elizabeth who
was reminded that there were more effective ways of communicating than
flying into a tantrum. And Kathy learned that a temper tantrum would not
get her out of a situation she did not want to face.

In every case the child feels that he is treated fairly and like a valuable
person even though limits may be imposed on him. And though some of
his behavior may be unacceptable, his basic relationship with the adult is
unaffected by any confrontation. He also experiences the adult's respect
and acceptance of his needs to behave in certain ways, while he is given
help in controlling the situation and in holding on to whatever healthy potential there is in him.

The following case study serves to underline some of the points made
in the preceding sections.

> *Bruno was an angry little fellow. He was always frowning*
> *and his speech was limited to a growl. He was totally negative*
> *and very compulsive. As he progressed in treatment, he started*
> *to develop a good relationship with Miss Simons. He laughed as*
> *well as frowned, and his growls became understandable words.*
> *He was a born architect who drew blueprints and built intricate*
> *buildings out of Lego blocks and other building materials. He also*
> *built highways and airports and seemed to have a special interest*
> *in flying.*
>
> *Over time, Bruno started to become aggressive and came up*
> *with all sorts of naughty behaviors. The most difficult one to handle*
> *was when he began to throw plates, with or without food on them,*
> *at the dinner table. Putting him out of the room was no help, since*
> *he would fly into violent temper tantrums, hit, kick, tear clothes,*
> *and throw anything that wasn't nailed down. He would also stop*
> *eating. It was clear that the situation had to be dealt with where*
> *it occurred: in the dining room.*

The first solution was to serve Bruno's meals on paper plates to make sure that no one got hurt when he started to throw them across the room. He threw paper plates with just as much gusto as regular plates, and one day he hit a child with a plate full of spaghetti. It became imperative to limit his behavior in some way.

Trying to capitalize on Bruno's interest in airports and flying, Miss Simons suggested that he might become a decent pilot, if he had less cargo loading down his planes. She told him the food was the cargo and it kept his "planes" from flying properly. The idea interested him, and from then on he only threw his plates after he had taken the cargo off by eating his food. Throwing an empty plate he again hit a child and was told that he would lose his license as a pilot if he could not steer better. This made him a lot more careful and he contrived to "fly" his plates over the children.

One day when it was raining hard outside, Miss Simons told Bruno that the airport was closed on account of bad weather and that no planes could fly that day. He accepted this. Some time later the airport was closed again, because of fog and then again because of rain. Miss Simons suggested that now that he was such a good pilot they should look for a better and bigger airport that would not be closed down so often. So they removed the "airport" from the dining room to a larger play area. Here Bruno demanded more paper plates. He counted them and gave them names which he printed on them.

Eventually geography was added to the game using names of cities and countries to which he could fly. Then he started to use crayons to color the planes and scissors to give the planes different shapes. Writing, coloring, cutting with scissors and the other skills and interests Bruno developed through his passion for airplanes were carried over into the classroom and were worked with there and expanded in different contexts.

A little later Miss Simons bought some Frisbees, which flew a lot better and further than Bruno's paper plates. Bruno was fascinated by them but he was told these airplanes could only be used if the pilot shared them. One child was the pilot one way; another flew the plane back. He accepted this, and through his desire to play with the Frisbee, Bruno was involved for the first time in positive interactions with other children.

Instead of leading to an exhausting power struggle over his naughty behavior in the dining room, Bruno ended up with a number of new skills and relationships on which further treatment could build.

SIX
✦ ✦ ✦

Compulsions

INTRODUCTION

The behavior of many autistic children is governed by an obsessive need for sameness. The children's desire for an unvarying routine and their insistence on maintaining a static environment is thought to be a way of assuaging a deep-seated anxiety and helplessness by trying to control events that may be incomprehensible and therefore confusing and threatening to them.

We have already mentioned the fact that autistic babies may at first experience the world as a jumble of meaningless sensations from which they retreat or against which they have to put up defenses. Rituals, routines, a tightly circumscribed environment, and a reduction of activities to one or two compulsive behaviors can all be seen as part of this defense system.

It is seldom possible to identify the specific aspects of the environment that a particular child finds hardest to cope with. Sometimes, close observation of a child's reactions in a given situation may provide a clue. More rarely, a child may, at a later date, be able to talk about what it was that triggered a particular reaction, fear, or compulsion. This was the case with Lee who had suddenly developed an extreme phobia that centered around an armchair in his living room.

This particular chair had always been a favorite object of Lee's. But suddenly he began to scream, gag, and become self-abusive every time he looked at it. When the chair was removed, Lee showed great distress; when it was brought back he seemed equally upset. Years later he was able to dispel the mystery. What had happened was that he had heard his parents talking while they were screened by the big chair. It seemed to the boy, who had no

*speech at the time, that the chair itself was talking. Yet he knew
that objects did not talk. The confusion he felt about this strange
phenomenon provoked panic and fear that he could neither communicate nor cope with by himself.*

Seemingly unprovoked tantrums, illogical fears, and all sorts of phobias
are ways in which some of the children react to the threats an unpredictable environment holds for them. More common are behaviors that reflect
the children's need for unvarying routines and a stable environment.

Many autistic children seem to carry a detailed map of their surroundings in their heads and react with dismay to the most minute changes that
would be unnoticeable to anybody else. If a piece of furniture is out of place
when a child comes in the morning, he may immediately put it back in its
original position. To test the extent of awareness of one especially obsessive
little boy, Jeanne Simons once marked the position of a record player that
he was particularly preoccupied with. With a very sharp pencil she made
two tiny dots at the corners, then moved it by less than a quarter of an inch.
As soon as the boy entered the room he repositioned the record player and,
when she checked, she found that it was exactly back in line again.

Any disruption of his routine, or the loss or displacement of an object, causes the child great distress and has to be corrected before he feels
comfortable enough to go about his business. The reader will remember
Lee and his collection of objects, all of which had to be arranged around
him before he could go to sleep. He immediately noticed the loss of a tiny
bead and had a major upset until it was found and the collection made complete again.

A desire for sameness can be found in normal children as well. At certain ages, notably around two or three and again at school entry, children
delight in repetition to the point of exhausting the patience of any adult.
They never seem to tire of the same little games; they ask for the same
story over and over again and will not tolerate even the slightest deviation
from the original version; they demand the same, limited menu and tend
to eat it in the same order. Plans, once made, cannot be changed without
greatly upsetting some children who are otherwise not particularly difficult.

Especially at times of heightened tension or anxiety, rituals tend to increase and be used like incantations against the threat of the unknown. In
the evening, the stuffed animals need to be arranged in a set order to make
the child feel safe and protected. A special pillow or blanket, a teddy bear,
the ritual of the good-night kiss or the drink of water before lights out,
may be needed to ward off night terrors and bad dreams.

The list is endless and imperceptibly blends into adult superstitions:
the lucky outfit worn to important interviews, the rabbit's foot fondled for

good luck, and a host of repetitive, ritualistic actions in specific situations whose meaning rests somewhere in the dark recesses of the unconscious.

In autistic children the need for sameness is not a passing phase, and their rigid adherence to routines and repetitive activities governs their whole lives and tends to restrict their opportunities for new experiences. They are especially unhappy in situations that contain strong elements of unpredictability. Mark, for example, used to demand the weather forecast from his mother every morning and would get extremely upset and angry with her if the predictions turned out to be wrong.

Even scheduled events that disrupt the daily routine, and especially those long-heralded, once-a-year occasions like Thanksgiving or Christmas, produce heightened tension and are experienced as unpleasant by many autistic children. Even while he was stuffing himself with the special cupcakes and candy provided as a treat on Halloween, Wallace insistently pleaded "Trick-or-treat all over now." The candy was clearly not worth the upheaval and excitement of the day to him.

As long as the disruptions are minor or temporary and the environment remains reasonably stable, as long as toys and furniture are arranged in order and their routine is maintained, autistic children can move about relatively freely and function within the limits of their capacity. In extreme cases, however, the children may exhibit a need for sameness that is so strong that it dominates their lives to the exclusion of all other activities, interests, or attachments. This kind of extreme behavior is called a compulsion and severe compulsions have a much greater impact on a child's development than the cleaving to routines and sameness described above.

Such compulsions can literally paralyze a child. They can preoccupy him to the point where they keep him from being aware of the environment and prevent him from developing other, more functional age-appropriate behaviors, preferences, or skills. Clinging to compulsions, a child is not only cut off from any involvement with the environment and other people, he may also not develop an awareness of self. Sometimes a compulsion, such as spinning or flipping objects, is the only activity an autistic child engages in. At times a compulsion may be confined to a certain time of the day or to a certain situation, such as an obsessive and exclusive focus on certain foods at meal times. For some children a particular object seems to take on the role of a talisman, and they can only function when they carry it around. Such children may even be prevented from doing other things because they cannot let go of it.

Other children may have to go through intricate routines before they can do things, like Toby who had to touch the door frames and doorknobs in a certain way before he was able to go through a door. Or they have to finish something they started before they can change course and go on to another activity, like Leo who was coming down the stairs when his teacher called him back. He hesitated for a brief moment, then deliberately continued his descent and remounted the stairs only after he had stepped off the bottom stair with both feet.

Among the most common compulsions are those that involve stereotypical movements, like rocking, spinning, head banging, rhythmical finger flapping, or the tapping or twirling of sticks, strings, straws, or other objects in front of the eyes. Equally characteristic are compulsive behaviors that have to do with spinning objects, such as bottle tops, wheels, toys, plates, or even chairs.

Almost every autistic child displays a compulsion at one time or another and just about anything can become one. Sometimes compulsive behaviors have no immediate visible connection with normal behavior, such as Philip's licking objects around the yard. But often compulsions are simply extreme manifestations of everyday behavior, such as an exclusive attachment to or excessive involvement with household objects or ordinary activities.

Some children endlessly repeat jingles, commercials, or fragments of conversation. Others are preoccupied with dates or numbers, time tables, or the calendar. Some engage in repetitive activities with specific toys or objects, like endlessly turning the pages of a mail order catalogue. Some children obsessively chew on things or sniff them. Some sit silently and without moving or mumble to themselves, while others run around or swing or rock untiringly. Flushing the toilet or washing hands can become an obsession, as can taking off clothes or shoes, stacking or throwing things, drawing or writing. One child, for example, had a compulsive need to draw pictures of freeway cloverleafs.

Some of the compulsive behaviors already described may also be found in children who have already become more aware of their own actions and of the environment, like Bruno with his plate throwing. But while such behaviors may reflect a need strong enough to make it compulsive, this kind of naughty behavior has a different origin and a different meaning to the children than "honest" compulsions. Children who experiment consciously and are naughty deliberately are at a different level of development from children whose only behavior is a compulsion or whose compulsive behavior is outside their own awareness or control.

As we have seen, it is ineffective to attack obsessive naughty behavior head on, because one may well end up in a destructive power struggle but it is even more futile to move on a real compulsion before its function to the child has been determined and before there is a signal that he is ready to let go of it. The very intensity of the involvement that characterizes the compulsion makes it resistant to extinction, and often, when one disappears, another one pops up in its place. The variations are endless and are as individually different as the different children.

Compulsive children are extraordinarily inventive and ingenious in getting what they want and cleverly circumvent attempts to limit their behavior.

Jackie was extremely compulsive about shades and blinds. Whenever he felt like it, his family would have to live in the dark because he would insist that every shade in the house be drawn. The room in which Jackie's group played had eleven windows. This was heaven for Jackie, who promptly proceeded to pull down the shades on all of them. However, since the windows were very tall, it was possible to roll the shades up to the point where they were out of the little boy's reach.

Jackie watched solemnly while the therapist secured the shades, then he walked off, seemingly resigned. But after barely five minutes he returned to the window, carrying a piece of soft wire which he bent into a little hook at the end. He climbed up on the windowsill, but was unable to reach high enough, so he climbed down again and fetched a pile of eight wooden puzzles which he piled onto the windowsill. The therapist, who had been watching him without interfering, warned him about the hot radiator, which was not protected by an enclosure at the time.

Jackie climbed down again, fetched a pillow, and covered the radiator with it. Then he scrambled up again, balanced on the puzzles and pulled down the shade with his hook. Not content with this, he attached a string to the shade which he weighted down with a block tied to the other end. Clapping his hands in evident satisfaction he beamed at the therapist who told him that he had won and gave him a big hug.

Jackie soon discovered that there were shades all over the house but he was told that he could only play with those in his own room and he was firmly prevented from interfering with other windows.

When Jackie became less compulsive and started to engage in other activities, he only pulled down the shades when something bothered him. Then he might yank them so hard that they ripped. As soon as he got what he wanted, he chuckled and was willing to open the blinds again. At that point Jackie was told that the other children did not enjoy playing in the dark and that lights were for evening only. He was given one window for his own, on which he could pull down the shade whenever he felt like it. But the other windows belonged to everybody and had to be left alone. Jackie accepted the limitations, and it was then also possible to set similar restrictions at home, to the great relief of his family.

DEALING WITH COMPULSIONS IN THERAPY

At Linwood, compulsions are initially treated like any other behavior a child displays. They are neither labeled as undesirable nor is an attempt made to stop or change them, unless they represent a danger to the child or the environment. This holds especially true in cases where the compulsive activity is the only one a child engages in.

To try to suppress such a compulsion, even if it were possible, would rob the therapist of the most natural, and possibly the only, opportunity of making contact with a child. No matter how obsessive or limited a child's activities are, they are a sign of his inner life and may denote an area of interest, skill, or strength that can be developed. His compulsion can be seen as the little finger the child extends to the outside world, and skillful maneuvering may eventually gain the therapist command of the whole hand by which he can lead the child toward new and more useful behaviors. The following case study embodies the principles that guide work with compulsions at Linwood and demonstrates how even seemingly negative or meaningless behaviors can become a starting point for constructive activities and growing social involvement.

Gregory's only activity was to hold and slap a piece of paper. He paid no attention to anything else that was happening around him, and he never let go of his paper. It was impossible to interest him in a game or toys and he even held on to his paper while he ate. Whenever anybody got too close to it, he would withdraw, become extremely upset, and clutch it more tightly.

One day all the other children were drawing and Gregory just sat there looking on. By that time he already had a sort of relationship with Miss Simons. She decided to try to use his interest to engage him in an activity, and when he came over where she too was drawing, she gave him a crayon and asked him to make a line on his paper. He took the crayon and smiled, but then let it drop. Miss Simons put the crayon back in his hand, slightly held Greg's wrist down, and pressed the point of the thick crayon against the paper. Greg immediately withdrew the paper and in doing so pulled it under the crayon, making a line. He looked at the line with some interest.

After some days, Miss Simons repeated the exercise with different colors and eventually Greg could be induced to draw lines on his paper by himself. For a long time that was all he did. Then

*one day another youngster took Greg's paper away from him. He
was very upset and looked pathetic and forlorn. Miss Simons gave
him a replacement and told him that it might be helpful to have
his name on the paper since most pieces of paper look the same.
That way it would be clear which one was his and people would
be less likely to take it.*

*Stimulated by his compulsion, Greg did indeed learn to write
his name, though the only place he would write it was on his piece
of paper. Seeing that he was not yet ready for any other kind of
educational activity, Miss Simons devised learning activities that
continued to center around his primary interest. When it was possible to unobtrusively take his paper, she brought out a much larger
sheet and a pair of scissors and had him help her cut off a strip
by guiding his hand. When he seemed reluctant to cut, she showed
him how to tear strips off, and eventually he enjoyed coloring,
cutting, and tearing paper.*

*One day the other children were out in the yard. It was a
windy day. "Let's take your paper outside and I will show you how
it can fly." Miss Simons helped Greg make a hole in his paper and
showed him how to thread and tie a string through it. He greatly
enjoyed the paper flapping in the wind and began running around
with it as if it were a kite.*

*He was still a loner and would not share his paper with
anybody. Then came the day on which Miss Simons distributed
several little pinwheels to the group. Now the other children too
had something to run around with that spun in the wind. Gregory
was fascinated by the pinwheels and coveted them. When it was
his turn he carelessly dropped his paper and ran off with the new
toy. It was the first time in months that he had been without his
piece of paper.*

*Since there were not enough pinwheels for everybody, the
children had to take turns playing with them. Gregory learned to
share and eagerly awaited his turn. However marginally, this involved him with the other children in the group and eventually
led to further interactions around other activities.*

Gregory's example is typical of work with a child whose compulsion
is the only sign of activity that can be observed. Several elements of his
case will surface over and over again in our discussion on how to deal with
compulsive behavior.

First, there has to be a relationship of sorts between the therapist and
the child before any kind of work can be done on compulsions. For another,

compulsive children have to be observed over a long period of time to assess the strength of the compulsion and its role in their lives. Premature therapeutic efforts to alter a compulsion only tend to sustain or even prolong compulsive behaviors.

It is also important not to get roped into a child's compulsive circle. Because severely compulsive children often become highly distressed or disruptive when their compulsions are interfered with in any way, adults often find themselves becoming even more compulsive than their charges in an effort to prevent upsets. They are more careful of the child's toys than the child himself and will go to absurd lengths to assure that he has the exact food, nipple, blanket, or toy he craves or that routines and schedules are meticulously maintained. The tyranny of a child's compulsion can thus easily enslave a whole family who does not dare to move without his approval and whose living space and activities are governed by his needs.

When an adult gets snared by obsessive behavior he becomes a participant in it which makes it almost impossible for him to help the child escape from its grip. It becomes even more difficult, but also more important to stay detached from a child's compulsion as the relationship between adult and child develops. The feelings the child experiences when he opens himself up to a relationship, create intense anxiety which in turn generates stronger compulsions as a defense. Only by staying outside this vicious cycle, can the adult help the child deal with his fear.

A child's compulsions often stand in the way of other activities and of his further development in general. By expanding his range of interests the autistic child has a better chance of increasing his skills and of participating and functioning in the outside world. Once the barriers of compulsive activities are weakened, the child may be more able and willing to engage in a relationship. He becomes gradually more comfortable with others and with himself and more truly part of the human race.

Sometimes it becomes clear that his compulsions are burdensome to a child and that he would welcome help with limiting them.

The reader may remember Larry, the compulsive little boy who at a later point in therapy threw trucks around. When he first joined Miss Simons' group his only occupation was to screw and unscrew a little bottle top. If the top rolled outside his reach he rarely pursued it, since he was at first unable to leave the small area in the middle of the room, where he seemed imprisoned within invisible boundaries. If he was unable to reach his screw top he would stretch out his hand and guide Miss Simons' arm towards retrieving it for him. Even with her help he was at first unable to leave his charmed circle to go after the cap himself.

After a while Miss Simons observed that Larry started to deliberately throw bottle and cap beyond his reach, and even seemed to want to have them out of sight. He aimed them at the piano or the radiator and became tense when they rolled back. He would throw them again and again and become more and more agitated as they rolled back out. As soon as the objects remained invisible he would relax but not before he had made sure that he could not see them from any vantage point within his living space.

One day he did not manage to aim the bottle right and he became so frustrated and upset that Miss Simons took it away and told him that she would hide it for him. She took it to the bathroom and locked it in the medicine cabinet. Instead of calming down, Larry threw a fit, trying to hurt himself by knocking his head against the wall and trying to scratch Miss Simons. She asked him what he wanted her to do, and he pushed her toward the bathroom door and into the bathroom itself. There he insisted on being picked up so that he could look at all the shelves and into the medicine cabinet.

Larry's attempts to get the bottle out of sight convinced Miss Simons that the time had come to help him shed his burden once and for all. She opened the bathroom window and threw the bottle out. Larry almost followed it out the window. She lifted him up and let him hang out of the window as far as was safe so that he could assure himself that the bottle had indeed disappeared and could not be seen any more. He searched every inch of the yard with his eyes and not seeing the bottle gave a big sigh and returned to the playroom. For the rest of the morning Larry was satisfied and relaxed and after that he was rid of that particular compulsion.

Sometimes, though rarely, a child may even be able to verbalize the relief he feels when he is helped to limit compulsive behaviors, as in the case of Lee with his morning routine.

In working with compulsions, it is important to take into account where the child is in terms of overall development, what awareness he has of his environment, what other interests or skills he may have and how important the compulsion is to him.

With some children, a particular compulsion is the predominant activity in their lives and their only interest. Depending on the compulsion, on the intensity of their involvement with it, on their level of development, and on the strength of their relationship with the therapist such an exclusive compulsion can be worked with in two different ways.

A strong compulsion can be left completely untouched and other activities gradually interjected. In this case the compulsion functions both as a device to keep the child going on an even keel and as a motivator.

At first the child's compulsive activity may only be interrupted for a very brief time and he will be allowed to continue with it before he can get upset. Later the interruptions may be of increasingly longer duration to allow some other skill to be developed. Every time, the return to his compulsion is the child's reward for the intervening performance. If done cleverly, the child may not even realize the way he is gradually weaned from his compulsion and oriented towards another activity.

While a child uses one hand for his compulsive playing with string, for example, the therapist can help him to drop an object into a box with his other hand. Lightly encircling the child's hand from above, the therapist can exert enough gentle pressure on his fingers to give him a feeling of holding the object, which drops as soon as the therapist opens her hand. While this goes on, his other hand is restrained momentarily, so that his only involvement is the short contact with the block, puzzle piece, or bead he has been helped to hold. Over time, the "working" hand becomes more active. The child will need less help in actually holding the piece and will begin to manipulate it independently. This kind of behavior can lead to more focused work with a form board or simple puzzle, to stacking blocks or to some other new activity.

As the child's skill and interest in the new activity increases, his exclusive focus on the string tends to decrease to the point where he may only play with it intermittently when he is bored or upset for some reason. The string may be put away and only brought out as a reward if the child has performed some other small activity. Eventually he may lose interest in it altogether.

An excellent example of breaking into a child's obsessive behavior and changing and redirecting it in almost imperceptible steps is provided by a Linwood anecdote noted by Dr. Charles Ferster in an unpublished paper.[15] Excerpts of his detailed observations follow to illustrate the way a child can be weaned from a certain behavior by seemingly minimal interventions.

The child described in this incident is Kathy, a little girl described in other contexts. When she first entered Linwood she was mute, but cried almost continuously. She also had an obsessive attachment to a little doll which she clutched tightly and carried everywhere. The following episode took place shortly after Kathy joined the program.

> *On this day, for the first time, Kathy was placed on a rocking horse, while Miss Simons sang to her and rocked her. The sing-*

ing and rocking temporarily stopped the crying. Miss Simons began introducing brief periods during which she sang, but did not rock Kathy to see whether the child would rock herself without crying. These interruptions of the rocking were short and always ended before Kathy had resumed crying. A little later, Miss Simons stopped the rocking when the child cried. Her doll was placed on a nearby table which was moved close enough so that Kathy could reach it and could take it back any time. This all occurred within a span of ten seconds or so and was the first time in which the environment was changed in a way that made a demand on the child.

Kathy quickly took the doll back and in doing so rocked herself slightly. Now, Miss Simons sang only when the girl rocked. Consequently Kathy rocked herself more frequently. Miss Simons repeated the sequence of taking the doll out of the girl's hand, placing it on the table and allowing the girl to take it back again. Throughout she continued to sing only when the child rocked. The manipulation of the doll, which under different circumstances would probably have produced fits of screaming, was not only tolerated by Kathy, she even placed the doll on the table herself at one point.

Miss Simons increased the rocking motion and adjusted the intensity of her voice to the intensity of the rocking. Kathy reacted by not resuming her crying and by not reaching for the doll. For the first time she had been without it for over a minute. At this point Jeanne Simons occasionally failed to sing when the child rocked. Kathy tried to take her toy back, but accidentally dropped it. She started to cry again. Jeanne Simons said, "Do you want to pick it up? I'll help you."

She lifted the child off the horse. The child picked up the doll and Miss Simons asked, "Do you want to get up?" Kathy lifted her hands and was put on the horse again. There she resumed rocking without any singing from Miss Simons. She dropped the doll again and the same routine was repeated.

At this point Jeanne Simons initiated an even more vigorous motion of the horse and Kathy responded by rocking more vigorously herself. Now Miss Simons moved the toy to the couch which produced a slight interruption in the rocking while the child watched. The therapist picked up the doll and tapped it. The child looked at her, vocalized and then rocked in the rhythm of the tapping. The doll was then returned to her.

When Miss Simons next took the toy away, Kathy cried but

> *continued to rock. The therapist sang, which stopped the crying, and then took the child off the horse, allowing her to get the toy from the couch where they then sat together, the child on Miss Simons' lap. Now the child tried to climb the horse by pulling on the therapist's arm in the direction of the rocking horse. She was picked up, but not put on the horse.*
>
> *For a brief time she was on and off the therapist's lap. Then Miss Simons moved to a small chair, taking the rocking horse along. Kathy stood next to it, played with it, and gestured to be picked up. Jeanne Simons eventually did put her back, after placing her briefly on the couch which she tolerated without crying.*

Kathy was motivated to stop crying, to let go of her doll, and to become more active by singing to her and rocking her which she obviously enjoyed. Once her attention was caught and the grip of her compulsion was weakened, the child was ready to expand her behavior. She began to communicate her wishes in more positive ways and even tolerated interactions on which a beginning relationship could eventually be based. Without making excessive demands and with a minimum of talk the little girl's behavior was changed noticeably within the span of a thirty minute episode.

Rather than leaving the compulsion itself untouched but gradually interspersing it with other activities, the compulsive activity itself can be used, built upon, and expanded to develop new skills. In this case it is the strong interest in a particular object or activity that provides the motivation. As the child expands his range of activities, his involvement with the original compulsion fades and eventually disappears.

We have discussed this process in the chapter on motivation and have demonstrated it in a variety of case studies, like Dale and the keys and the one at the beginning of this section of Gregory and his pieces of paper.

There are as many variations on this technique as there are children and compulsions. By close observation, the therapist determines the opportune moment and the most fruitful avenue for the first, cautious steps towards changing the compulsion. Creativity and close observation of the child's reactions suggest the next steps.

At times, a child may become more compulsive because too-rapid progress or feelings produced by emerging relationships make him anxious. His compulsions provide a refuge and give him a feeling of security. During such times the child needs his compulsions, and rather than interfering with them, they should be a signal to cut down on the anxiety-producing activities, to slow down the work done with the child, and to make sure that he gets as much pleasure as possible out of his activities.

As he becomes less tense and has time to consolidate his gains and to become more comfortable with new feelings or experiences, work can be resumed. Following is another example of working with a child whose only interest centers around one object.

> *We described in a different context Terry's strong attachment to a red sock that he carried around with him at all times. Otherwise he only ran around more or less aimlessly, sometimes humming to himself tunelessly. As their relationship grew, the therapist was able to take the sock away from Terry for a few seconds and eventually long enough to hide it while he was watching. At first the hiding places were easily accessible: under a chair, under a magazine, etc. Later Terry had to climb to get to the sock, learn to open cabinets with different fastenings and to untie knots when the sock was tied to a chair leg. In every case, possession of the sock was Terry's reward but in the course of these games he not only learned many new skills, but his obsessive attachment to the sock faded to the point where it could be put away for long periods of time while Terry was involved with other activities.*

Sometimes the only way to reach a child is by joining him in his compulsive activity for a while and then gradually introducing small variations into it, until the compulsion has lost its exclusive hold on the child.

> *Kirk's only observable activity was outside on the porch, where he endlessly tapped the boards with a block. Miss Simons made a point of staying in his vicinity and when he did not move away, she too tapped a couple of times a little way away from him. Startled, he briefly interrupted his own tapping then resumed it again. Encouraged that her interference was not going to make him stop his activity, Miss Simons repeated her tapping over the next few days until Kirk had become accustomed to her presence and her tapping. After a while, Miss Simons introduced a very slight variation in the rhythm of the tapping and was pleased to notice the child picking up on it. This convinced her that he was attentive to her and was actually engaging in a first, tentative interaction.*
> *Now that she had his attention, Miss Simons slowly moved herself and her tapping down the length of the porch. The child followed. Then one day she started tapping on the edge of the porch but then walked over to a picnic table she had stationed nearby and continued to tap there. Again the child followed. When he had become accustomed to the new place, she changed posi-*

tion again and over a period of five or six weeks, slowly led him through the whole yard, ending up by the swings. By now the child was definitely more alert and after a short period of tapping on the swing, he climbed on and allowed himself to be pushed on it, the first real activity he had ever engaged in outside of his tapping.

Some children have strong compulsions, but they also engage in some other activities that can be used as a basis for further learning and development. Even though such compulsions may occupy the child a great deal or may be difficult to cope with, they do not really require intervention and are ignored as much as possible. They usually fade out as other behavior develops, or they may persist in a milder form that does not interfere with either the environment or the child's overall progress. Ryan's stick twirling fits into this category.

When Ryan came to Linwood at age four he was mute and withdrawn. He insisted on wearing earmuffs as if to close out the sounds of the outside world, and in all of his free time did nothing but march up and down inside the fence, twirling sticks in front of his eyes. Nevertheless Ryan made progress and eventually began to communicate. His pacing decreased and his earmuffs eventually came off. The more involved he became in other activities the less compulsively he twirled his sticks but he did not give them up until he was almost ready to go to school part-time outside of Linwood. Even today, as an adult, he still remembers his compulsion.

Some compulsions, while they do not hinder a child's possible progress, may interfere with others to an intolerable degree, or may be potentially harmful to a child's health, as is the case with children who take off their clothes and shoes in winter.

Where a child's behavior infringes too far on the comfort or safety of other people, limits are set almost immediately.

When Mel first came to Linwood his favorite activity was to spin every object he could lay his hands on, including chairs. He did this throughout the whole house and he finally came up to the office where he tried to dislodge Miss Simons from her chair so he could spin it. She firmly told him that this was her office and her chair and that she wanted to sit in it undisturbed. He was welcome to visit her but this was one chair he could not spin. He readily accepted this and eventually was further limited and only allowed to spin his own chair, until he gave up spinning all together.

In this kind of limit setting it is important not to get into a power struggle with the child. By keeping the demands manageable and the steps small, or by acknowledging the child's urgent need to behave in certain ways, it becomes possible to ask some concession of him and to achieve changes that benefit both the child and his environment.

> *Jack, an indefatigable spitter, was eventually given a wastebasket of his own to spit in. It meant that he had to put some controls on his urge, though he was still able to indulge his compulsion. Later, further limits were put on his spitting. He could not do it at mealtimes, though at first snack times were exempt from that restriction. Still later, he was limited to one particular snack a day, then spitting at the table, whether for eating or working, was out. Some years later, Jack still spits a little, mostly when he is otherwise unoccupied. But he usually limits himself to wetting parts of his pants or shirt and can be fairly easily distracted and stopped when he tries to spit elsewhere.*

Some children have compulsions that seem to run away with them and they need help with coping with them.

> *Owen was a regular little pack rat. He accumulated things and needed to take them with him everywhere. To help him transport them more easily, he was given a paper bag. But this only allowed him to carry more stuff around and he soon had a whole collection of bags which had to be lined up within his sight or he couldn't function. He would not tolerate other children near his bags, yet as their number increased they were becoming a major obstacle in the hallway, the dining room, and the play area.*
> *Owen's anxiety over his belongings and his need to keep them close and safe were beginning to become so burdensome to the little boy that he had to be helped. He was told to select what he really needed near him and was told that from now on he could only bring two bags with him. He was also given a place for them where they did not obstruct traffic to make it easier for the staff to protect them from the interference of other children. This deal satisfied Owen and reduced his overall anxiety so that he was able to function more normally again in other respects.*

Another example of an escalating compulsion is provided by Jimmy who played exclusively with toy cars and trucks.

One day Jimmy brought a miniature plastic car with him to the dining room, placing it next to his plate. Within the next few days his fleet increased and as time went on he brought larger and larger trucks with him, until he began crowding everything else off the table.

The staff insisted that Jimmy bring only one toy to meals at a time. He had a terrible tantrum, but the staff held firm. Finally he chose the largest truck he could find and placed it smack in the middle of the table, looking at the adults with an expression that seemed to say "What are you going to do now?" A staff member told him that he should take the truck off the table and put it somewhere where it was safe from the other children and where he could see it. First he put it on a smaller table that had four children sitting at it, but he was reminded that he didn't like it when other children touched his toys and was asked to look for a place they couldn't reach. He moved it to a serving table and then to a staff member's chair. With his truck he was controlling the whole dining room. The other children were upset because dinner could not be served until Jimmy had found a suitable place for his truck. Finally he was told to put it on top of the refrigerator which could be seen from his seat and which was safely out of the reach of other children.

Screaming, he took a chair and placed the truck where he had been asked to. For several days he insisted on using a chair already occupied by another child to stash his truck away, but the staff firmly kept him to his own chair. After a few days he seemed to lose interest and stopped bringing toys to the dining room.

Dealing with Jimmy's compulsion could easily have ended in a power struggle. By accommodating his desire to have a toy in the room that could not be touched by anybody else, but at the same time limiting the number and the placement of the toys when they began to encroach on the comfort of the people around him, it was possible to avoid an escalating conflict. Rather than arbitrarily forbidding his activities, Jimmy was actively engaged in the limit-setting process. His ability to reason was appealed to, and instead of treating him like an infant whose needs were unimportant or unreasonable, the staff worked with Jimmy to find a solution.

The willingness to compromise, to take a child's needs seriously and to go slowly, are all part of successfully helping children deal with their compulsions. And even before it seems as if they could possibly understand, rules are explained to them and their reason is appealed to. Other people's discomfort with certain behaviors, other children's needs, restrictions imposed by a concern for their safety, all of these are pointed out to the child as he is led away from some dangerous, unacceptable, or compulsive behavior.

Though many compulsions can simply be ignored and relied upon to fade out by themselves, others may be too intrusive, disruptive, unpleasant, or embarrassing as is the case of children undressing in public or of children publicly masturbating. Their behavior may be ignored at first but eventually they will be taught that there is a place for everything and that certain things can be only done in private or in certain places, like the bathroom.

Children who habitually take off their shoes, may have to put them on for specific activities, to go up the stairs to the bathroom, or to go outside. While they may be admitted barefoot to the playground at first, the driveway may be out of bounds for unprotected feet, and a child who takes off his shoes or clothes in the car or on an outing may be taken home and be told that he is not yet ready to leave Linwood.

LIMITING COMPULSIONS THAT HAVE BECOME WEAPONS

From observing children's reactions to limit setting and from watching their compulsive behavior change in certain situations, it sometimes becomes clear that a child is beginning to become aware of his effect on the environment and that he is using his compulsion to exert some control over others. That was certainly the case with Jimmy and his trucks. When a compulsion becomes a weapon, steps have to be taken to limit it before it gets out of hand.

> When Barry came to Linwood he acted as if he were a machine. He had all kinds of strings in his hands and a whole lot of stuff hanging from his pockets. He planted himself in the middle of the room, surrounded himself with little bits of paper and with chairs and "plugged himself in." There he was, with all kinds of visible strings and invisible wires attached to every object around him, and if any of his arrangements were interfered with, he started to scream and yell. When Miss Simons tried to move him and his objects out of the way, he strongly objected, which alerted her to the fact that Barry's behavior was at least in part an attempt to control the environment.

In cases where a compulsion is beginning to turn into an attempt to control the environment, it can usually be limited or even terminated fairly quickly and effectively.

> In Barry's case, Miss Simons emptied a whole large corner

of the room and told him that this was his place, where nobody would disturb him or inadvertently interfere with his wires. All his bits and pieces were put in the reserved part of the room, and the other children were specifically told that this was Barry's space and that he was to be left alone there until he wanted to come out.

At the time Barry did not talk, but he obviously understood what was said to and about him. For a little while he sat "plugged in" in his part of the room and the staff protected him from intrusions but otherwise ignored him. Within a very short time Barry came out of his corner, leaving everything but one little piece of string with a bead on it behind. For a while he carried this remnant around with him wherever he went and even plugged himself in with it at the dining room table, but the intricate network of wires was gone and his compulsion no longer interfered with anybody's activities.

Barry's obsession with wires did not originally develop in an attempt to manipulate his environment, but as it expanded, others became more affected by it and were forced to take note of it, until it had the potential to become the focus of every group or situation the child was in. As he became more aware of his environment, he also became more aware of the effect his compulsion had on others and on its attention-getting potential. Had it been allowed to continue unchecked, he would soon have had everybody dancing to his tune, subjugating their needs to his compulsion.

On the other hand, Barry's compulsion and that of other children whose behavior encroaches on their environment is strong and real and stems from an urgent inner need that has to be respected. If it is necessary to limit these behaviors or even to stop them altogether, it has to be done in a way that proves to the child that his behavior is accepted. He needs to know that he will be allowed to indulge his compulsion and may even be protected from outside interference, even though certain limits are imposed on him. This was the case with Barry.

It also worked with Nancy, whose particular compulsion was beginning to make it difficult for people to move freely around the house. Nancy had a strong compulsion about the way she went up and down the stairs. She had to march up in a straight line and down the same way, like a soldier. Sometimes, when she was on her way, she would suddenly start to scream and get terribly upset. It took weeks of observation to realize that this happened when somebody else was on the stairs while she was making her way to the bathroom.

Since there weren't that many children at Linwood at the time, it was relatively easy to arrange free passage for Nancy. When she had to use the stairs, everyone else was asked to stop and wait so that she could walk up and down without an upset. After a while, Miss Simons noticed that Nancy was beginning to time her visits to the bathroom differently. She now used the stairs at those times when traffic was heaviest, such as lunchtime, or at times when children or staff were scheduled to go to and from the yard or to the dining room or dormitory. This meant that the other children were kept waiting at meals and other crucial times. In effect Nancy had it in her power to make activities at Linwood come to a full stop any time she wanted to.

It became clear that her moves were calculated to have the greatest possible effect on her environment and that something had to be done about it. Though Nancy herself spoke only a few words, Miss Simons judged that she could understand what was said to her. She took Nancy out to the stairs and told her "Nancy, I know that you don't want anybody to cross your line when you are on the stairs." Nancy looked at her with a startled expression on her face. "I am going to help you. You can walk alongside the wall and then nobody will be able to cross your line." They went up together, and Miss Simons demonstrated how Nancy was "safe" as long as she kept close to the wall. "Or, if you want to walk in the middle, you can do it at certain times during the morning and afternoon." (She was given times when no one else was likely to need to use the stairs). Nancy looked up with a smile, marched down the stairs and from that time on never screamed on the stairs again. It was as if her compulsion had been cleanly cut through.

From accumulated observations, there was good reason to suspect that Nancy had become aware of the attention-getting potential of her compulsive behavior and that she enjoyed it. Though she may not have had control over her compulsion, she was able to control her environment with it. Her manipulations indicated a growing awareness of other human beings and of human interactions. While this is a definite sign of progress, it is necessary to help the child contain his compulsion. Unchecked, the need to control the environment becomes a compulsion itself, and it not only makes everyone else miserable, it also engulfs the child, whose total energy has to be spent in maintaining his grip on the situation.

Once it is clear that a compulsion is mainly used to attract attention or to dominate the environment, measures to limit it have to be taken. As in the case of "naughty" behavior, described earlier, children are usually allowed to enjoy their mastery for a while before it is made clear to them that they have been found out and that others are no longer willing to submit to their tyranny. As we have seen, this can be done by limiting the child's opportunities to dominate the living space or routine of others. In extreme cases it may be possible to cut even more directly through some behavior that is clearly aimed at attracting maximum attention.

> *Though Nancy had lost her compulsiveness about the stairs, she still continued to scream and yell throughout the day. In fact, her screaming seemed to have increased. There never seemed to be an observable reason for it, and since she hardly communicated at all, she was unable to tell anybody the possible causes of her discomfort.*
>
> *Nancy screamed and yelled in the room, outside, in the dormitory, and in the hall. There it was the most unbearable because it echoed up through the stairwell and affected every single person in the house, including the staff who had offices on the top floor. Attempts to get Nancy to confine her screaming to a room were unsuccessful, and as time went on Nancy clearly began to favor the hall and screamed and screamed in it until everyone's nerves were on edge. Again, she had found the most dramatic way of interfering with the comfort of the maximum number of people. Something had to be done.*
>
> *So one day, when she had a screaming fit again, Miss Simons took Nancy into the dining room. The staff was instructed not to interrupt her or call her for any reason, because she wanted to have unlimited time to work with Nancy. When they were alone, Miss Simons told the little girl, "Nancy, I think the time has come for you to do something else than scream. It's time for you to talk. But you still have an awful lot of screaming to do first, so I'm going to be with you here and help you." While she was talking, the girl briefly interrupted her screaming and seemed to be listening to her. "I'm going to sit here with you, and you are going to scream as long as you want to, because this is the last time you are going to scream anywhere." Nancy screamed and screamed, while Miss Simons calmly read a magazine.*
>
> *After a while Nancy stopped and looked at Miss Simons who said, "You still have a lot more screaming to do," and returned to her reading. Nancy screamed again for a while, then stopped, came up to Miss Simons and smiled at her. Again she was told "That's not long enough, Nancy, you have an awful lot more to do." So Nancy screamed and screamed, and kicked and screamed for about two hours. Miss Simons assured Nancy that she would*

*stay with her as long as necessary, even if her ears hurt from the
screaming, that nobody was going to call her, and that the other
children could do without her, because she felt that Nancy needed
her more at this time.*

*After about two hours Miss Simons felt that the child was
beginning to get exhausted. She said, "Nancy, if you are really
through screaming you are now going to talk", and Nancy said,
"I want a cookie." She was promptly given one and ate it contentedly without further screaming. From that time on the unprovoked
screaming disappeared and Nancy only screamed when there was
a clear reason for an upset.*

As was the case with Nancy, a compulsion that has been cut off in this
fashion does not reappear, at least not in the same guise. Though autistic
children do regress at times, as we have discussed earlier, the reappearance
of an earlier compulsive behavior, such as screaming, should not
automatically be dismissed as a relapse into old behavior patterns that need
to be curtailed again. Children do have legitimate reasons for screaming,
crying, or temper tantrums and the first order of business has to be to
carefully examine the environment for possible stress factors that might
be causing their behavior, as the following story illustrates.

*It was a great relief to everybody when Nancy's endless
screaming and temper tantrums gradually diminished and disappeared. Though she was still essentially mute, Nancy began to
understand speech and to react to it. She was also able to identify many pictures of objects and animals on flashcards.*

*One day at lunch Nancy suddenly, and for no visible reason,
went into one of her famous tantrums again. The staff was
dismayed, fearing that this might mean a resumption of her old
behavior patterns. But Miss Simons reminded them that children
often had legitimate reasons for being upset and that Nancy's tantrum, seemingly out of nowhere, might well be her way of trying
to communicate something definite.*

*Instead of dealing with the tantrum by sending Nancy from
the table, Miss Simons invited her to show her what was upsetting her. Nancy ran from the table and pointed to the cupboard
in which her flashcards were kept. As soon as she had them, she
selected one with a bird in a tree, then pulled Miss Simons by the
hand, indicating that she wanted to go outside. Card in hand she
excitedly pointed to a live bird sitting on a tree in the yard, then
ran back inside and this time selected a card with a fish on it. Back*

*in the dining room she put the card beside her plate and scream-
ing pointed first to the card, then to the fishstick on her plate.*

*The message was clear. While the bird in the tree outside
resembled the picture on the card, the fishstick she was given
looked nothing like the fish in the picture. So she screamed out
her confusion and her anger. Nancy was promptly taken to a store
that sold fish to show her the real thing, and the process of turning fish into fishsticks was explained to her in simple terms. This
satisfied her.*

This story accentuates the need for extreme caution in interpreting a
child's behavior. Even if past experience with a child might suggest reasons
and ways of dealing with him, it is always better to approach each situation as a new one and to observe the child carefully, instead of prejudging
him or of jumping to conclusions.

Autistic children's obsession with sameness and their compulsiveness
which have been discussed in this chapter, are striking symptoms of a severe
developmental disorder. They can be interpreted as an expression of the
overwhelming anxiety these children experience as they move through a
world that makes little sense to them. Their compulsions provide a tiny
island of certainty and predictability in a sea of sensory information that
they are not equipped to decipher properly, to organize, or to learn from.

Their peculiar style of functioning is described and analyzed in all the
literature about autism. The question remains what neurological malfunc-
tion is forcing children to behave as they do. Some professionals see autism
as a special form of mental retardation which particularly affects language
and cognition. These processes and the therapy techniques designed to deal
with them are examined in the following chapter.

SEVEN
✦✦✦

Language and Thought Processes

INTRODUCTION

It is easy to give credence to a view of autism as primarily a language disorder since aberrant language development is a predominant, pervasive, and persistent part of the syndrome. Autistic children who use or develop speech before they are five or six years old usually have a better prognosis than those whose speech does not recover early. Mental retardation has also been associated with autism, since only 20% of people with autism have measured intelligent quotients of 70 or above. The majority show an extreme variability of intellectual functioning, especially on formal testing, performing poorest on tasks requiring abstract thought, symbolism, or sequential logic. Many professionals consider the IQ level the single most relevant predictive feature in an autistic child's mental, intellectual, and emotional make-up.

Despite its obvious importance, the question remains whether the language disorder autistic children display is indeed the main root of their problem, or is itself only one of the areas affected by malfunctions in an underlying brain structure. Such an area might be the reticular activating system, located in the cerebral cortex and involved in widespread activities throughout the brain, especially in language and emotional states. Another theoretical model links early brainstem damage with improper development of the mesolimbic portion of the cortex.[12]

A structural impairment in any area of the brain involving emotions and other sensory information as well as language would explain why deficiencies in communication show up from birth onward and affect every aspect of interactions, verbal as well as pre-verbal and nonverbal ones.

Many autistic children seem to lack the ability to elicit, perceive, or interpret facial, as well as vocal cues. They themselves rarely develop the rich body language and the repertoire of gestures, facial expressions, and sounds that are the earliest forms of communication and of social interaction. Almost from birth on, they either shy away from physical contacts or fail to react to them. Autism is thus often perceived as being a disorder of social and emotional processes as much as one of language deficiency.

Regardless of causation, there is clearly a connection between social and language development which at later stages shows up in mutism or the absence or distortion of communicative speech, especially in social settings or around emotional issues. Delayed and erratic language development, idiosyncratic usage, and abnormalities in understanding and using language, as well as impaired thought processes are major concerns in the diagnosis and treatment of autistic children.

In normal children, language unfolds in set, sequential stages as part of the overall cognitive, social, and emotional development. At first, a baby's only signal is of discomfort. But as early as the second month a child "answers" the mother with little sounds of its own when she talks to him while caring for him. This voice contact is parallel to the eye contact the child establishes with the mother while he is being fed and which leads to the first social smile around six weeks of age. Sounds are thus both a means of communication and of social interaction long before they become words with concrete meanings.

Gesturing also develops as a precursor of spoken language in the early months of life. Nonverbal cues, such as head shaking or nodding, stroking, patting, pulling, or pushing gestures as well as facial expressions, smiles or frowns with or without accompanying sounds, are the predominant means of communication between the child and his caretakers. In these exchanges, the child is an active partner. He not only reacts to signals, he generates them spontaneously himself and evokes them in others, indicating his emotional and physical needs as well as taking obvious pleasure in the interplay of human interactions.

PATTERNS OF LANGUAGE DEVELOPMENT

In most autistic children many of these precursors of speech are absent. Gestures as well as eye contact either do not develop at all, or gesturing is clearly not part of two-way interactions. If gesturing develops at all, it is only aimed at satisfying an immediate need. An autistic child does not reach out to another human being from whom he expects solace or satisfaction. He reaches out to an arm or to a hand that he can use like a tool to help himself obtain what he wants.

As sounds develops into speech in normal infants, the first words are a product of imitation. Copying is one way in which children learn, and early games of pattycake, of waving good-by, of handclapping, and the many other little interchanges involving mutual imitation of gestures, facial expressions, and sounds are the forerunners of many later skills, including speech.

Many autistic children lack the ability or the inclination to copy. They do not engage in the imitative games of normal infants and may never pass beyond the stage of spontaneous babbling. These children may already have shown abnormal crying patterns and a general lack of nonverbal and pre-verbal communications such as smiling, cooing, or reaching out. They may have seemed closed off and out of touch to the point of appearing deaf.

In a number of children, early development was unalarming, seemingly uneventful, and in some respects even precocious. They imitated sounds, words, and even first sentences, but language development came to an abrupt halt around 18 months to 2 years of age. Already acquired speech disappeared, until the children were either completely mute or used only isolated sounds or words in inappropriate ways, so that again, deafness was suspected. A majority of the children presently at Linwood were first seen at a language and hearing clinic around 2 to 4 years of age where it was discovered that their hearing was normal.

Other autistic children do talk, some at an early age, but that doesn't mean that they communicate. They seem to have an unusually well developed auditory memory and are able to repeat words or sentences spoken within their hearing, either immediately or days and weeks after the fact. This phenomenon is called echolalia. Children may parrot single words or lengthy phrases, jingles, TV commercials, songs from the radio, or anything else that sticks in their minds, without any apparent comprehension.

Some children start talking in this fashion so early and imitate what they hear so perfectly, that they may even fool their parents for a while into thinking them particularly precocious.

Dawn knew the whole score of the "Sound of Music" by heart at age two. She also taught herself to read around the same age from Reader's Digest Magazines. Despite her fluent speech, she did not interact normally with her family and worried her mother by a seemingly willful and stubborn refusal to ask for things she wanted. The parents were somewhat reassured when she responded to their insistence on good manners and proper speech and repeated requests in the required form, "May I have a cookie, please, Mommy?" until she was sent to fetch a beer for her father one day at a family picnic, and was heard to address the stranger presiding over the beer thusly, "May I have a beer, please, Mommy." It was at that moment that the mother's diffuse unease sharpened into certainty that there was something seriously wrong with her unusual little daughter.

Children who exhibit echolalia or hyperlexia—a premature ability to read, coupled with a lack of comprehension—sometimes intersperse their echolalic utterances with meaningful language. There may be a striking contrast between the facile recitation of lengthy texts and the clear pronunciation of complicated words that are part of echolalia and the often tortured delivery, low tone, and distorted diction of predominantly monosyllabic words children use to express needs or answer questions.

There are also children who have a set repertoire of words or phrases that they either use to communicate with or with which they interlace their regular conversation. One boy, who talked to himself constantly in an echolalic fashion, started out with a single meaningful phrase with which he addressed people trying to interact with him, "Scratch my back." Another boy routinely greets adults with the phrase, "Orange juice is a breakfast drink." He demands confirmation of this statement before he continues any interchange.

Some otherwise mute children hum or sing. While they seem able to pick up melodies very quickly, they either can not or choose not to reproduce the words of a song. Their musical ability and the often almost uncanny way in which they are able to imitate voices and the exact phrasings, intonation, and pronunciation of words or sentences also contrasts strongly with their own speech patterns. The speaking voice of most autistic children usually lacks inflection, and the children tend to talk in a low monotone which may alternate with a sudden, staccato delivery in which some words emerge with explosive force.

The language of some children who have had previous speech and language training is characterized by the presence of rote expressions that are applied mechanically and often inappropriately. It becomes quickly apparent that these children have learned their vocabulary like parrots and cannot apply what they have been taught to real life situations. The following exchange was observed during an intake examination.

> Therapist: "What's your name?"
> Child: "Danny."
> Therapist: "What's your sister's name?"
> Child: "I'm fine, please."

The boy had obviously expected the routine second question, "How are you?" and responded with the set phrase to this that he had memorized.

The forms of deviant language development described so far differ in important ways. The various categories may be indicative of differences in intelligence, in causation, in the overall severity of the autistic impairment, or in the degree to which the child's ability to process language in particular is affected. But there is a highly significant feature that they have in common. In all of them, it is the communicative and interactive aspects of language that are either missing or most strikingly deviant.

LANGUAGE AND SOCIAL–EMOTIONAL DEVELOPMENT

The fact that a goodly number of children stop developing further speech, or even lose the vocabulary they have already developed, at the point at which language becomes associated with people and social interactions, suggests that there is a close connection between the two. It is possible that around age two both language and social processes start to become so complex that the children are no longer able to handle them. It may also be that it is the relationship aspect of language that is especially difficult and frightening to autistic children, and that mutism and retarded language development are at least in part a defense against social and emotional contacts. This view is supported by examples of children who were mute and seemingly unaware of activities in their environment, but turned out to understand a lot of what was said to them or in their presence, like Lee at his first meeting with Miss Simons.

Many children clearly understand what is said to them but communicate only under duress and only in the most primitive one-word sentences around their most immediate needs. Other children with a good command of the language either cannot or do not want to talk, but write at a very advanced level, often with a large vocabulary and perfect spelling.

Lee used to dictate long stories by spelling them letter by letter at high speed. Later he talked more normally, but would still run the words together without pause, creating interminable sentences that were almost impossible to understand. He not only corrected the spelling of these stories, he also remembered word for word exactly what he had dictated and would get upset if something was missing, such as one repetition of "Knock, knock, knock."

Frank's way of communicating with people is to ask them to spell out words for him or, in his turn, spell his way through a list of words that are always in alphabetical order. This seems to be a residue of his earlier training where he was taught the alphabet with flashcards of objects. When a new adult establishes contact with him, Frank will demand that the adult spell out his name at every meeting, preferably by tracing the letters on Frank's stomach.

Many children who have developed speech sabotage its communicative aspects in other ways. They may mumble unintelligibly, run words together, distort sounds, or hum words instead of pronouncing them normally. In writing, they may scribble letters or words on top of each other, thus hiding what they have written and making it illegible.

In some children language ability seems to fluctuate. When they are alone and talking to themselves or are relaxed and comfortable, they speak more freely and with a better vocabulary than when they are tense and under pressure. Some parents compare their children to a kind of radio receiver that fades in and out, depending on the atmospheric conditions. Autistic children clearly tune out at times; or perhaps they either do not make an effort to tune in or have greater difficulties in doing so at some times than at others.

A kind of tuning out can be clearly observed around specific topics. Many autistic children and even adults who can make their needs known in appropriate ways and can converse freely on factual topics revert to mutism or almost monosyllabic answers when they are asked to address issues with emotional overtones.

Language is not only a tool of social interactions, it also mirrors the emotional development of children. As a normal child begins to experience the world as something apart from himself, and as he becomes more and more independent, he develops a sense of self that expresses itself in changes in his language. From defining himself as others do, "Bobby wants a cookie," he eventually acts and talks like a separate individual who interacts with others on his own terms: "I want a cookie."

In autistic children this process of separation and differentiation is either absent, delayed, or distorted, as we have discussed in the chapter on relationships. The result is that these children generally have a great deal of difficulty in making verbal distinctions between themselves and others, even when they have already reached a fairly high level of speech development and generally function on a higher level.

They frequently confuse possessive pronouns, and there is a marked delay in the correct use of personal pronouns as well. Even youngsters who are almost ready to leave Linwood may introduce themselves correctly to a stranger and then ask him to reciprocate by saying, "What's my name?"

A girl of twelve who was seen for diagnostic purposes was chatting more or less appropriately as she went through various tasks like reading, writing, puzzles, and drawing. Whenever she ran into difficulties she would stop and say with the faintest questioning inflection, "You need help"?

As the above example also indicates, autistic children have difficulties in making the distinction between a statement and a question. In answering questions, they often simply repeat it in the form of an assertion. When asked why he was crying, Matthew replied "Because why." Such an answer may partly stem from a confusion about the nature of questions as requests for information. They may also be influenced by the echolalic tendencies of autistic children that we have already talked about. But in good part the difficulty results from the children's inability to reason, on the one hand, and from their inability to understand or describe their motives and feelings, on the other hand.

Autistic children also have problems with listening to others and of relating the experiences of others to their own. All of these elements are present in the partial transcript of a group session with three boys, given below. It was called because one of them, Mark, had gotten self-abusive when he was teased by another boy.

Q: "What happened, Mark?"
M: "I hit a wall."
Q: "Why did you do that?"
M: "Because why."
Q: "Who teased you?"
M: "Jan teased."
Q: "What do you do when somebody teases you, Calvin?"
C: "Hit him back."
Q: "Listen, Mark, what does Calvin do?"
M: "I hit you."
Q: "No, you don't hit me. Harold, do you hit your head against a wall when you get angry?"
H: "Hit your head against a wall."
Q: "Do you hit your head?"
H: "Yes." [He doesn't]
Q: "Calvin, tell Mark what to do when he gets angry."
C: "What do you do, Mark?"

On their own, autistic children rarely ask questions. Their speech is mostly restricted to requests, commands, and denials. While they eventually learn to assert or defend themselves through the use of language, and to say "no" to something instead of throwing a temper tantrum or becoming physically aggressive, they have an almost impossible time learning to say "yes." A child who is asked whether he wants to do something tends to repeat the question as if falling in with a suggestion rather than making an independent decision. "Do you want to go swimming today, Danny?"

will most likely be answered with, "Want to go swimming today," instead of a simple "yes."

Because they do not understand their own emotions or are frightened by them, autistic children sometimes talk in riddles when the subject matter is fraught with emotions. However, autistic children do not fantasize the way schizophrenics do, or make up stories and fantasies like normal children. Their sometimes bizarre and fantastic statements always hide realistic thoughts or feelings they are uncomfortable with or anxious about.

> *It took the staff three weeks to figure out what Benjamin was saying when he periodically went about muttering "Once a month a sweetmeat." From observations and from putting two and two together, they came to the conclusion that he was obliquely referring to the monthly appointment his parents had with the social worker, at which time they brought a treat along for him.*
>
> *The same boy was impressed by the violent temper tantrums of Clark, a big boy, who tended to throw himself against walls and yelled and roared in a voice that filled the whole house. At various times Benjamin made seemingly incomprehensible statements, such as "A brown Dodge hit the wall this morning," or "Do you hear the sounds of the Grand Canyon?" which were actually comments on Clark's tantrums. (Clark's father owned a brown Dodge.)*

Since the children are either unaware of their own emotions, or afraid of them, talking about them in this cryptic way allows them to express feelings without having to face them openly or deal with them. Asking children for explanations of what they have said, or offering interpretations, would therefore not only be intrusive, but threatening to them.

Intelligent autistic children, especially those who have developed speech before the age of five or six, often catch up in their language development to the point where they can express themselves fluently on any familiar subject. Many children who were initially mute end up going to school and are able to function well in situations that demand a fair degree of literacy. But often the language of even the more advanced children and adults retains characteristic peculiarities that reflect the fact that their social and emotional development lags far behind their language skills. They typically talk at people in repetitive ways about their own preoccupations or special areas of expertise and have a hard time listening to what somebody else might have to contribute to the conversation.

The language of autistic individuals abounds with facts and is empty of emotional content. The same goes for their memory. The way they remember or describe events consists of the enumeration of facts. It is usually a compilation of minute details, presented in exact sequence, regardless of their importance. Many autistic children are fascinated by numbers, dates and technical information. They are interested in anything that is factual, exact, and quantifiable, like maps, mechanical drawings, historical events, addresses, and the like.

In 1981 Brian, who was then eleven years old and attending a regular middle school while living at Linwood, wrote an essay entitled "The Seven Year Story." Following are excerpts from the beginning of the story that goes in chronological order from 1974 to 1981.

> *When I first came to Linwood in 1974, I was predicting I would go to public school in five years. I thought this would be a long career for me. But when I got off to a terrible start there, they thought they had put me in too quickly. I could have waited another year or two. When I first went swimming, I banged on lockers. On my first Christmas party in December, I bought [he means "got"] a Flintstone Box Game. I went to the Howard County Public Library in February, 1975. I kicked and hit people when I usually get mad at those staff members. I went to Patapsco State Park for my first picnic in June, 1975. [. . . . .] Kenneth went to Ellicott City Elementary School in September of 1975 and it was located on College Avenue at that time . . . .*

In reading through Brian's account, one is struck by the feat of memory it represents, by the details of dates and events he is able to recall, as well as by the way occurrences that were obviously highly emotional are described objectively and are casually slipped between information about dates and facts, almost like afterthoughts.

The emotional poverty and over-emphasis on facts are recurrent and characteristic features of the language and thought processes of autistic children. Their emotional and social development influences the content as well as the style of their speech, but the concreteness of their language and thinking also stems from a lag in cognitive development and not only from social and emotional deficiencies.

LANGUAGE AND COGNITIVE DEVELOPMENT

Normally a child learns about the world by experimentation and by being exposed to a variety of routines and experiences from which he gradually begins to extract information about the properties and characteristics of things, events, and people around him. A normal child's inborn ability to screen sounds and to make the connection between them and things, activities, or emotions makes language an important part of the cognitive processes.

For specific sounds and words to acquire meaning, they have to be connected repeatedly with sensory information the child consciously experiences. The smell, taste, look, and texture of a certain substance, for example, becomes associated with a particular sound and thus becomes identifiable as "milk," "water," or "cookie." The totality of touch, voice, facial configuration, and smell and the sensations of having physical needs satisfied make up the impressions the child has of his caretaker. They soon blend into a unique "gestalt" that eventually becomes associated with the word "mother."

Once words have meaning, they can be used for more effective communication. Language consists of a system of common symbols, governed by a set of rules that make it possible to convey and exchange precise information. Apart from its importance for social interactions, language also enables people to store information, to organize, rearrange or recall it, to speculate about it, apply it to new situations, and add to it.

Although thought and language are mutually interdependent, they are not identical. Even before a normal child has the means to express his thought processes verbally, he can solve problems in his mind for which he previously had to find solutions by trial and error.

The first manipulations a child engages in are purely exploratory. Babies bang objects together, they shake them, squeeze them, lick them, chew on them, smell them, drop, poke, or throw them. In the course of these activities, the child begins to discover some of the characteristics as well as the common properties and differences of the things he handles. Later experimentation becomes more purposeful and play more functional. Objects are used in the various ways to which they lend themselves. Sticks are used to hit or poke with, balls are rolled, bounced or kicked, buckets are filled or emptied.

At this stage, and for the next few years of the child's life, his view of the world is based on his own, very concrete experiences, and his language, as well as his thought processes reflect this fact and are equally concrete. In time, language helps to free thought processes from their concrete, experimental base and thus facilitates abstract representation, symbolic play, and logical reasoning.

If meaningful language is rooted in a child's own actions and experiences, it is easy to understand why autistic children who are out of touch with the environment and have difficulties processing both sensory and auditory information would suffer impaired thought processes. There are a significant number of autistic children, however, who do reach the stage of pre-verbal reasoning.

In a number of examples in previous chapters we have had demonstrations of the children's cleverness in solving complicated practical problems, such as reaching a rolled-up blind with a bent wire, or short-circuiting an outlet without getting hurt. At an age when they were either totally mute or were talking at the most elementary level, these children had an understanding of the way things function that showed intelligence at or above their age level.

Some autistic children, however, never get to or past the most primitive exploratory play and even the more advanced children rarely advance beyond the stage of concrete thinking and language. Autistic children are commonly deficient in concept development and abstraction and their play rarely becomes representational and almost never reaches the level of symbolic "make-believe." Sticks and stones remain just that and do not represent roads, houses, or trees in the sandbox. Doll play is rare, "let's-pretend games" practically unheard-of.

The language of autistic children mirrors their thought processes. In talking, they tend to stick to facts and they interpret what they hear in its most literal sense.

> *A small group of children was taken to an orchard where peaches were sold at a roadside stand. Ned, who seldom said anything, was preoccupied, as usual, with twiddling a small object between his fingers and did not seem to be paying much attention to anything. He stayed in the car and the only thing the counselor noticed was that he briefly, but deliberately, blew out twice, as if to blow bubbles.*
>
> *The following week the expedition was repeated. As the children were loaded into the car, Ned, without looking up or stopping his twiddling, mumbled "The blow-twice stand." He did not answer when he was asked what he meant but enlightenment came when the counselor noticed a sign on the stand that said "Blow Twice." It was an invitation to customers to blow their horns if the stand was unattended and they wanted service.*

Sometimes it is relatively easy to figure out a child's reactions, as in Ned's case. Often the children's reactions can be traced to their literal interpretations of metaphor. One child who overheard a conversation about somebody having had a "change of heart" was convinced the person had had a heart transplant. Expressions like "catching a bus," "hold on to your pants," or even "give me your hand," are also taken literally by autistic children, often with comical results.

Sometimes instructions seem straightforward, such as the assignment to "draw the woods" after a nature walk. In this case the result was a picture of several sticks, (plural of "wood"). In another case, a Linwood pupil who was already attending public school on a part-time basis, was chided by a teacher for not doing an assignment. At Linwood he was asked whether he had now completed his homework which consisted of writing a story. Readily he produced a sheet of paper on which he had written: a story.

Most normal children go through a phase in which they take great delight in riddles and jokes based on the literal meanings of words. This happens when they begin to shed the bonds of purely concrete thinking and are becoming aware of the metaphorical uses of language. An example is the perennial favorite "What did one wall say to the other?" to which the answer is, of course, "Meet you at the corner." Autistic children would fail to find any humor in this exchange.

Being stuck at a level of concreteness and literalness can also prevent children from being able to adjust to situations they have not previously encountered.

> Benjamin, who already visited public school daily from Linwood, walked to where the school bus picked him up, about a ten minute walk. When he first started this arrangement, he had been given ten cents to keep in his pocket and told that he was to call Linwood from a public phone with this money if ever there was an emergency.

> One day he did call from school to say that there was something wrong with his eye and that he could not see with it. An examination showed that an embolism in the eye had damaged it beyond repair. Benjamin was asked when this had happened, and it turned out that he saw a flash of light and then darkness on the steps of Linwood. He was asked why he hadn't come back in. Puzzled he said, "But aren't you proud of me? This was an emergency."

> Harvey had to walk a quarter of a mile to the school bus that took him to a regular school near Linwood. One day the principal called at noon to say that Harvey had only just arrived and that children had seen him in the morning walking the streets. He would not or could not tell them where he had been. At Linwood, Harvey explained that he had missed the bus that morning and had had to walk to school. It should only have taken him fifteen minutes at most, but he had faithfully retraced the route the bus took each morning picking up children throughout the neighborhood instead of going the direct way which he also knew.

Autistic children generally use speech to convey factual information or to express their wants rather than ideas. For them, language is at best a means to an end. They use a word to request something, such as a desired object, attention or assistance, or to direct somebody to either do or stop doing something. Some of the words the children use in these contexts are conventional ones that they have picked up or have been taught. Some are idiosyncratic in nature, and their meaning has to be inferred from the context in which they are used. Frank, for example, cries out "soofa," anytime anybody intrudes into his space, attempts to take something away from him or tries to hug, push, or hit him.

At home, Sidney used to get a cookie to console him whenever he fell or bumped himself, even though at that time he never showed any reaction to such accidents. After a year in treatment, Sidney became aware of pain. Whenever he got hurt, he would cry "cookie." But when he was given a cookie he was not really interested in it. Instead of eating it, he would take it to the first aid cabinet and ask for a bandaid for his "cookie." Once, Sidney had an infected finger which he showed to the therapist saying "cookie." When a cookie was offered him, he refused it. He led the therapist to the kitchen, got a bowl, and pointed to the water kettle on the stove. The therapist poured some warm water in the bowl and Sidney, satisfied, soaked his finger. To Sidney, "cookie" meant "hurt."

The same little boy was four and a half years old when he started to print words. At that time he hardly talked and most of his vocabulary was his own. The word he used for "green," for example, was "dye," but when he started to write, he spelled it correctly "g-r-e-e-n." If somebody else called green "dye," however, he got absolutely furious.

The concreteness of their thinking and their lack of spontaneity hamper many autistic children in expressing themselves appropriately. They may repeat set phrases they have been taught in one context or another, like Saul in this letter to Miss Simons.

"Dear Miss Simons,
How are you? I'm fine thank you."

Even when they have made great progress, autistic children generally exhibit a lack of imagination and creativity that is reflected in their language. Their grammatical speech is either overly pedantic, or they use complicated or inappropriate terms. A typical example is the round-about and almost tortured way in which twenty-four-year-old Terrence, who worked as a messenger at the time, expressed himself in a letter.

Dear Jean Simons,
Oh well, in this letter I will be saying a few lines about the follow-ing news and other things. [. . . .] How is everything been doing with you these days for yourself? [. . . .] I am kind of interested in for me to find out about the certain things what had been go-ing on with you these days. [. . . . .] I wish some day for me to come and visit you soon. Your best regards. . . .

While the development of language and reasoning of autistic children generally follows that of normal infants once they start improving, there are several ways in which the patterns may diverge. For one, the first words of autistic children are often not those that make up the usual vocabulary of normal infants. As often as not, they do not start to use language around food or everyday activities. Instead, their first words frequently express some primary interest or compulsion. The only word of one child, for a long time, was "pocket book." Trixie understands a lot and shows it by following instructions or identifying pictures, but the only thing she regular-ly says is "Friday," expressing her obsession with going home.

Another typical phenomenon is the unevenness of cognitive functioning of autistic children. They may perform at a very high level in one area, and be clearly retarded in their performance in another. Sometimes this divergence is linked to an inability to understand basic concepts. Some children are able to add long columns of multidigit figures at great speed, yet seem unable to grasp the concept of counting. Some children who cannot perform the simplest addition can apply mathematical skills to a practical situation, like Ricky who couldn't do arithmetic but was able to draw a scale model of his room that was exact to the fraction of an inch.

Children who have never talked have been known to teach themselves to read or at least to distinguish writing in situations that are of special in-terest to them. Martin was able to differentiate between jars of baby food containing various meat and vegetable mixtures that looked identical in every respect except for the legend on the labels. Kirk could pick out his favorite records from a whole stack that all had the same green centers and tiny gold lettering.

THE SPEECH AND LANGUAGE TREATMENT PROGRAM

Before devising a treatment program for a child, it is important to assess the level of his verbal functioning and identify areas of a particular strength or deficiency. Children enter Linwood at levels that range from mutism to proper speech, though the latter is a rare exception. In the case of children who have a certain amount of functional language, it may be possible to conduct a conventional evaluation based on intelligence and language tests, but with the majority of children, assessment is a long-term process, based on observations of their general functioning, their way of relating and communicating, and the use they make of sounds and words.

Spoken language is of such importance in human interactions and in cognitive development that it is one of the principal elements by which development levels are routinely judged. It is deemed so critical that often too much emphasis is put on speech too early in the treatment of autistic children. There is, indeed, a certain urgency about speech training, since there seems to be a consistent correlation between the first appearance of language proper and overall treatment outcomes. Children who start to talk before age five are considered to have a better prognosis than those who do not develop speech until later.

Despite this, language training cannot be hurried. It always must be part of a total treatment approach if language is ever to serve its proper functions. Communicative speech is an integral part of overall functioning in both normal and autistic children. But while it parallels and facilitates normal development, it often lags far behind the development of other skills in autistic children. A child who is not yet interested in relating to others, has no use for language. Pushing language on a child before it makes sense to him to use it may be futile, or produce drilled-in responses that can only be maintained by rigorous conditioning techniques.

Premature or exclusive focus on speech in isolation also tends to ignore an autistic child's many other, often more pressing needs. It may curtail development in other areas and even interfere with the establishment of relationships, because of the pressure put on the child to perform.

When a child first comes to Linwood, speech development may therefore not be a priority in treatment. Self-abusive children, who do not relate at all or those who are socially and emotionally still at an infant level as well as children with some critical, pervasive problem, such as a severe eating disorder may have to be treated in those areas before they are ready to learn to communicate. Also, before an autistic child can communicate through language, he has to develop some basic language prerequisites. He has to have a sense of himself and of his body. He has to feel the heat and the cold and be able to distinguish tastes, sounds, sights, and smells. He also has to be willing to open up to the world and to tolerate some contacts.

The first communications are usually nonverbal, just as in normal babies. But while in babies the precursors of speech grow naturally out of the daily contact with their caretakers, these have to be taught and practiced with autistic children. Speech and language therapy, therefore, starts long before a child is taught his first word. The whole treatment approach is aimed at developing the child to the point where he can understand language and can integrate it into his life.

It starts with gaining the child's trust and with establishing relationships within which he feels safe, and proceeds through developing preverbal skills like gesturing, motor and vocal imitations, turn-taking, and the different phases of play. The approach moves from isolated to parallel, imitative and finally interactive play. Within these activities the child builds up a first receptive vocabulary and a willingness to follow instructions. Only then is expressive speech, a child's ability to talk, addressed.

Once a child has progressed overall to a level comparable to that of a nursery school child, speech and language therapy can start concentrating on developing language. Since most children in treatment are not toddlers and come in with varying skills at vocalizing, no attempt is made to recreate normal speech development, in which sounds, such as vowels, usually appear in a certain, more or less set progression.

In normal speech development there is a hierarchy of usage with ascending levels of complexity of both thought and sentence structure. Different juxtapositions of words express different concepts, only some of which even the verbal autistic children use routinely. Once observation has pinpointed the ways the children use sounds or combine words to express meaning, speech and language therapy can expand a child's vocabulary and teach him new combinations that allow him to express more complex concepts.

If a child already uses words, the thrust of the treatment will be on teaching him that they have definite meanings and uses. If he only babbles, therapy will pick up on the sounds he produces spontaneously and expand on them. And if he is mute, some other activity connected with the mouth may be introduced or practiced and eventually associated with sounds, such as blowing soap bubbles, or spitting, in which the "sp" sound can be used as a basis for teaching the "p" sound.

One of the triggers for communicative speech is want. There has to be a reason to speak, and the more reluctant a child is to communicate, the more compelling the reason has to be. Compulsions, or any other strong interests or needs a child exhibits, are useful to motivate him. If he is especially interested in keys, for example, or he badly wants a cookie or a special toy, the therapist first establishes the connection between certain sounds and the desired object by emphasizing the word whenever the child sees or handles it. He is urged to imitate the word, or even just the beginning sound, "k-k-k-key" and any sign of cooperation is promptly rewarded by letting him have the desired object. By reinforcing increasingly closer approximations of the correct sounds, the word is eventually shaped and the association between the word, the object, and the effectiveness of speech is made.

Sometimes a desired object may be useful to motivate the child to develop other words. If a favorite toy is kept in a locked cupboard, for example, the therapist may use a key to open the door, emphasizing the word key or open while doing so. When the process of repetition has set up the association between the object or action and the word, opening the door may be delayed, while the word or its first letter is stressed, "k-k-k-key" or "o-o-o-open," and the child is encouraged to imitate the sounds. As before, any attempts or approximations are promptly rewarded, and as before, closer and closer approximations and eventually the whole word are required before the closet is opened and the child gets what he wants.

Children often develop imitative speech before they are engaged in a relationship, but once a child can talk and discovers that language can be a useful means to an end, he naturally tends to use it to get what he wants and in the process interacts more with people, so that language eventually becomes part of developing relationships. Once these are firmly established, more pressure can be put on the child to use words to communicate his needs.

Even within a strong relationship, however, speech training must never be pushed to the point where it becomes so intrusive or unpleasant that it turns a child off speech altogether. On the other hand, when a child is able and motivated to talk, and when speech is the focus of the interaction, other behaviors must not be allowed to interfere with the main task.

Once it has been decided that a child has to use speech to get a special toy, asking for it must be the only way for him to get it. A child may become impatient, frustrated, and temporarily upset by this insistence that he produce a sound, a word, or a sentence to get what he wants. He may turn to other activities, start acting out or even throw a temper tantrum. If the therapist lets himself be sidetracked by this behavior, attention shifts from the task at hand, and the wrong behaviors get reinforced.

The best way to handle these upsets is to ignore them. Depending on how seriously upset the child is, the interaction can be broken off, and the child involved in some other activity until he is judged ready to address the task again. Or the child is simply allowed to work off his spleen and when he is finished throwing things or tired of screaming or running around and again indicates a desire for the toy in question, the demands for the sound or the word are calmly repeated and success quickly rewarded.

This kind of speech training takes patience and a light hand. There is a delicate balance between pressuring a child too much and pushing him just enough to keep him moving forward. The way speech training is approached at Linwood helps avoid excessive pressure and at the same time strengthens the relationship aspects of language.

When a child seems ready for speech and starts working on a sound or word, he usually does so with only one person and in a particular, limited situation. He may be encouraged to imitate a sound, name an object, or ask for extra food in the speech therapist's room, or use a word to communicate a need to some other person on the playground or in the dining room. He may get the same things from other people or, in a different situation, even from the same person, without having to use speech.

Once a new skill is firmly established, it may eventually be required and practiced at other times, until it has become an integrated and permanent part of a child's behavioral or language repertoire. Once a word is used appropriately in the original situation and with different people, the usage of the word may be expanded to other situations or to other functions, and practice then centers on the transferability and generalization of a word or a concept.

> Larry has learned the word "open" in the speech therapist's room, but he only associated it with the action necessary to open the tin of cookies with which he is rewarded at the end of each session. Once he uses the word easily and routinely in that particular context, the therapist stores the tin in a cabinet that has to be opened to get to the cookies. Larry is shown the place where the tin is kept and is allowed to fetch it himself. Every time he opens the cabinet door, the therapists stresses the word "open."
>
> Then one day the cabinet is locked. Larry looks at the therapist for help. "What do you want, Larry?" You want me to open the door?" Larry nods and the therapist says, "O.K. let's open the door." On subsequent occasions the door is locked again and now the therapist demands that Larry tell him what he wants him to do. Soon Larry says "open" both for the cabinet door and for the lid of the tin.
>
> Next, the therapist may teach Larry that "open" can also be applied to the door of the room. Eventually Larry will be asked to use the word he has learned during the speech and language training sessions in selected situations in his regular room, until he uses it routinely whenever he is in an appropriate situation.
>
> In time, the one word sentence will be expanded from "open," to "open door," or "open the door." An expanding vocabulary makes the original word ever more useful. Further demands may now be made on Larry. The cookie tin will only be opened if Larry indicates what he wants. First "cookie" alone will be acceptable.

Eventually this will be expanded to "want cookie" and later to "I want cookie" and this sentence can then be generalized to other objects, as in "I want milk."

At this point it becomes important to provide a variety of experiences on which words and concepts can be based and to structure situations so that the child will have to use language to make things happen. Pictures depicting actions (running, sleeping) are introduced, sorting objects leads to quantifying (another..., more...) etc. One of the basic techniques of speech and language therapy is to give language an experiential basis, to associate the child's own activities and experiences, touch, smell, and movements with language in the same way that thoughts, language, and actions are connected during the early development of infants.

Any behaviors or words that show up spontaneously can be used in teaching language, but it is important not to pounce on anything when it first appears or the child is likely to give it up again. He has to have time to experiment on his own and feel comfortable with something new before demands are made of him to use it on command or in specific situations. And he must never feel that something that he does voluntarily is being used to pressure him. Just as with other behaviors, newly emerging manifestations of speech are at first seemingly ignored or acknowledged only casually. Later they are slipped into interactions almost accidentally and only occasionally, before being introduced into activities that are intrinsically interesting to the child. In speech development, as in every other aspect of treatment, the child is never punished for progress by being hurried along too fast or being pressured too insistently.

Language development is viewed as an ongoing process. The speech and language pathologist is part of the Linwood team. He not only works with individual children if and when they are ready to profit from more intense instruction, he gets to know them in their groups and during free play. The language therapist and the staff share their observations and incorporate them into an overall treatment plan of which language is only one component.

Depending on a child's developmental level, the staff may at first concentrate on the nonverbal prerequisites for speech, such as the ability to play next to others and to tolerate some social interactions, to imitate, to take turns, and to follow simple instructions. The children are also encouraged to communicate without speech. If a child throws a temper tantrum because he wants something, he is reminded that "You can show me what you want." Or if he gets agitated because another child comes too close, he is shown how to communicate his displeasure, perhaps by pushing the other child away.

It is also preferable not to focus on speech development when other oral tasks are being worked with. If the priority in treatment is to broaden food intake, for example, language therapy is de-emphasized. On the other hand, it may be decided to ignore a child's dietary idiosyncrasies for the time being and concentrate on the development of speech using strong food preferences as a motivator.

> *The reader may remember the boy who came to Linwood eating only marshmallows and crackers and was later introduced to peas and other foods. While he was still new to the program, however, his food habits were not interfered with, especially since he did eventually add milk to his intake and seemed to be doing all right on that diet.*
>
> *What seemed more important was the fact that the boy who had originally been mute was observed to start mumbling words that sounded like "crackers" and "marshmallows." Since he was giving indications that he was ready for speech, regulating his diet was deemed of secondary importance. Instead, his interest in his favorite foods was used to teach him some words like "cracker" and "marshmallow" and later have him ask for those foods that were locked in a closet by verbalizing, saying "open," "door," "key." Over a period of months he developed some primitive speech around foods he especially liked. Only when speech was firmly established was the task of expanding and normalizing his diet dealt with.*

One of the earliest interactions that babies engage in is intent gazing at their caretakers. Eye contact in normal children is an integral element of communication and one of the precursors of speech. At Linwood, eye contact is not deemed absolutely necessary for speech development. It may be helpful, but experience shows that insistence on it may actually slow down the process of language development, since some children may be very resistant to the intensity of a direct gaze. Many children develop speech long before eye contact and are only taught to look at people once they have established good relationships and a more secure sense of self.

In a few cases spoken language may not appear despite a structured speech and language program or may remain rudimentary. Signing is an alternative explored with such children either as the only form of communication or as a supplement or a bridge to regular speech.

The following case study may serve to illustrate various phases of beginning speech therapy. It is typical in many ways, most particularly in the way therapy picks up at the point at which a child comes into therapy, builds on observed, spontaneously occurring behaviors, and patiently follows the child's lead and lets him set the pace of treatment. The particular things this child was taught however, as well as the sequence and the techniques that were used with him, differ from other cases as would the toys, activities, or rewards used to motivate each child. The case study summarizes, in brief, the milestones of treatment over a four year period of an extremely withdrawn, self-abusive, aggressive boy given to sudden, violent mood swings.

> When he first came to Linwood at age nine, Dorian wrapped himself up in his shirt and jacket and bundled into additional towels or blankets which he drew over his head. His hands were covered by his sleeves, and he roamed around restlessly, or sat hunched into his protective shell like a tortoise. When something or somebody upset him, he would strike out unpredictably, but with great accuracy, speed, and force, then draw back into himself.
>
> When he started in residence, Dorian was given free reign over his environment. He avoided contacts and engaged at most in isolated activities that scarcely deserved the name of "play." There were few limits imposed on him, but over an extended period of time he was encouraged to do things by and for himself, such as reaching out for something he wanted, or eating with his hands, rather than lowering his face into his plate.
>
> When Dorian was able to accept other people's activities in his vicinity and began to tolerate parallel play with some favorite toys, he was deemed ready for one-on-one speech and language therapy. This was about one and a half years after he entered Linwood. In individual therapy he regressed, obviously uncomfortable with the intensity of the situation, and some of the prerequisites, like parallel play, had to be redeveloped in the new setting before anything further could be attempted. At first Dorian's play activities during therapy were, at most, accompanied by humming and the therapist, too, kept his comments to a minimum during the sessions. Eventually it was possible to introduce some turn-taking into the sessions and from there to proceed in slow stages to imitations, at first mainly gross motor ones like jumping, clapping, or stomping on the floor.
>
> It was at this time, approximately one year into the weekly individual sessions, that Dorian's humming began to change and he started to produce some recognizable tunes, some of them children's songs, some pop tunes that he had obviously heard on the radio. Interactions between the therapist and the boy now

began to include sounds for the first time, with the two of them taking turns singing. At this point, the therapist started to take a slightly more active role. For example he introduced a sound during a therapy session which the boy had experimented with while playing by himself on the playground. The therapist waited a few days before repeating the sound and did so casually while engaged in some other activity. From Dorian's reaction it was clear that he recognized the sound as something special. He seemed startled, stiffened, and glanced up at the therapist who pretended not to notice his reaction. A little later Dorian imitated the sound while his back was turned to the therapist.

Taking turns with this sound led to the introduction and imitation of new sounds. At first Dorian had to face away from the therapist, or pulled his shirt over his head to hide his face from him; later the exchanges could take place more openly and were accompanied by occasional eye contact. As a basis for further imitation the therapist also initiated oral-motor imitations, such as tongue clicking and different mouth movements. By and by, sounds were incorporated with these imitations, until the child started producing strings of sounds of his own, which the therapist imitated.

At this point Dorian seemed ready for speech, and the therapist started to integrate some words into the play activities which the child eventually imitated. Slowly his vocabulary increased, and after a further one year period he started generating words that he had not been taught explicitly. Outside of the therapy sessions, Dorian still uses speech infrequently and mostly to indicate something he badly wants, such as food. Some requests he utters almost ritualistically. They come out with varying emphasis, depending on his mood, from whispers, to loud, explosive demands: "go home."

DEVELOPING CONCEPTS

Once the children have started to talk and have expanded their vocabulary enough to function in everyday situations, they are encouraged to practice their speech in various settings, including more formal teaching sessions. The focus of treatment shifts from teaching simple vocabulary to concept formation and later to developing the ability to reason and think logically. As we have mentioned, autistic children have great difficulties with abstractions. Time, as a sequential entity, for example, is hard for them to understand. Again Lee, the boy who lived with Miss Simons, provides a good example of the difficulty autistic children have with the time concept. The following anecdote also shows how understanding grew out of the child's own experiences rather than resulting from someone else's explanations.

> When Lee became more aware of what was going on in the world around him, he began to enjoy activities such as special holidays or celebrations. The first occasion Lee wholeheartedly enjoyed was Easter. There were about six painted eggs hidden in the yard that he hunted for. The day was very special, and when it was over, Lee became upset and could not understand where Easter had gone. That it would come back in a year had no meaning for him, since he had no concept of either past or future.
>
> The next celebration he enjoyed was Christmas, but again he had difficulty coping with the fact that it only lasted a certain time and then was over. He thought that these occasions were actually stored somewhere and went throughout the house to look for them.
>
> One day Lee told Miss Simons that he had the present back. She asked him to explain that to her. Lee said, "All the stories I asked you to type are in the past. I like living here with you—now I have the present back." He said that he had lost it long ago (he refused to give a date) when he had visited an aunt in New York. He liked his aunt and felt very comfortable there. When he had to return home he had been very upset, because he had wanted to stay with his aunt. His mother told him that the visit was in the past. This was how he lost the present.
>
> While he was living with Miss Simons, his parents took Lee on a trip. "Will I be sad when I come back?" Lee asked. Miss Simons told him that she didn't know, but that there might well be another trip in the future after he came back. He didn't seem to like to hear this or to understand it and wandered away.
>
> Upon his return, he was very happy, because he was in the present again. But he was worried about the future. "What is the future?" he kept asking. "Tomorrow, next week, next month, or next year." He did not seem to register this. At last he said, "I am a little sad now. I do not have the future in my mind yet."
>
> Several months later, he was taken on a trip again. When he came back he was jubilant. "Miss Simons," he cried, "I have it. I understand. The present becomes the past and the past can become the future. I have it, I have it."

Causation, logical deductions and the reason for events, are especially difficult to grasp for autistic children, since they do not always have an immediate concrete basis. For the same reason, the "where," "who," or "when" of a situation, and questions in general, often confuse the children.

Lisa was asked, "Where do you go to school?" Her answer was, "On Monday."

Therapy, therefore, concentrates on teaching these abstractions in the most concrete form possible, by using immediate, real life situations. Discussions are kept to the level of the understanding of the children. At first they may involve things like the weather and the date. Later, events the children were involved in, outings that are planned, and even upsets and confrontations can be discussed. All of these discussions have the goal of giving an experiential underpinning to language and provide a base for the teaching of concepts and language.

> *One incident that proved useful, for example, involved a broken glass. A group of children was engaged in a discussion of possible consequences. These depended on whether the boy involved had broken the glass on purpose, or not. In the course of discussion, the teacher discovered that the children did not have a very clear idea about the concepts of "on purpose" and "accidental." She promptly proceeded to act them out, by "accidentally" stumbling over a chair and by deliberately dropping a pile of books.*

At every stage, teaching techniques are aimed at forcing the children to apply what they know, or to learn new skills, not just for the sake of learning them but because the knowledge helps the children function in their world. As in every other situation we have discussed, the motivation to learn, talk, read, write, or do arithmetic is strongest when it leads to some concrete, desired result.

One child, who is especially interested in food, is allowed to copy the daily menu and put it up on the bulletin board in the dining room by selecting the appropriate letters from a box full of type and composing the words with it.

Other children keep a book on the money they earn for chores and decide on their own whether they want to spend it every day, what to spend it on, a soda, or candy, or what to save up for.

> *A group of older boys who had made excellent progress but were not interested in schoolwork approached Miss Simons one day and requested a "club room," a place of their own they could use in their free time. Instead of assigning them a space in the house, Miss Simons suggested that they build themselves a club*

house. Their imagination was kindled, and they fell in with the plan enthusiastically.

Executing it involved a lot of measuring, figuring, and writing. The boys were forced to draw up plans, to calculate the amount of wood of different sizes they needed and the number of nails necessary. They had to go to stores to find out the prices of these items so that they could figure out the cost of the supplies. They had to make out lists of tools and material that had to be purchased and handle the financial transactions. And finally, they had to learn how to translate their plans into reality by using the appropriate tools. With the help of the handy man, they ended up building themselves a little cabin that they proudly occupied and greatly enjoyed.

Without noticing it, these boys developed all the skills taught in a regular classroom, and more. The difference was that they might have balked at working this hard on paper only, and indeed some of the boys involved were totally uninterested in scholastic activities. With a practical goal of their own choosing, they were involved, motivated, and stayed on task.

It is not always possible to find a task that is as multifaceted or as motivating as the project described above. But whenever an opportunity naturally presents itself or can be created that is intrinsically interesting and meaningful to a particular child, it is used in treatment to further language development or to develop other cognitive and social skills.

EIGHT
✦✦✦

Social and Emotional Development

INTRODUCTION

Even graver than the delays and deviations in the language and thought processes in autistic children is the impairment of their emotional and social development. It is often already noticeable during the first months of life and is usually the last symptom to respond to treatment. The following anecdote, told by Miss Simons, illustrates several typical characteristics of these children's emotional functioning which will be examined in this chapter.

> *It was close to Halloween and I had promised four of the older boys that they could come with me to get pumpkins. One of them, Adam, was already attending a regular school from Linwood and spoke fluently. Of the other three, Ryan sometimes used a few words, while the two others understood quite a bit, but hardly ever used words themselves to communicate.*
>
> *As we were driving, we ran into a heavy thunderstorm. As quickly as it had begun, the rain stopped and the sun came through again. Suddenly Adam got very excited and asked me to stop the car. I pulled over and stopped in a safe place. Adam jumped out of the car. "Look, Miss Simons, a rainbow," he shouted. He danced around the car and with great excitement he said, "Miss Simons, something is happening to me. It started here (he pointed to his chest) and it's going all over. It feels so good. We have to celebrate it." He kept jumping up and down with a joyful expression on his face. It was the first time he had displayed any real feeling, except for occasional anger. "What is it, Miss Simons? It feels so good. Let's celebrate!" He wanted donuts and some cookies and he wanted us to go to my house and to eat them in front of an open*

fire. While we were feasting he kept asking again and again what had happened to him. "You think it can be called happiness, Adam?" I suggested. "Yes, yes. The rainbow was so beautiful."

The other boys did not respond much. When I asked them if they had ever been happy, Ryan, who habitually wore earmuffs over his ears and obsessively twirled a stick, said nothing. He gave the impression of not hearing what was said.

Weeks later, Adam came to me, very upset. "Miss Simons, something started here again (pointing to his chest), but it did not feel good." I suggested a group meeting with the four boys and what eventually came out was that Adam had gotten the bad feeling when another child got a certain privilege. We discussed the incident and identified the feeling as jealousy.

A couple of years later Ryan too was able to go to public school. He had made great progress and was getting good marks at school. One day he came to me and said, "Miss Simons, I think Eddie was jealous today," and he explained why he thought so. I asked him whether he had ever been jealous, and he said "yes." He mentioned an exact date four years previously, a time when he had still spent most of his time walking back and forth along the fence, wearing his earmuffs and twirling his sticks.

I asked him why he had been jealous at the time. He told me that it was because I had taken one of the other boys out to lunch alone. "Did you know that you were jealous then?" I asked. "No," but two years ago (again he mentioned the exact day and date of the incident) Adam talked about something here (pointing to his chest) and later talked about jealousy. I knew then that on such and such a date I had been jealous. I had a strong feeling here (pointing to his chest)." "Did it bother you?" I asked him. "No, not long. I didn't know it was my chest."

PATTERNS OF EMOTIONAL DEVELOPMENT

This introductory story illustrates several important points. For one thing it shows by how much the emotional development of autistic children lags behind the rest of their development. At the time Adam discovered the "strange feelings" in his chest, was able to feel and express joy and later learned to distinguish the good feeling from jealousy, he was already functioning at a relatively normal level in most other areas. The less advanced boys had no way of identifying with his emotional experiences, though Adam's description of jealousy gave Ryan a label to put on something he himself had felt without understanding what it was, or even that it was part of himself.

Only after years of treatment and at a time when he was almost ready to leave Linwood, was Adam able to experience joy and describe his experience. From Ryan's example, we can deduce that the delays and difficulties in the emotional development of autistic children are not due to a total absence of emotions, but rather reflect the fact that feelings are at first undeveloped and undifferentiated.

Early, inexplicable outbursts of emotionality, seemingly unprovoked screaming, tearless wailing, temper tantrums, or short-lived fits of glee at odd moments, support this hypothesis. Their sensitivity to the moods and feelings of others is another proof that autistic children have emotions. Though they are at first unresponsive to verbal as well as nonverbal cues, they often react strongly to emotionality in others, even if it is controlled or hidden.

At first they may simply observe the environment and since they have no way of relating what they see to experiences of their own, the behavior of others as well as their emotions, their tears or laughter, concern, or anger are simply part of the host of phenomena that inundate the child and against which he has to keep up his defenses. It is as if he were sitting behind a one-way mirror, looking out into a world full of puzzling impressions but himself hidden from view.

The more conscious the child becomes of the world and of people around him, and the more he engages in relationships with them, the more reactive he becomes to their emotions. If he senses their anger or concern, it makes him anxious and agitated and he may either close himself off more completely or become negative, aggressive, or self-abusive.

It is unlikely that children would notice the emotions of others or react to them if they could not relate them to something they themselves had experienced at some level or other. One young man, looking back to a time when he did not yet speak, insists that he felt that there was something wrong with him long before he could speak. In part it was simply a feeling of discomfort that he is still unable to define or describe properly today. In part, he thinks that he was registering the distress and concern of his mother.

For another child, an early positive experience fueled his eventual recovery.

Saul, a severely autistic child, became extremely demanding as he began to open up a little and to form relationships. No matter how much his favorite therapist did for him, it never seemed to be enough. When he was given something, he wanted more, escalating his demands as they were being met.

After several years it seemed as if Saul had gotten as much out of Linwood as he was likely to, and he was placed elsewhere.

It was expected that he would remain institutionalized for the rest of his life. But Saul fooled everyone. After six years, when he was in his early twenties, Saul suddenly started to improve dramatically, and within a relatively short time he was living at home.

One day he came to Linwood for a visit. While there, he asked Miss Simons whether she remembered the occasion when she had taken him to get a soft ice cream and he had asked for two scoops instead of one. He reminded Miss Simons that she had told him that cones for soft ice cream were designed for one scoop and that everything might fall down if two scoops were piled on top of each other. Saul had insisted on two scoops, but had asked what would happen if the ice cream did indeed fall down. Miss Simons' reply was that if he was as careful as he could possibly be and some ice cream fell in spite of his care she would get him another portion. "Boy, was I careful," Saul told Miss Simons. He also insisted that it was the memory of this particular incident that had made him feel that he did not belong in a hospital. Once he was determined to go home, he improved rapidly and soon managed to leave the institution for good.

Observations and experience suggest that autistic children feel emotions, just as they see, hear, taste, and have the sensory apparatus to register heat, cold, and pain. But just as their sensation and perceptions are often isolated and seemingly disconnected from their own bodies, emotions too, are not registered or recognized for what they are.

Normally it is the self that interprets and organizes perceptions. If it is lacking or feeble, as in autism, both cognition and emotions remain undifferentiated and disassociated from the child's own body and mind. As we have seen, words they hear are often sounds without meaning to autistic children. They do not recognize their communicative or interactive function and repeat them without comprehension, or ignore them completely until they are taught the connection between specific sounds and objects or activities.

The same holds true for physical sensations. In the absence of a proper body image, an autistic child may hurt himself over and over again, without withdrawing from a situation or avoiding it. Only to the degree to which they become more generally aware of themselves and their body, does their seeming insensibility to pain disappear. It took Larry four years to reach that stage.

Larry had always liked to play records and could sit for long periods of time listening to them. Sometimes, when the record player was too close to the wall, the lid would tip and fall on his fingers when he tried to change the record. There had never been the slightest reaction from Larry that indicated that he felt any pain. Without flinching, he would simply open the lid again. It was impossible to move the record player to a different place since Larry accepted no changes in his environment and would always move the machine back to its original position.

One day when the cover had again fallen on his fingers, Larry did not immediately lift it off but looked intently at his hand and then at the record player. Then he lifted the cover carefully and deliberately let it fall on his fingers again. After he had done this several times, he removed his fingers, put the cover back, and slapped the record player. Then he looked at his fingers and slapped them as well as his forehead. It seemed as if Larry had not only figured out the connection between the falling lid and sensations in his fingers but had finally become conscious of the fact that the fingers belonged to him and that he was somehow responsible for them.

A true feeling of self develops even more slowly than a body image. Depending on the degree of impairment and the extent to which treatment has succeeded in drawing the children out and in awakening an awareness of themselves as separate individuals, symptoms differ. Furthermore, not all children progress at the same pace or reach the same level of emotional and social functioning. In fact, difficulties in social relations and with appropriate emotional reactivity often persist in autistic adults who otherwise function at a high level.

Early on, most autistic children actively shy away from contacts and emotional involvement. They are either exceptionally "good" babies who make no demands or are impossible to comfort and stiffen when they are handled. When emotions surface they are at first clumped together in an unidentifiable mass and since the children's repertoire of expressions is very restricted, any type of feeling may produce the same, often inappropriate responses. Children may become self-abusive, or hit, or bite somebody when they are pleasurably stimulated as well as when they are upset. Or they may laugh when they see another child hurt himself even though they will later show that they understood that something bad had happened.

When he was four years old, Josh saw a little boy struck by a car. He laughed excitedly, but later became extremely anxious and often referred back to the accident even though he was reassured that the child recovered from it.

Because of their inability to process sensory information, autistic children may also feel overwhelmed and powerless in the face of a flood of unconnected and unpredictable events. In an attempt to keep things simple and manageable they cling to routines and compulsions, and when these are interfered with, the children may literally fall apart. Asked as an adult whether he remembered why he kept twirling his sticks, Ryan said, "Because I liked it; it made me feel safe."

The children's inner lack of cohesion and their feelings of helplessness are also evident in the drawings of themselves autistic children produce. Often limbs are floating around in a disjointed jumble, or pieces of the body—most often arms or hands—are missing.

Cathy, the little girl in Chapter 3, began by drawing pictures of houses. Her first drawings of people, two little girls, resembled the stick figures drawn by three- or four-year-old nursery school children; a circle for the head with smaller circles for the eyes and dots or lines for nose and mouth. The legs were immediately attached to the head, but there were no arms. Cathy said they were hidden and that she liked it that way.

As time went by, Cathy drew many pictures of children, both boys and girls, adding more and more details, including a variety of hairdos. But it wasn't until almost four years later that she began to give them arms and name the figures as representing the other little girls in the group. Herself she continued to draw armless. In the meantime, Cathy's mother was pregnant again, and the staff began to prepare Cathy for the arrival of a sibling. Cathy showed great interest in the baby and drew pictures of it, always with both arms and legs.

A few days after the baby was born it suddenly turned blue and was in critical condition for several days. Her father and grandmother, who stayed with Cathy while the mother was in the hospital, tried not to show their worries to her.

At school the staff noticed that Cathy was becoming very withdrawn again and did a great deal of daydreaming. It was suggested to her parents that she was very much aware of the tension in the family but felt left out and anxious because she did not know what was happening. Overprotecting Cathy meant underestimating her strength and would do her more harm than good. Cathy had shown on many previous occasions that she wanted to share her thoughts and feelings with her parents and that she profited from openness.

The father accepted the staff's recommendations and told

Cathy what was happening with the baby in a way that she could understand. When she came in the following day, Cathy drew the first picture of herself with arms.

As we have seen, children often do not know what is happening to them even while they feel strong emotions like joy or jealousy. When Lee saw the door with the keyhole separating his room from that of Miss Simons, he was clearly terrified though he was unable to say what was bothering him.

At another level, a child may experience a strong sensation without being aware of the fact that there is a connection between a specific event and his feelings, as happened to Lee when Miss Simons invited her first weekend guests.

Often it is impossible to tell that a child is feeling something because he himself does not understand what is going on and is therefore unable to express any feelings. Ryan was only able to identify the discomfort he had felt as a much younger child when he recognized the description of jealousy in a group meeting years later. In the same way, children are often able to understand and verbalize past events only long after they happened. At the time they seem totally out of touch, confused, or resistant to attempts to draw them out, as in the case of Garth.

Garth already went to public school. Like all children, he spent the weekends at home. One weekend he suddenly refused to eat. He also didn't sleep. In a sort of catatonic trance he sat stiffly upright in bed both nights, unable or unwilling to tell his mother what was happening.

Concerned that he might collapse if he didn't eat or sleep, Miss Simons, with whom the boy had a good relationship, offered to have him stay at her cottage with her overnight, and he eagerly accepted. She poured out some Rice Krispies and fed them to him, even though he was perfectly capable of eating by himself. It was the first food he had eaten in three days. Then she prepared a bed for him in her spare room. He went willingly, but sat up, just as he had at home. "Here you have to stretch out," he was told, and he did. Garth insisted on having all the lights out and the doors closed, but Miss Simons told him that at the cottage there was always a light left on in the hallway. Before she left the room, Garth asked her to sing to him. She sang softly, but chose a regular song, rather than a baby's lullaby.

The next day Garth returned to Linwood, where he resumed his regular routine. Miss Simons offered him the opportunity to come back with her at the end of the day, but he elected to stay with his group. Garth did not refer to the incident or discuss it in any way, but years later, he gratefully told Miss Simons "You saved my life!"

The staff later conjectured that Garth's state might have been due to blocked anger. Up to then he had never expressed any strong emotion but shortly after his stay at the cottage, he erupted violently and for a while had outbursts that would last for hours. A little later still, during the week-long summer camp session, Garth was able to talk about the death of his father that had occurred two years earlier.

He also revealed the fact that he had been able to deal with a compulsion that had gripped him for a long time. He used to tie magazines into bundles and stack them along the walls of his room. As the stacks grew, they began to encroach on his living space until he felt that his compulsion was going to choke him. While he was in treatment at Linwood he had finally been able to rid himself of his compulsion and to throw out the magazines, but had not told anybody about it at the time.

As the children begin to relate, they not only become more aware of the world and of themselves, they also have to face dealing with change. What is seen as progress by the outside world may be a negative, frustrating, or frightening experience for the children themselves. Consequently, the first identifiable emotion autistic children display is often anger. Since at first the children may still fail to make correct connections between cause and effect, their anger is often misdirected. It may surface in the form of self abuse, or a child may hit a table, kick a chair, or strike out at an adult.

Though the children show no visible empathy with each other for a long time, especially excitable children may be "set off" by the emotionality of other youngsters. It is as if the strong feelings others display weaken the hold they have on themselves. A child may totally lose control and go into fits of screaming, hit out, or throw things if another child is especially disruptive. If the adults remain nonreactive, most children eventually react to their calm in the same way that they picked up the negative emotional cues from other children.

To help them pull themselves together and to feel safe, the children may have to be physically held for a while. Later a touch or a word or the mere presence of a trusted adult may be enough to prevent them from "going off." Some children eventually even become aware enough of their own feelings that they come for help when they feel themselves slipping. Often the restraint they need is mostly symbolic.

Philip has a mat in the hallway on which he lies when he becomes overly agitated. One little girl brought her therapist a towel whenever she felt herself losing control The towel had originally been introduced by the therapist as a gentle way of helping her to keep her arms folded and thus prevent her from attacking people and scratching them bloody when she had one of her upsets.

What emotions autistic children do display are usually immediate and concrete. They have no wishes, for example, only needs. Wishes not only involve emotion, they also require imagination and a concept of the future, all of which are usually absent in these children. Their almost passionate attachment to certain objects, their cravings for certain foods, or their obsessive involvement with certain activities are part of their way of dealing with the world and of keeping things the same and safe rather than an expression of positive emotions. Their activities, or the fulfillment of their needs, usually give them little visible joy. Only a disruption of their routine may bring on strong reactions since it threatens the established order and with it their defense mechanisms.

Rather than dealing with emotions, autistic children invest their energies in activities that are precise, factual, and carry no emotional content. When language is used expressively, the children may talk in riddles, especially when dealing with emotional issues, as we have seen in the previous chapter. Feats of memory involving numbers, dates, schedules, and maps contrast strongly with an inability to remember simple recent events in daily life.

Their concrete memory is highly developed, whether it is the auditory or the visual one. One boy could draw detailed maps of the roads he had been driven on outings, many children can remember events years back with exact days and dates, as in Lee's case, or remember every outfit anybody ever wore in minute detail, names and addresses of all doctors they visited, birthdays of everybody they have met and menus or the weather dating back for years. But an autistic person's recollection of past events usually falters abruptly when an autistic person is asked how he felt at a particular time. In my talks with autistic adults I got many recollections about their life and special events at Linwood, but whenever I asked them what they thought had been especially helpful to them, made them feel good, or had been difficult during that time, the flow of recollections stopped and the most I got after a long uneasy silence was something like "That's hard to say," or "That's a difficult question."

Letters that former students write to the Linwood staff are equally bare of allusions to social or emotional events. They may deal with recollections of some special past event or contain a list of factual information about current happenings.

After the most perfunctory introduction, Bruce used most of his letter to describe a favorite building set of his at Linwood and included detailed, three-dimensional scale drawings of the elements, especially the interlocking joints.

He went on to say: "I liked Lego best." and then in an abrupt switch: "I like to hear your voice over the phone. However, it's expensive for me to hear your voice for that long distance call especially we're in an inflation economy. . . . "

THERAPY APPROACH TO EMOTIONAL AND SOCIAL DEVELOPMENT

Emotions are a product of living. In order to experience and develop an appropriate range of emotions, autistic children have to learn to identify and express their emotions in interactions with others and to recognize the connections between emotions and events in the outside world.

The first step toward helping children feel is to engage them in relationships in which they do not feel overwhelmed or threatened. We have described this process in some detail in an earlier chapter. Here it is important to stress again how important patience, reserve, and sensitivity are to success. The adult must turn himself into a nonintrusive part of the child's environment. By his presence and openness he makes himself available and invites interactions but he leaves it to the child to indicate when he is ready for them and what form they should take. Only by remaining somewhat distant, nonreactive, and calm can the adult initially reassure the child that relationships are safe.

Once first relationships have been established and the child becomes more aware of what is going on around him, a lot of anxiety may be stirred up. For a while he may become increasingly agitated and compulsive or release his tensions in brief, explosive, emotional episodes. At this point it is especially important to accept the child's behavior and emotionality, to ignore it as much as possible, or to deal with it calmly and to set a minimum of limits.

This does not mean that the therapist ignores either the child's needs or his limitations. Children whose feelings are not taken into account or who are pushed too far too fast react by either retreating into inactivity or by making their feelings unmistakably clear.

Larry, who had come into treatment shortly before he was five as a mute and withdrawn little boy, had improved remarkably after just one year. He had formed a good relationship with Miss Simons, and had become happy and more alert. He still did not talk, but communicated with sounds, the way babies do. One day, when he was in a gay and cuddly mood he was again vocalizing freely. Miss Simons asked him whether he didn't think that the time had come to start talking a little in words. At the time, Larry was skipping happily through the room, but when he heard her suggestion he stopped, turned around, stormed toward her and scratched her so deeply that she bled. Then he skipped away again. He was obviously perfectly aware of what had been said to him. He also made it unmistakably clear that he did not agree, and that he was not ready yet.

Above all, the child has to be convinced that it is safe to have and express emotions and that neither his feelings nor his outbursts endanger himself or others, and that they do not affect the relationships he is beginning to form. Especially at the beginning, when even small demands made on the child stir up his anxiety and when his emotions are still undifferentiated and uncontrollable, it is important to focus on them as little as possible and to keep the child active without getting sidetracked by emotional outbursts or temporary upsets. The following episode illustrates how it is possible to ignore a child's negative behavior or emotions without ignoring the child.

Elizabeth was sulking on top of a cabinet because she resented the extra attention paid to Karen who had had an accident the day before. When Miss Simons entered the room, Dana started to climb all over her. Miss Simons turned the climbing into a game in which everybody could participate. This was to give Elizabeth, who normally loved to cuddle with her, a chance to become reintegrated into the group and to come out of her sulk gracefully.

While Dana was having her turn, Miss Simons mentioned the names of other children who might want to participate in the game, including Elizabeth's name among the possible candidates. After a short while, she finished her interactions with Dana, calling a next child over, and while she was busy with him she casually mentioned the fact that "Elizabeth doesn't want to climb now, she is resting" and offered another child his turn next.

After a couple of prompts like these, Elizabeth began to stir a little, looking furtively in Miss Simons' direction and watching the other children having a good time. After a few children had had their turn, she finally climbed off her shelf and began to play with Miss Simons.

If an adult is unable to handle an anxious, angry, or jealous child properly at this early stage, it may leave the child feeling even more anxious or insecure, and make a lasting impression on him. Nat, for example, still remembers as an adult the way his insistent and negative attention made his favorite counselor, Pauline, run away from him. On the other hand, children gratefully remember the help and support they received during times of emotional upheavals, even though they did not seem to register anything at the time.

> *Alfred came to Linwood when he was five years old. He was diagnosed as brain damaged, retarded, and autistic. He didn't talk, never looked at anyone, and never smiled. He had a furious temper and was very self aggressive. When he was in one of his fits he would climb on anything he could reach, chairs, tables, stairs, or cabinets and plunge down head first. Since he would not tolerate anybody touching him, Miss Simons devised a method of holding him safely with the help of a wide belt made from a rolled-up sheet. In this way she could prevent him from hitting the floor when he jumped, without physically touching him.*
>
> *Alfred developed some speech while at Linwood, though he had a speech defect. Eventually, he went on to an institution.*
>
> *Ten years later, Miss Simons met Alfred at a workshop. As soon as he saw her, he became very excited and started talking a blue streak. He asked about various staff members by name. Then he asked her whether she remembered how she had helped him not to hurt his head. He reminded her that she had made a thick belt from a sheet and slipped it under his arms. He seemed to especially remember the fact that Miss Simons had been very solicitous of his comfort and had pulled his shirt down and made sure that the sheet was not too tight. He recalled that the arrangement had left him free to thrash around and to jump without hurting himself.*
>
> *He then told her that he remembered how one day after he calmed down, Miss Simons had sat down with him to draw. He remembered that she had had a brown crayon and had given him a green one and that they had taken turns drawing circles, little ones first, then big ones. He beamed when he recalled these events and also said that he would like to come and visit Linwood, the place that held so many good memories.*

Children who are not yet ready to express their own emotions may be reassured that emotions are safe by seeing the staff deal with temper tantrums or aggressive outbursts of other children. Even so, they themselves may at first only be able to experience strong emotions vicariously, like

Nathaniel who delighted in watching another boy throw blocks at the window and break it. Still later, they may express them indirectly or obliquely, rather than coming right out and engaging in a direct confrontation. A nice example of this mechanism is the cartoon which Erwin drew of himself and Clive. In the picture the character representing himself says to the other boy, who has a bandaged hand, "I'm sorry Clive! I'll never stab you with my pen again." The other character is seen to reply, "Okay, Erwin!"

As we have discussed in the relationship chapter, autistic children may be so afraid to express anger directly that they hit a favorite counselor with whom they feel safe, or an inanimate object, such as a table, instead of another child that provoked them. Despite the fact that their anger is misdirected, both the feeling and its expression are concrete and immediate. Just as autistic individuals do not use language as metaphor and do not engage in symbolic play and "as ifs," so their feelings do not contain hidden meanings. There is therefore no sense in trying to analyze what an autistic child says or does or examine it for symbolic content. If a child hits out, it is because he feels anxious, pressured, frustrated, or angry about something in his immediate environment. The recipient of his aggressiveness may not be the original cause of his emotions but he or she is also not the symbolic representative of the mother, for example.

When children do get emotional but are unable to take appropriate action, they are eventually helped to recognize the true cause of their anger. Their aggressiveness is redirected, rather than interpreted, and they are also shown how to deal with it in ways that reflect their levels of development.

In the following episode, a boy who had an upset earlier in the day is confronted with his reactions in a group meeting.

Therapist: "Every time you are angry, you throw a chair, but you can't throw chairs all your life. So why don't you yell it out? Say it!"

John: "I was trying to bang a table, but I didn't."

Th: "Why not?"

J: "You are not supposed to."

Th: "You can do a lot of things here, you are still at Linwood."

It is interesting to note that while the intent of the interaction was to encourage John to verbalize his anger rather than giving in to destructive urges, the emphasis shifted to reassuring him that his impulses were safe and that any attempt to limit or change his habitual reactions were acceptable at Linwood. At the same time, he was reminded that there was a world outside of Linwood to which he had to adjust when he was ready to.

Autistic children may have strong emotions, but they may not recognize them for what they are and may have to be helped to identify them correctly.

> *Mark, an adolescent who is already leaving Linwood several times a week to work at a nearby library, was teased by another boy and expressed his anger by punching a hole in a wall. As a result he was barred from the weekly outing to the shopping mall, which is one of the bigger boys' privileges. In going over the incident in a group meeting, Mark was asked what happened. He was extremely reluctant to discuss his anger, evaded answering, rolled his head back and forth and gave only one-word replies. When he was reminded by the therapist of the consequences of his actions he grimaced and giggled.*

Therapist: "It isn't funny."

M: (laughs)

> *The discussion moved on to a different subject. While the other boys talked, Mark sat quietly. Suddenly tears are began to roll down his cheeks, though his expression did not change.*

Th: "Why do you cry?"

M: "Don't cry."

Th: "Yes, you can cry. Why do you cry?"

M: "Go home tomorrow."

Th: "Are you sad?"

M: "Yes."

Th: "About what?"

> *Mark didn't answer and the therapist asked the other children why they think Mark was sad. Finally it was suggested that he was*

sad because he couldn't go out with them that evening. When asked directly Mark agreed that this was so, and stopped crying.

As was the case with Adam, a child may have a feeling without knowing what to call it or what caused it. Group meetings are a good way of linking events and feelings, and of defining and naming emotions. More advanced children provide examples or definitions, which may throw some light on experiences or emotions other children had or will have. Less advanced children can remain passive. Some of what passes may well be beyond their level of understanding at that time, but they may remember it later, as did Ryan.

Talking about emotions and acting them out in the safe, controlled environment of the group also may make it possible for some children to face or express them without feeling too anxious or threatened about their own emotionality. But despite all of the reassurance within the therapeutic milieu in general and especially designed group sessions in particular, many autistic children are unable to deal with feelings or to apply them in social interactions, until they have made great progress in treatment in other areas. All therapeutic interventions are therefore aimed at convincing the children that emotions are safe and at teaching them how to come to grips with them and how to interject emotions into their lives without frightening consequences.

Those children who do not speak yet are given harmless substitutes for throwing or hitting. They are also taught appropriate gestures of refusal, how to push another child away rather than hitting out at him, how to hold on to a toy rather than give it up to anybody who tries to grab it, and eventually how to say "no."

Those who already have speech learn to make their wishes or their anger known verbally. They may also be shown various ways of defending themselves or of physically responding to provocations. Group meetings are a good forum for this kind of "rehearsal." In a group discussion with four older boys the therapist asked John, who had been provoked by Eddie, what it meant to be angry.

John: "I'm afraid to talk about it."

Th: "You have to let it out."

J: "No, N—O!"

Th: "Are you afraid of being angry?"

J: "I don't know."

Later in the same session the therapist encouraged the boys to settle their differences by telling each other about their emotions "without getting too angry." One way of doing this, which was suggested to them, was to hit each other "where it is safe. Not in the face." At this suggestion John ran away, screaming. He collapsed in a heap outside the door of his room, screaming and sobbing as if in terrible agony. Back in the room, he hung on the therapist's shoulder crying in deep, wrenching gulps. It was the first time in his life that he had been able to cry or seek comfort. The episode was painful to watch, but it was a breakthrough for John. Throughout the therapist reassured him.

Th: "Why did you run away? Are you afraid of being angry? When you are with us, you never have to be afraid of it. You may yell it out."

Anger is not the only thing children have to learn to identify and express appropriately. Positive emotions toward another person may also be hard to deal with for some children. We have already discussed the fact that many children use the safety of a good relationship to vent their anger more freely, so that the people to whom they are the closest bear the brunt of their anxiety and negativism. Disliking physical closeness, or lacking social skills, children may also use negative means of interacting with a person they are attracted to, rather than expressing their feelings in the normal way through smiles or cuddling. Emotions like sadness or joy may have to be formally rehearsed with some children.

In one group session an attempt was made to teach one of the boys to cry as an alternative to outbursts that were destructive and less emotionally satisfying. This particular boy was fascinated by the tears of others but was afraid to cry himself because he had heard the expression that "somebody cried their eyes out." Taking the saying literally, he did not want to take the risk of losing his eyes. At an appropriate moment, Toby was encouraged to express his sadness by crying.

In a session in which the boy ran through a whole gamut of screaming, tearless sobbing and halfhearted attempts at keeping up an angry demeanor, interspersed with humming, chuckling and "asides," such as "are we almost finished with our screaming and crying?" Toby eventually managed to produce tears. This seemed to strike him as a very satisfactory feat, but at the same time as a strange phenomenon from which he still remained somewhat distant. After asking, "Are we almost finished? That's all the tears.

Can I go downstairs now?" he added with genuine curiosity, "Did the tears come out really slowly from my eyes and cheek? Because I tried...."

DEVELOPING EMOTIONAL MEMORIES

Children unused to dealing with emotions or afraid of them often have a difficult time recalling events that involve feelings. To help them develop an emotional memory, it is necessary to build up a fund of positive, non-threatening experiences that do not have too heavy an emotional content. Recalling such events provides the children with practice in dealing with past emotional issues, pleasant ones first, negative ones later on.

One way of keeping situations light and emotions nonthreatening is to inject humor into them. Humor not only relieves tension, it provides distance without cutoff. Humorous episodes make perfect memories, because shared laughter is a joyful experience without the emotional intensity that may be attached to some other interactions.

To develop a sense of humor in autistic children, who are very literal, the jokes have to be literal too. They have to involve concrete experiences so that the children have an actual situation to remember, rather than only abstract words. It is also important to stress the difference between a joke that is funny and in which one laughs with a person, as opposed to a trick that may be hurtful and in which one laughs at another person. To help children experience humor, several staff persons may cooperate to set up a situation in which an everyday interaction gets a humorous twist.

> *On an occasion when dessert was being handed out, a child was sent to staffers in another room to ask whether they would like another piece of cake. One adult replied that she would like a piece, but only a tiny one. The child was sent back to the person with a large plate on which there was a miniscule sliver of cake. At seeing the absurd way in which her request had been interpreted and fulfilled, the staffer burst into laughter and invited the boy and others to share in the joke that had been played on her.*

It is very likely that the child will be eager to repeat such a joke at some future occasion, and it also makes a good story to recall every time somebody asks for a piece of cake or a helping of some other favorite food. Gentle teasing of this kind not only helps develop a sense of humor, it also encourages children to interact with adults and with their peers in a way that keeps contacts pleasant but light and provides a balance between the intense extremes of emotions which human interactions often involve.

Therapy aims at building up positive memories by providing

pleasurable experiences wherever possible and by talking about them. We have already mentioned how diligently the staff searches for things a child seems to enjoy and of the special privileges the children get. Once a child begins to react and to differentiate between people, his environment is structured in ways that assure as many positive experiences as possible by taking advantage of his preferences.

> *Bruce has a strong attachment to his former teacher, Miss Bessie, even though he has not been in her group for some time and he did not react to her especially while he was with her. Every time he sees her, his face lights up and he strains toward her. In his own room he is often very passive. Whenever he is left to his own devices he prefers to curl up and go to sleep. He doesn't talk, and it is hard to get him interested in anything: snacks, toys, or activities. As a treat, and also as a way to use his feelings for Miss Bessie to activate him, he is regularly taken to visit her. He is allowed early into the dining room and watches while Miss Bessie sets up for lunch. He recognizes her name, knows when it is time to go visit her, and changes from a sleepy, withdrawn little boy into a perky, smiling child.*

At this point, Bruce's visits with Miss Bessie are "freebies." He does not have to do anything to earn them. They are simply meant to give him pleasure. But it is hoped that through his interest in Miss Bessie, he may become interested in what she is doing and that it may become possible to eventually involve him in some activities she demonstrates, like setting the table for snack time.

JEALOUSY

To the extent to which children make overall progress, their emotional repertoire expands. With relationships come feelings of attachment and joy but also of jealousy and rivalry. Jealousy in autistic children is a sign of growing emotional awareness. Normal children too, go through phases of sibling rivalry and jealousy. How long it lasts depends in good part on the way children are treated. The more secure a child feels as a unique and valued individual in his group or family the less intense, lasting, and disturbing jealousy will be.

If a first born, for example, loses out because of the birth of a sibling, never has the mother to himself anymore, has to give up his crib to the new baby, or is sent off to nursery school because now he is a big boy and the baby needs to be taken care of, the state of being "big" may well seem unattractive. Most likely the child will blame the newcomer for his discomfort and be jealous of him.

If instead, the child is moved into a bigger bed before the baby is born or is allowed to attend nursery school as a privilege he will experience these things as positive consequences of his growing status instead of feeling dispossessed. An older child should always have distinct privileges and be protected against the encroachment of younger siblings. Once he realizes that he will always be the oldest and that he gets as much gratification from being a big child as from being a baby, he will no longer be jealous of the mother spending time caring for the baby or try to imitate him.

In the same way, children at Linwood soon discover that there is no need to be jealous of their peers. Despite the fact that children within the same group are treated differently, that some have fewer demands or limits placed on them, while others have specific privileges not shared by the group, it is very rare to encounter open jealousy among these children.

One reason, of course, is that jealousy is an emotion and that emotions, as we have seen, are generally undifferentiated in autistic children until relatively late in treatment. Only a very few, atypical, children already exhibit strong jealousy when they come to Linwood. This diminishes as they learn to trust the staff and as they develop a sense of their own uniqueness and come to take pleasure in the special privileges and rewards that set them apart from other children.

Sometimes a child who is coming alive emotionally and has developed a close relationship with a therapist will go through a short stage of normal sibling rivalry and jealousy.

> *Linda had graduated from having to be fed and eating with her hands to handling utensils neatly and eating by herself. Some time later a new little boy came in who could not yet eat independently. Linda, observing "her" teacher feeding him, dropped her spoon, started to whimper, and demanded to be fed also. Rather than reprimanding her, the therapist placed her next to her, and every so often fed her a little piece of graham cracker that was not part of the regular food, while continuing to assist the child on her other side. In this way, Linda had the gratification of being fed, without losing the skills she had already acquired. Her rivalry with the little boy quickly faded and she resumed her independent eating habits without any further show of jealousy.*

The major reason why jealousy is no real problem among the children at Linwood is probably due to the very fact of the individualized treatment they receive. While the expectations are that they will eventually conform to certain standards of behavior, the children are not subjected to a system of conditioning that is applied in a blanket fashion to every child in the program. They are accepted as they are, and demands as well as privileges are tailored to their specific needs and developmental levels.

> *Karen, a little girl who was handicapped by a serious defect in language expression, also was extremely withdrawn. One day she began to show interest in carrying the refreshment tray to the other children for their evening snack. The staff was delighted by this, but Elizabeth got very upset and said, "Karen gets to do everything—I can do things too."*
>
> *At first the staff thought to deal with Elizabeth's obvious jealousy by letting the two girls take turns carrying the tray, but after some discussion it was decided that both children would profit more if Karen would retain sole rights to carrying in the tray and some other activity were found for Elizabeth that would be hers alone.*

Being treated as an individual with special privileges and limits confirms the child in the feeling that he is unique. He also experiences the fact that he does not have to compete for attention or gratification, so that he does not need to begrudge the attention or the privileges other children receive. Budding signs of jealousy are usually quickly defused by pointing out to a child that "This is what Johnny gets, or needs, to do, you have already done this," or "You are the only one who gets to drive in my car," or whatever other special privilege the child may have. Sometimes it is even the children themselves who point out the needs of their peers with insight gained from their own experiences.

> *When Gabriel first came to Linwood, he would not touch white milk, but loved chocolate milk. Whenever there was only a little chocolate milk, Gabriel would get it all, even though some of the other children liked it too. Eventually Gabriel began to eat a more varied diet that included white milk. Quite some time later, another little boy came to Linwood who also drank only chocolate milk. He had not been there very long when one evening the supply was a little low and the therapist said to him, "Oh, Kenny, can't you drink white milk this once?" Gabriel immediately rose to Kenny's defense and admonished her, "Kenny isn't ready to stop drinking chocolate milk yet. When I came here, I drank chocolate milk for a long time."*

Sometimes a child will ask a staff member, "Do you like me?" When he is told that he is liked, he will ask the same thing about another child and then end up with the question, "Do you like me better than Johnny?" The answer is always "No, I don't like you better, I like you differently. There is only one Johnny, even though there may be other children with that name, there is only one Johnny X, and that is you, and that makes you very special, and that's the way I like you. And there is also only one Bobby or Peter, and that's the way I like them." Obviously saying these things alone is not enough, but if they are backed up by the constant demonstration that each child is indeed an individual whose skills are appreciated and whose wishes are respected, the message will come across and the children will begin to think and feel about themselves in the same terms.

SHARING

The subject of sharing, which often takes on great importance in early sibling relationships, is closely related to jealousy. It too depends on the existence of a sense of self as well as feelings of attachment toward people or objects. It presupposes an awareness of others, since it implies that there is someone to share with. A child also has to have something he cares about or want something somebody else has, before he can understand what sharing is all about.

At first autistic children lack both a sense of self and the necessary interest in the environment to make the concept of sharing real to them. They may be compulsively attached to a particular object and may become distressed if it is taken away from them. But generally, they do not notice at all when something they are playing with is taken away from them and simply pick up another object instead. They also are usually not at all interested in things other children have.

For sharing to have a meaning to these children it has to be taught to them as part of an integrated approach toward developing social and emotional awareness. The first experience the children usually have with sharing is when another child tries to take something away from them. If they are at a point where they have developed differentiated likes and dislikes and feelings of ownership, they will resist the takeover attempt. The therapist backs up their claim by telling the other child something like "Johnny is not ready to share this toy, why don't you take something else?" This makes the child feel protected and underlines his special claim to the toy he is playing with.

The next step is reached when Johnny in his turn becomes interested in the toy of another child. At that point that child in turn is given a chance to decide whether he wants to relinquish his possession. He is asked, "Do you want to share this with Johnny?" Only if he agrees will Johnny get the toy.

In this way the children learn that it is possible to let go of something without losing it for good. Eventually they can be introduced to the experience of using the same toy to mutual advantage. There are many things that are more fun when they are used by more than one person. A ball can be rolled, kicked, or thrown back and forth, a toy car can be rolled from one person to another, two people can draw together, etc. This kind of cooperation eventually leads to games that are specifically designed for several people, like board games, and also introduces the concept of taking turns.

Sometimes there is only one toy to be shared, like a bicycle, and again taking turns becomes an important part of sharing. Children who have a hard time sharing something, can be shown the advantages that come from sharing and the disadvantages that may result from keeping things to oneself, if and when they are far enough along in their development. The following example shows how a group activity was used to demonstrate the principles of sharing while avoiding a power struggle or negative confrontation with a child who was determined not to give up sole possession of a toy that was meant to be shared.

> *Wayne showed a marked preference for a toy road truck loaded with all sorts of signs, such as "Children at Play," "Men at Work," and "Stop." He had been playing with it exclusively for several days, and by mistake he was allowed to put it away in his private cabinet so that he came to regard it as his exclusive property although it was intended for the use of all the children. Kirby was intrigued by the truck, and wanted to play with it too, but every time he tried to do so, Wayne threw a terrific temper tantrum.*
>
> *After this had gone on for several days, the therapist decided to step in. First she suggested to Kirby that he try asking Wayne for something from the truck, like the stop sign he especially wanted. As soon as he heard this, Wayne flew into one of his tantrums, screaming and kicking. The therapist removed him from the room, telling him, "Here we play, we scream in the hall." The therapist stayed with him in the hall, where he continued to thrash around and scream. After a while she told him that she needed to get something upstairs and asked whether she could leave him alone for a moment. After further screaming, he agreed.*
>
> *When the therapist came back downstairs with a mysterious box under her arm, Wayne quieted quickly and said, "I'm all right now, can I come back in?" He followed the therapist into the room where Kirby, having taken advantage of Wayne's absence, was playing with the stop sign. The therapist said to him, "Kirby, let's*

play with something else as long as Wayne isn't ready to share. He thinks that's his truck, so you let him play with it." Then she announced to the group, "Here is a toy that all the children can play with."

Everybody crowded around, including Wayne, who said that he wanted to play too. When he got no reaction from the therapist he fetched the truck, handed it to Kirby and said, "Here Kirby, you have the truck, I play with the new game." The therapist quietly insisted, "No Wayne, that's your truck, but you can come and watch what is in the box. This is going to be for all the children." She proceeded to unpack a little train set, handing every child, except Wayne, a piece of the track and instructed them to put it together. The tracks included a very colorful turntable which all the children wanted but they were told that they would have to take turns with it. Wayne wanted to know whether he could have a turn too and was told that "each child can have a turn."

When the tracks were set up, each of the children got to choose a train. The therapist made sure that Kirby got first choice, and that a couple of other children had their turn before Wayne. The children then played with the set for about five minutes, taking turns with the turntable. Meanwhile the truck had been sitting neglected some distance away. After a while the therapist said to the group, "It would be nice to have a stop sign, so the children know when a train is coming." Wayne went for his truck and said "I have a stop sign." He brought all the signs over, keeping the stop sign for himself, but spontaneously sharing out the other signs among the rest of the group.

Soon everything in the truck was included in the game, and within fifteen minutes the signs changed hands several times. When it was time to tidy things away for lunch, Wayne asked another child for help in putting away the signs in the truck. The therapist suggested that the truck be put with the train so that everything would be ready for another time. The next day Wayne shared not only the truck, but also some blocks, without difficulties.

Learning about emotions and developing emotionally and socially is a very slow process. Rarely is there the kind of dramatic breakthrough we saw with John or with Adam, where a child seems to be literally struck by a new emotion. For most autistic children emotional growth comes late and by a painfully slow process. Even autistic adults who have "made it," are integrated in society, and function at or above the intellectual norm, often still struggle with the social and emotional aspects of their lives and may have great difficulties in making and keeping close contacts with their peers.

Sometimes it becomes clear that positive emotions growing out of developing relationships may be even harder to face than negative ones. In the concluding case study, told by Jeanne Simons, we follow the development of Nathaniel from a withdrawn, compulsive little boy to a loving adult.

NATHANIEL AND THE TREASURE

Nathaniel's problems started at birth. He was born by Caesarian section. For six weeks he suffered from severe colic and had to be carried around twenty-four hours a day. Even after the colic subsided, the screaming continued. The parents hired a practical nurse to help with Nathaniel's care. She dealt with the situation by letting the baby "scream it out" for two or three days. From then on, Nathaniel was a "good" baby. He liked to be left alone and only got upset when anything in his environment changed. He also reacted with real terror to the sound of low-flying airplanes landing and taking off from a nearby airfield. He would scramble desperately at his mattress as if trying to burrow his way in to escape from the noise.

When Nathaniel was three months old, his parents were in desperate need of a vacation. They left Nathaniel with his grandmother. He reacted to the change with obvious fear and screamed endlessly for the whole three weeks he was there. When his parents returned they found him completely withdrawn. He was terrified of strangers and this lasted until he was two years old. At that time his fear of strange adults subsided somewhat but he was still very much afraid of children.

Nathaniel started to talk when he was a year old. He soon had a large vocabulary and clear diction but he talked in a monotone and did not use speech to communicate. He simply repeated what he heard. He also never looked at people. He had never displayed any affection and did not want to be cuddled by anybody. When Nathaniel was almost four years old, he was diagnosed as autistic by Dr. Kanner and shortly thereafter he joined my group at Children's House.

Nathaniel was a good looking little boy who was dressed to perfection. But his face was too serious. He seemed unable to smile. For days he sat by himself in front of a French window. Whenever another child came anywhere near him, he would cling to my sleeve or skirt. Other than that he did not show any interest in anything that was going on in the room. As long as he was left to himself, he seemed perfectly satisfied. The way he occupied himself was by multiplying large numbers and mumbling them to himself.

As time went on, it was possible to take him by the hand and lead him toward a group of children. At first he clung to me but by and by I was able to station myself at a little distance from him. Though Nathaniel didn't play with any of the other children, he did begin to show some interest in one particular boy, Allen, who was hyperactive, full of mischief, and often quite destructive. Nathaniel would watch his antics with fascination, even egging him on at times to do things he himself did not dare to do, like throwing objects at a window.

By keeping Nathaniel closely by my side, I could get him to play next to Allen, and eventually they began to interact. At first I had to be the intermediary, helping Allen build something with one hand, encouraging Nathaniel to bring the building down. As Nathaniel became less afraid, it was enough to initiate a game and then leave the two boys alone. After two years at Children's House, Nathaniel had gained enough independence to enter a private school. Academically he did fairly well, but he kept to himself, ignored the other children, and never joined in any group activities.

At home Nathaniel was still very difficult to live with, always demanding, never giving. He could not accept affection from his parents and never displayed any toward them. He had never hugged either parent. He called them by their first names, rather than addressing them as "mother" and "father." This was especially difficult for his mother, whose whole life was given over to the care of her only child.

During that time he still had many problems and I continued to see him on an individual basis. He would get upset if it rained when the weather bureau had predicted good weather, when he had a cold, or when his hands or clothes got dirty. He had severe allergies and that made him angry at the pollen and the wind. He always had to talk about how often he had to sneeze. It sometimes appeared as if he wanted to control the whole world.

When things became easier at home, we sometimes interrupted our sessions for several months. Then another problem might crop up and he would call, or his parents would ask for help. At one point Nathaniel was building a harpsichord and a telescope with his father. Nathaniel's father enjoyed working with him, but gradually Nathaniel began to take over all the available space at home, getting very upset if any of his tools or parts were moved. The parents were slowly being backed into a corner and his mother called to say that she was at the end of her endurance.

Nathaniel came to discuss the situation. I told him that his mother was obviously at the end of her rope. He was intrigued by the expression and wanted to know what it meant. After I had explained it to him he said, "Well, then it is my turn to make a move now." Nathaniel, his parents, and I met and discussed how the available space should be divided equitably. Both parents had hobbies. The father loved photography and had a darkroom in the basement. The mother painted. They had a large room in the house which they all used as a hobby room. Nathaniel agreed that his mother should have the largest space because of her big canvasses. He allocated himself a smaller area and after that never intruded into his parents' part of the house anymore.

During his sessions with me, Nathaniel talked incessantly to himself, never looking at me. Everything was in numbers. How often he had sneezed, how many times he would sneeze that year. How many stones had been put down in the new patio, how many stones were smaller, how many larger. . . .He never listened.

We interrupted the sessions by drinking milk and eating cookies. Sometimes we practiced "listening." I told him that he could talk about numbers and I would listen, if in exchange he would listen to me for a few seconds. When he agreed, I introduced some toys or books and we briefly "talked" about them.

The more spontaneous and warm Nathaniel's relationship with me became, the more obsessed he seemed to become with numbers. Distances, heights, depths all ran into trillions and trillions. He would bring pages with numbers that had ten and twenty zeros. He expected me to listen to him, but he never "heard" me when I asked him about the meaning of all of those numbers. This went on for months and months. Then one day Nathaniel asked for milk and cookies at the beginning of our session. This departure from the firmly established routine he insisted on at other times alerted me to the fact that he might be ready for a change. I decided to tackle him about his numbers once more.

"Okay, Nathaniel, we will have our milk and cookies, but first tell me what all the numbers are about. I am getting tired of all these numbers." This time he not only heard me, he responded.

"It's a treasure and it is trillions and trillions of miles deep. I am going to dig for it."

Between drinking his milk and eating his cookies, Nathaniel pretended to dig. He did this for several sessions, but any time he got a little deeper, everything would "cave in" and he had to start all over again. It was June. In July he would go to summer camp and our meetings would be interrupted for several weeks. I told him that the treasure would have to be dug up before he left for camp. He became very anxious and had a nosebleed. He became even more anxious when I figured out for him how many miles he would have to dig every time he came, even though I had done away with the trillions and substituted numbers in the thousands.

On his last visit before leaving for camp he became very upset. He could not dig today, he told me. He had had to sneeze too much, the medication was not working, and various other excuses. He had some milk and cookies and I told him that I would help him and dig extra hard to get to the treasure. He felt better and we "dug" the last few hundred miles. He bent down and panto-mimed lifting something with great effort. "Oh," he said, "It's a box and it has millions and trillions of locks on it."

"Nathaniel, you must be very much afraid of what's in the box that you put so many locks on it."

"Yes. I am."

It was the first time that I heard him say "yes."

"Let's leave it here, Nathaniel, until you come back from camp."

At first he didn't seem to hear me. He walked carefully around the imaginary box and mumbled to himself. Then he walked over to me and handed me the treasure. "Put it in a safe place until I get back from camp."

When he returned from his summer break, we took the treasure and put it on the table.

"Miss Simons, I am not strong enough to get the locks off. It will take a year."

"I am strong, Nathaniel," I assured him. "I will help you."

"All right. You start."

I ripped off a lock and he pitched in to help.

"I can do it alone now." He became more and more excited as the locks came off. There was no sign of his previous anxiety. At last he gave a big sigh.

"The locks are off now." He opened the box. The lid made a squeaking sound. Then he looked into the box. A beautiful smile illuminated his face.

"Look, Miss Simons, it's all wrapped in cotton." He put his hand in the box and took out the treasure.

"Hold your hands up, Miss Simons." Carefully he walked toward me and put the treasure gently into my outstretched hands.

"It's love, Miss Simons. It's for you."

I held the treasure carefully.

"Are you sure, Nathaniel, that it is for me?"

"No," he said, "It's for El—M.O.T.H.E.R." He took the treasure out of my hands and slowly walked to the room where his mother was waiting.

"Here, El—M.O.T.H.E.R, it's love, and it is for you." He almost choked on the unaccustomed word, but he hugged his mother. Then he asked me in a normal voice to practice saying "mother" with him.

I said "mother." He looked at his mother and repeated the word. We did this several times, then he returned to the therapy room to drink his milk and eat his cookies to terminate the session. When he left he asked me how he could practice saying "mother" at home. His mother was overwhelmed but managed to keep her emotions under control. She told him that she would help him.

During the following week his mother called to tell me that Nathaniel had started calling her mother at bedtime but never during the day. Then Nathaniel himself called to ask whether he could come for a session with his parents. "You know," he said, "You can't have a 'you-know-what,' without a 'you-know-what.'" The family arrived and Nathaniel asked me to help him practice "you-know-what." I said "mother." He repeated it. Then he looked at his father. I said "father." He repeated it. We did this several times. Then he looked at his parents and said, "Now we have to decide if I will call you Father and Mother, or Mom and Dad." He finally decided on Mom and Dad.

After this incident I saw Nathaniel a few more weeks. Soon he would be twelve years old. I had been working with him for eight years, and I asked him whether he wouldn't like to start seeing a male therapist.

"You have done well, why change?" he asked. I explained that it might be interesting for him to see a man.

"Could be," he said, and that was the last I saw of Nathaniel for months. I had a few calls from him in which he complained about his new psychiatrist. What bothered him was that whenever he asked a question he was asked what he thought. "If I knew the answer, I wouldn't ask the question," Nathaniel reasoned. Nathaniel saw several psychiatrists over the next few years and continued to make progress, but he never formed a close relationship with any of them.

When Nathaniel was sixteen he got a car. He called to ask if he could come over and give me "a spin." He knew all the rules and followed them to perfection. He also knew his car inside and out. He graduated from high school with As and Bs and went on to college. Academically he had no problems but he did not seem to be able to make friends. Though he made an effort to socialize, people tended to leave him alone after a few encounters. He was very upset about this and called me for advice. I told him that he was a "talker rather than a listener," and that it might help if he could learn to listen once in a while. I also practiced "listening" with him over the phone.

At last Nathaniel found a friend who was a great help to him. He moved away from home and shared a room with his friend. His roommate even arranged a double date, but it turned out to be a fiasco. Nathaniel called to say that his heart was broken. He graduated and held several jobs until he found a good job in a bank.

A few years later, when he was twenty-five, Nathaniel called me one day and asked whether he could come over. He had a surprise for me. He sounded very happy. When he came, he had a girl with him. He was radiant.

"You are the first person I trusted. I trust her as much as I do you."

The girl could not believe that Nathaniel had had so many problems. She asked me questions about his past. I told Nathaniel that he could answer those questions himself.

"Yes," he laughed, "but she doesn't believe me. You better tell her."

Nathaniel put his arm around her shoulder and said seriously, "You know what I did? I asked her to marry me. I completely forgot that we weren't even engaged yet."

The girl looked at him with great warmth. "Nathaniel, I do not know if we will ever get married. We will always be friends, even if I marry someone else. You are the dearest, most honest friend I ever had."

One year later, Nathaniel called and invited me to his wedding. I have never seen a more radiant groom. At the reception his mother gave a toast. I whispered to him to hug his mother.

He lifted his arm up hesitantly, as if he didn't quite know what to do with it. He needed a tiny nudge to his elbow to help him forward, then he briefly hugged his mother.

Nathaniel has been married for eight years. He recently changed jobs and now works as a cost analyst in Washington.

NINE
✦✦✦

Mysteries

INTRODUCTION

In the preceding chapters we have examined the typical characteristics of autistic children and how to help them improve their chances to develop and become functioning members of society. Although autism is one of the most difficult disorders to work with, there are also indications of unusual abilities and behaviors in many autistic children that suggest hidden potentials and offer a glimpse into a world of experiences that is mysteriously different from our own.

Especially intriguing are clear manifestations of preverbal memories and demonstrations of a variety of skills that reveal extraordinary talent in specific, often isolated, areas. They raise questions to which none of the existing theories about possible causes of autism offer satisfactory answers. We are simply left with a feeling that there is more to these children than meets the eye.

Other developmental disorders that have a clear organic or psychogenic base are characterized by developmental delays and deficiencies that result in children performing below the norm in predictable ways and in clearly defined areas.

Autistic children, too, function below par, often considerably so, but many of them exhibit behaviors or skills that not only put them above the norm, but that may never be encountered in normal, or even in especially gifted children. Occasional dramatic cures of severely autistic children, but especially the flashes of brilliance that pierce the darkness surrounding the autism syndrome and its origins convince an observer that he is in the presence of something truly unique. Following are a series of anecdotes that illustrate this fascinating aspect of autism. They are told here without any attempt at explanation or interpretation, simply because they happened.

221

EARLY MEMORIES

In the story of Lee we have already come across evidence that some autistic children remember incidents that go back to the earliest moments in their lives. Lee not only remembered his hospitalization before the age of eighteen months, he recalled minute details of the intravenous feedings he received there. He also dictated stories that obviously happened before he had any understanding of spoken language, and he talked about being given a bottle in his crib rather than on somebody's lap when he was a little baby.

Another boy, Keith, talked in a group session about how he shrank from the nearness of his mother when he was still small enough to be in a crib. Unable to describe emotions that flooded him long before he had any words for them, he nevertheless conveyed the panic and the pain he felt when his mother bent over his crib and her face slowly came closer and closer to his own.

Even more dramatic was the anxiety attack Gordon suffered while he and a group of older boys watched the movie "A Child is Born." At the time, Gordon was doing well at Linwood and was already attending public school. The film was shown to the boys during one of their regular group meetings as a basis for a discussion about the beginnings of life. The film depicts all phases of fetal development and discusses a variety of prenatal complications and their medical treatment.

At the actual moment at which the baby was born, Gordon panicked. He jumped up on a low coffee table where he stood, trembling and white. "What if the baby gets angry if the mother touches it," he gasped. "What if he cries?" He was clearly in the grip of an overpowering emotion.

The therapist lightly touched him and said, "I will tell her to be very careful and gentle with the baby." This assurance was enough to calm Gordon and he was able to watch the rest of the film with the group.

RELIVING THE BIRTH EXPERIENCE

In some cases, the memories seem to go back to birth itself or even to the time before birth.

Cindy was three when she came to Linwood and one of the most severely autistic children who ever entered the program. She was mute, never looked at anybody, and could not be interested in anything. From the moment she came in until she left she would screech and scream and only quiet down somewhat when she could sit on somebody's lap. There she would huddle on her knees, with a dull expression on her face, sometimes whining softly. Her arms were always folded across her chest and she tucked down her head, pressing it against the adult's stomach. Burrowing into the person holding her it seemed as if she was trying to return to the womb.

At home she behaved the same way. If she was put down, the screeching would start immediately, and she followed the adults, hanging on to their clothes with hands and teeth. Often she would burst out into a sort of desperate rage even while she was being held, biting, bumping her head against an abdomen or breast, and trying to rip off her own clothes or those of the person closest to her.

Over the course of months, it became clear that despite every attempt to give her all the cuddling she could want, she was not getting what she needed. The snatches of sitting in various people's laps were not enough to assuage her desperate need to find a place where she could be at peace. It was time to try something new. So one day, after about a year in treatment, when Cindy again started to cry and pull at people, she was undressed and gently lowered into a bathtub filled with lukewarm water. Though she protested at first, she quickly quieted down and submerged herself in the water until only her mouth and nose showed. The therapist put some toys in the water, but Cindy paid no attention to them. She just lay there, knees slightly drawn up, submerged and quiet. The therapist sat next to her, humming wordless tunes, letting her enjoy the water without interference.

After twenty minutes when the water had cooled, she quickly took Cindy out of the tub and wrapped her in a soft blanket that she had pre-warmed. Cindy made contented little baby sounds and also eagerly drank from a baby bottle filled with juice. Then the therapist started singing about a little girl and how she needed a shirt to put on her. After a moment, a little hand emerged from the cocoon, reached for the shirt on the radiator and handed it to the therapist. In the same fashion she handed over every piece of clothing that was mentioned. Once fully dressed, she seemed satisfied and relaxed and was undemanding for the rest of the morning.

The same procedure was followed several days in succession. Then the bottle was replaced with the contents of Cindy's lunch box. At first Cindy always lay perfectly still and submerged in the water. One day she sat up in the tub and began to play with some of the toys swimming about. That was the signal to start tapering off the sessions, skipping a few days and after about fifteen times discontinuing the baths altogether.

After that Cindy still liked to sit on laps but not more so than other children in the group. She also didn't scrunch herself up in a fetal position anymore, but sat more like a normal child. She became more animated and soon everybody was commenting on her beauty and grace. She also began to use more words and was able to show affection both to the staff and to her parents.

Cindy needed help to be able to go back to an early period in her existence, to experience its gratifications and to slowly emerge from it more content and more able and willing to perform at the level of her real age. Other children recreated the birth experience spontaneously, but in their cases too this could be seen as a breakthrough to the outside world and to more functional behavior. We have already mentioned Johnny, who wanted to be a baby again when his sister was born.

Johnny always carried a rope with him. Most of the time he would stay in his particular corner of the room and make designs with his rope.

One day Johnny took his rope over to Miss Simons. He pushed her into a chair, standing in front of her and making designs with his rope. Suddenly he picked up a teddy bear and held it against his stomach, with the rope wound around the bear. Then he started to groan, as if in terrible pain. "It's coming, it's coming." His face was distorted as if he really suffered. He pushed the bear down until it was between his legs with the rope firmly held against it. He groaned louder and louder, until the bear fell to the floor. Then he threw the rope down, jumped into the therapist's lap and cuddled down there whimpering softly. "It's a girl. I'm a little girl. I'm hungry," he cried.

Miss Simons indulged Johnny for a while, then indirectly asked him to help her with a task that only a bigger child could perform. Johnny readily complied and after this he came out of his corner, and began to take more of an interest in things other than his rope.

A similar reenactment of the birth process freed Larry from the confines of the boundaries within which he forced himself to live. Larry was the little boy at Children's House who did nothing but play with a bottle top within a narrow circle in the middle of the room. As the weeks went by, Larry slowly enlarged his original space, by holding onto a hand — any hand — and carefully pacing out an ever larger circle within which he could move freely. If it was necessary to leave the room, to go to the bathroom, for example, or to go home he had to cling tightly to an adult's hand and had to be lifted over the doorsill. It was impossible to get him to go out into the yard. After several weeks he would occasionally permit himself to be carried outside, where he immediately set up his boundaries.

> *After Larry had been in treatment for several months, one day he took Miss Simons' hand and guided her into the hall. He closed all the doors leading to the hall, took her to the darkest corner and placed himself in front of her, with his back toward her. Then he positioned her hands and arms so that one hand was on his neck while her other arm encircled him. He bore down on them until she held him very tightly. Then he continued to press on the hand on his neck so that his head was forced lower and lower. After a while he jumped up, tumbled around and ended up hanging upside down over Miss Simons' arm with his knees bent. He folded his arms across his chest, then guided her, still upside down, through the hall, the bathroom, and the playroom. There he let himself slide to the floor. He rushed her back to the hall, leaving all the doors open this time. Then he repeated the sequence, but more quickly and laughingly. Back in the room, he walked to the hall and the bathroom by himself. That was the end of his boundaries.*
>
> *When he had gotten rid of his boundaries, Larry also became less compulsive about his bottle top and was able to stop his compulsive play at times to go outdoors. He could be engaged in other activities and also started to develop more of an awareness of the people around him, showing a marked preference for Miss Simons' hand over that of the other staff members.*
>
> *Over the next three years Larry repeated this reenactment of the birth process several more times. Each time it preceded a tremendous gain he made, such as giving up baby food, making contact with other children, and saying his first words.*

ISLANDS OF BRILLIANCE

Autistic individuals usually show an extreme variability of cognitive functioning. A few even perform so brilliantly in certain isolated areas that they are called "autistic savants" (from the French "idiots savants," describing the phenomenon of mentally retarded individuals with extraordinary skills).

Autistic individuals often excel in areas that have some connection with numbers or dates. Several children who have passed through Linwood obviously carried a sort of perpetual calendar in their heads and, like Lee, were able to come up almost instantly with the day of the week any date fell on in the past or the future.

Others have performed incredible mathematical feats, such as multiplying multidigit numbers in their heads at a time when they had absolutely no numbers concept and could not have explained the meaning of one plus one. Many autistic children have impressive memories. Their recall is always factual, usually nonselective and at times photographic. If they have been somewhere once, they notice the most minute changes when they come back.

Stephen, at sixteen, could recall all the names of the doctors he had had contact with since he was two years old. He also remembered when and where he met them, how long they stayed with him and the clothes they were wearing. He was able to repeat verbatim what they had said, even imitating their voices. He remembered which bed he had slept in in various hospitals, in boarding school, and at camps the names of the children in the room with him, and which ones snored or were restless in bed. He remembered not only the birthdays of his entire extended family, but also those of acquaintances and even those of strangers he met in the street. Any record he heard once, he knew by heart.

Children register and recall things long before they make sense to them.

Fraser was brought to Linwood by taxi from the city every day. He was five years old, mute, and typically uninvolved in what was happening around him. One day his ride didn't come and a counselor had to drive him back home. Knowing only the general direction in which he lived she said to him, "Fraser, you will have to direct me." And Fraser did. Pointing correctly ahead, left or right, he charted their thirty minute ride and unerringly brought them to his front door.

In a different context we have told how Larry identified his jars of baby food by the labels before he could read.

Another boy, Lester, could read but didn't know the meaning of what he was reading. His visual memory was so acute, however, that he could walk past a row of boxes on the shelf of a supermarket and afterward reproduce everything written on the labels, including the ingredients listed in small print.

Even more amazing was Ronny. At five, he liked to play in the room where his father, an engineer, worked on his mechanical drawings. He never interacted with his father or showed any special interest in his work. One day, his mother found a series of drawings on small pieces of paper crumpled up in the wastebasket. They turned out to be copies of some of the father's blueprints which the boy had reproduced from memory. They were not only complete in every detail, they were reduced in scale and the relative dimensions were correct down to the fraction of an inch.

While Ronny's feat can be explained by an unusual capacity to memorize and reproduce an image in its totality, Sidney's ability went beyond anything attributable to memory alone.

Sidney loved to build with the small plastic "American bricks." He would pour the whole set out on the table. Then he would study them for a while, chin on hand and a frown between his eyes. After a while his face would brighten and he would start to sort out the bricks of different sizes, the tiny doors and windows, putting some in one pile, discarding others.

When he started to work, Sidney first laid out all of his materials as if following a blueprint. Then he began to put together the pieces with infinite patience. Sometimes he duplicated his own home, sometimes his designs were of imaginary buildings. Some had storm windows, others double doors or elaborate porches. When they were finished, all of the original pieces were used up, and Sidney was never short a single block. It was obvious that he had been able to visualize and analyze a structure that existed only in his imagination.

Though many of the amazing skills autistic children exhibit are connected to facts, figures, and concrete memories there are also cases of unusual artistic talent among this population. A case described in the literature was Nadia.[16,17] Linwood too, has had its share of artistically talented children, such as Barry who at ten produced reams of colored comic strips. He never sketched anything in or erased a single stroke, but, starting somewhere midway in a frame, developed each scene complete with commentary in bold, decisive strokes. Various other children exhibited great early musical talent. We have already described how Fred corrected a theme into which the piano player had slipped a false note. A similar thing happened with Silvio.

When Silvio joined the program he was three years old. The staff soon called him their "little sack of sand." Since he hardly walked, he had to be carried around most of the time. He was heavy as lead, and when he was put down he simply sagged, folded double with his head almost resting on his legs. There was little that was attractive about Silvio. He had beautiful eyes, but there was no life in them. His nose ran and he was always wet or soiled. The only thing he did was to throw little objects over his head. But early on it was clear that he loved music. When someone played the piano or records he always sat perfectly still and would stop throwing things or chewing paper.

Then one day, after several months in treatment, he suddenly climbed up on the piano bench, threw one chubby leg over the other, moved his hands over the keys until he found the right ones and played "chopsticks" with both hands. When it was over he looked at the audience that had gathered. The children had drawn closer, the staff was breathless, everybody stared at him in amazement.

Silvio seemed puzzled by the silence that greeted his performance. He clapped his hands. That broke the spell and everybody gave him an enthusiastic hand. So Silvio gave an encore and played the piece a second time. He was put into a regular little music group. He carefully watched the teacher as she played and was able to reproduce a simple tune after hearing it once. Silvio was still in many ways retarded in his functioning. But the music brought him alive. He learned to smile, to demand as well as give affection, and he became naughty too, a sure sign that he was developing a will and personality of his own.

Another child who showed an early fascination with music was Pierre, although he never touched an instrument himself. His father played the piano every day and Pierre could hardly wait until he came home. At five and a half, Pierre talked very little and was very withdrawn, but he recognized a great number of classical pieces by ear as well as by looking at the score and was able to turn the pages for his father after hearing a piece just once. Once he found a book in which a single bar of music was reproduced, and he immediately identified it correctly as belonging to one of Beethoven's piano concertos.

Though all of these behaviors and skills are spontaneous manifestations of a child's functioning and some of them are at times an important part of his life, they are with few exceptions isolated pieces that do not fit into the rest of the puzzle the child presents. And because they are not part of the general scheme, they rarely lead to anything more. They do not carry over into other areas or develop further themselves. They just *are*, appearing one day, full blown, like a volcanic island out of the sea, and sometimes disappearing the same way, when there is a further shift in the substructure.

In fact, almost without exception, the unusual abilities autistic children display disappear gradually as they begin to develop in treatment. Their mindless facility with numbers fades as they develop the basic mathematical concepts though they may preserve some of their skills like the ability to fix a weekday to a date. Their prodigious musical ability too, often does not survive their encounter with the demands of the outside world. As far as treatment goes, most of the children's unusual talents are therefore of limited value.

On the other hand, the existence of these extraordinary skills does prove that these children are neither deaf nor unable to take in their surroundings. And nobody who witnesses skills like Sidney's or Pierre's will be able to believe that these are basically retarded children. However, the promise of normal development and higher-level functioning they hold out is often not fulfilled. The behaviors remain isolated, inexplicable—mysteries.

TEN
✦✦✦

Linwood Today

Over the last thirty years Linwood has grown to its present capacity of between 30 and 35 children. Much has changed since the perilous beginnings.

Financial support by groups and individuals as well as the Board of Education allowed continued structural improvements and the addition of a separate dormitory building as well as an expansion of staff and an increase in the number of children that could be accommodated. With the passage of Public Law 94–142, Section 504, the rising educational costs for each child are no longer the intolerable burden on parents that they used to be. At the same time, licensing requirements by various agencies have introduced complications and red tape of which the early Linwood was largely free.

Generations of children have graduated and have moved on, many to enjoy a normal life. The staff has expanded and many who came to work and learn at Linwood from different parts of the country and from all over the world have left and have taken their training and their experience with them to places as far away as Japan, Holland, France, Germany, and Ireland.

PAST RESEARCH AT LINWOOD

In the course of the years since Linwood's inception in 1955, there has been continued interest in the work done there and Linwood has been involved, either directly or indirectly, in a number of research projects. One of the most important ones from the point of view of Linwood was a three year study (1965–1968) headed by Dr. Charles Ferster from the Institute of Behavioral Research in Washington, D.C., funded by a research grant from the U.S. Department of Health, Education and Welfare.

231

Dr. Ferster was a behavioral psychologist and his main interest lay in demonstrating that principles of behavioral conditioning developed in the laboratory with animals could be taught to the staff to make them more effective therapists with developmentally impaired children. Actually much of the work done at Linwood at the time was based on the principles of behavior modification. But the intervention techniques the staff used did not, on the face of it, look anything like the classic types of conditioning made famous by people like Watson and Pavlov or the operant conditioning techniques pioneered by Skinner and his school. They also differed in important ways from the kind of operant conditioning that has become the treatment of choice in many centers dealing with autistic children.

For one, the Linwood approach to shaping behavior relies on positive reinforcement of aspects of existing behaviors rather that on adversive conditioning or punishment. For another, the rewards and reinforcers that are used to motivate the children are not the usual and traditional ones of food or praise, but "natural" reinforcers, things derived from each individual child's own needs, interests, or preoccupations. Furthermore, there are no set predetermined treatment sequences in which specific behaviors, like establishing eye-contact, are worked on according to priorities selected by the staff. Instead, the *child* is allowed to set the pace and his need determines priorities. The staff manipulates the environment, rather than manipulating the child. In that way the structure of the children's natural, daily environment and consequences growing out of their own activities act as motivators and gradually produce new behaviors.

Before the Ferster study, the staff at Linwood had not thought in terms of theories or techniques. His observations helped them to see that most of the therapeutic interactions they used could be described as a series of carefully orchestrated small steps that gradually lead to observable changes in behavior. Before Ferster's involvement, the often dramatic improvements of children placed at Linwood were regarded by some as sheer magic, wrought by a uniquely gifted therapist who trusted mainly in her intuition to reach the children under her care. Charles Ferster not only identified the behavioral modification components and the unique ways in which they were integrated into a total treatment approach, he provided both a theoretical base and a language that made it possible to describe most aspects of the therapy process in more exact terms. What had mainly been passed on by example could now be taught in a more formal way and it was easier to help the staff become better observers and to apply what they learned about each child in therapy.

In conjunction with the Ferster study, Dr. Leo Kanner, who had been an early and enthusiastic supporter of Jeanne Simons and Linwood, undertook a study to evaluate all of the children then being treated at Linwood.

His study was carried out in two series of visits, one in 1966, the other, as a follow-up in 1968. His findings, together with notes by Jeanne Simons on each child's further development up to the date of publication, was published in 1973.[18]

Dr. Kanner divided the children into five nosological categories: true autism, schizophrenia, developmental and behavioral manifestations due mainly to organicity (neurological impairments and retardation) or to psychogenicity (disturbances of the emotional environment that produced deviant development and behavior), and dementia infantilis or Heller's disease (in which a smooth development during the first 1½ to 2½ years of life is followed by complete regression). In all cases, regardless of their diagnosis, the children originally exhibited behaviors that were characteristic of the autistic syndrome.

At the time of the evaluation, the 34 children had been in treatment for varying amounts of time. By 1973 ten of them, that is approximately 29%, had attained what Kanner called "a state of near-full or full recovery." They had left Linwood and were attending public schools with good success. Thirteen (38%) were functioning well enough to be placed in day care centers, while 11 (33%), including the two with Heller's disease, were institutionalized in centers for the retarded or in other private or state institutions.

Given the fact that only 20% of all autistic children have *measured* intelligent quotients of 70 or above, these figures are heartening. If nothing else, they have to be treated with caution. As Kanner himself wrote,

> It would seem that the present state of the art does not allow us to meaningfully relate the outcome of any case to either the diagnosis or to the duration of treatment at Linwood. Suffice it to say that of the 34 children whose stay at Linwood ranged from 1 year 10 months to 12 years and 9 months, only a few have failed to demonstrate visible progress. (p. 282–83)

OUTCOMES

As we have seen from Dr. Kanner's follow-up study, Linwood's success rate is relatively high, especially when the severity of the affliction is taken into account. Since that study was published no systematic follow-up has been done at Linwood. However, a survey of students who left Linwood since the Kanner study was published, provides some interesting information.

Most of this group of 57 entered Linwood after 1966. They were in treatment between 2 and 12 years, with an average stay of 5 to 7 years. For 4 of them no information is available. Of the rest, 19 went from Linwood into some other type of residential program (Level VI). Most of these children were either severely retarded or had multiple handicaps, though three of them were judged to be higher functioning by the Linwood staff. Of these one later left the institution, is presently competitively employed, and is looking into moving into an apartment of her own.

A further 18 went from Linwood into a Level V placement in public schools, where they were educated in self-contained classes for children that are either retarded or have multiple handicaps. A number of them have since gone on to some sort of vocational training and are presently enrolled in CSAC adult programs.

Four children were mainstreamed (Level IV) and of those, 3 are now also in CSAC programs. Altogether, 7 former students of the group under discussion who originally attended in Level IV or V public school programs are presently in special adult programs, work in sheltered workshops or under special supervision, and live in group homes or apartments.

Twelve children made the transition from Linwood into regular public school programs, either at the middle or at the high school level. Four of these are presently attending college.

A number of former students and their families have stayed in contact with Linwood so that information on them is more or less up to date. For others, data is mainly based on their records and concerns their placement directly from Linwood. It is possible that more former students have since moved on from their initial placement into more independent situations.

According to the third edition of the Diagnostic and Statistical Manual of Mental Disorders, published by the American Psychiatric Association, only one child in six, (16.6%) makes an adequate social adjustment and as an adult is able to do regular work. A further 16.6% make only a "fair" adjustment, while the remaining 66.6% remain severely handicapped and unable to lead independent lives.

Compared with these statistics, the Linwood figures are heartening:

• 22.8% of former students in this group now function within or above the norms of society, in school, colleges, or a job.

• 20.9% could be mainstreamed in public schools and/or live semi-independently and are able to work.

• 17.6% went into special classes (Level V). A number of these may eventually be able to make the transition into special adult programs and achieve semi-independence.

- Only 31.7% remained so severely handicapped that they needed institutional placement and, as far as is known, are still institutionalized.

So far, no correlations between specific indicators and therapy success can be demonstrated. In some cases children who initially seemed totally unresponsive or severely retarded could be reached after being in treatment for two or three years. In other cases children began to develop suddenly, after hope for progress had almost been given up. Some children with initial severe symptoms went on to lead normal lives, others, for whom prognosis had originally looked good, never developed past a certain stage. But there are only a handful of cases in the whole history of Linwood where no change for the better can be documented.

Parents whose children went from Linwood to other institutions generally talk about the Linwood experience with as much enthusiasm and affection as those whose children could be reintegrated in normal schools. All parents expressed their relief at having been given a definitive diagnosis by people they trusted. Talking about the most positive aspects of their child's involvement at Linwood, many parents particularly stressed the importance of having found a place where neither children nor parents were judged, where the child was accepted, respected, and appreciated as he was, where the whole program was geared to deal with the particular disabilities of autistic children and where they had a chance to develop whatever hidden or limited potential they might possess.

Over and over again the fact that the child is seen and treated as an individual with an emphasis on his strengths rather than on his limitations was mentioned by the parents as one of the outstanding assets of the Linwood approach. This view of the child, handicapped as he may be, humanizes rather than depersonalizes him. Indeed, anybody who is in daily contact with these children quickly discovers the clear differences in personality between them that shine through the overlay of their autistic symptomology.

Asked what the outstanding effect of the Linwood treatment methods was in her opinion, one psychiatrist said, "You know, when some of these children come in they are almost invisible and some of them act more like little animals than like children. But when you meet them after a while and when they leave, they are all really nice human beings."

THE EDUCATIONAL PROGRAM

Because it was almost the only and possibly the first center of its kind in 1955, children in the early years were generally no older than 5 years of age upon admittance, and some were as young as 2½ or 3. They usually did not stay beyond early adolescence. By that time they were either transferred to public school programs or channeled into other, more permanent placements.

During the last decade more services for autistic children have become available, with some districts opening up special classes for them in their public schools. Consequently, the children applying at Linwood today are frequently older than they used to be. They may have had years of alternate education, and it is often only after other placements have failed that they are brought to Linwood. For the same reason, they are, with rare exceptions, generally lower functioning than the earlier population.

Children today are also being kept at Linwood until they are older. Experience has shown that autistic cognitive and social development does not level off in adolescence as it does with normal children. Instead, progress continues into the second decade and beyond. Sometimes the first real breakthrough, especially in language development, only occurs during the teens. Mark, for example, did not use language to communicate with until he was 12 or 13 and had been in treatment for six or seven years.

Because growth continues to take place during a more extended period, continued and consistent treatment, tailored to the specific needs and characteristics of autistic adolescents is essential. If treatment is broken off prematurely, earlier gains may be lost and the individual may never fully develop his potential.

Linwood is spearheading the effort to create specialized centers for autistic adolescents, because it does not want to discharge youngsters who are not ready to enter regular public school and would therefore be faced with placement in centers or institutions that are not geared to treating them.

The fact that educational plans are required every year and that the children's placements are reviewed on an annual basis, puts a lot of pressure on the staff at Linwood. On the one hand they are committed to a method that stresses total development over a longer period of time rather than short-term gains and the acquisition of isolated, often meaningless skills. On the other hand, they have to document yearly progress to justify a child's placement.

Often, a child is claimed by the public school system for their own special classes as soon as he is beginning to show some progress. This means that the staff at Linwood never know how much time they have with a particular child to achieve long-term goals. A child may be placed elsewhere before he has developed his full potential and before he has consolidated his gains, especially in the areas of social and emotional development to which less attention can be devoted in public school programs.

Part of the task of the Linwood staff is to represent their students at hearings at which their scholastic future is determined and to demonstrate the benefits the Linwood program offers a specific child, because of distinctive features not found in any existing public school program. Following is a brief description of these programs.

Linwood offers three placement possibilities: a *day program* that covers regular school hours, an *extended day program*, until 8:00 P.M., that encompassed after school activities and includes supper, and a five-day *residential program*. Newly entering children are usually first placed in the day program. After an initial adjustment period their needs are reassessed to see whether they might profit more from one or the other two options.

The extended day program, for example, offers increased involvement in recreational activities, group games, arts and crafts, cooking and baking, and pre-vocational skills. Children in residence live in a child-centered environment and have the opportunity to develop closer relationships with a steady peer group and with a larger number of staff persons. Opportunities to practice self-help skills, hygiene, dressing and toileting, simple housekeeping chores, and other activities that are part of a normal daily routine are also emphasized according to a child's developmental level.

The decision to place children in residence is always discussed with them. It is made clear that they are not being "dumped" because they are bad or too hard to handle at home. Linwood is a place where children have to be accepted for valid reasons and these are explored in a straightforward manner with children who are advanced enough to understand.

> *In a group discussion on what it means to have emotional problems and why children come to Linwood, one boy said, "I was kicked out of several schools, because I was bad. That's why I had to come to Linwood." Miss Simons' reply was, "Well, we don't take bad boys at Linwood. We thought you had a problem and that we could help you with it."*

Within each of the programs children are grouped according to their level of functioning. In assessing children for grouping, academic ability is not the primary consideration. Where a child best fits in is mainly determined by factors such as his readiness for limits, his ability to control his behavior, his willingness to participate as a member of a group, his physical size, emotional development, and his use of language. The ideal group for any child is one in which he is stimulated, especially socially and verbally, without being overwhelmed.

As a child develops, he moves through the groups, the most advanced of which is "the schoolroom." From there, children whose progress continues are gradually eased into public school programs, or may be taken to a job, for example at the county library, where they can get supervised work experience.

Contrary to public schools, all of the programs at Linwood are offered on a year-round basis. Autistic children need consistent and ongoing reinforcement. Since progress is generally slow and takes a long time to generalize from one situation to another, a two or three month break in treatment may undo much they achieved during the rest of the year.

Another, and perhaps the most crucial difference between the Linwood approach and that of other educational programs is the fact that at Linwood treatment encompassed every aspect of a child's development. It is not limited to developing academic skills, but places great and continued emphasis on those areas that are especially handicapping to autistic children: social and emotional adjustment, involvement in and exploration of the environment, self-help skills, and the development of functional language and of a body concept. All ultimately aim at increased independence and the ability to fit into society.

To achieve those goals, treatment is not confined to a specific time or place. Instead, all activities a child is involved in throughout the day are structured to be educational and therapeutic, to influence his behavior, increase his skills and further his total growth.

Depending on their level, children engage in a lot of different activities in a variety of natural settings. The skills they learn encompass the whole gamut of a person's functioning. They may be very basic, such as self-care in toileting and feeding. They may concern social behavior, like learning table manners or participating in a group activity. They may have to do with physical development, gross motor skills, like kicking or throwing a ball or learning to balance on a balance beam or riding a bicycle, or with manual dexterity, like learning to cut with scissors. They may involve group interactions or cognitive development at various levels—recognizing shapes, matching colors, or learning to count, for example.

The opportunities for learning extend throughout the day. They occur at meals, during free time, at bath time, on outings, in group work, during individual treatment, during games, in physical education, at the pool, and in any of the other situations a child finds himself in during his stay at Linwood. And everybody with whom the children come in contact, teachers, aides, volunteers, bus drivers, clerical, professional, and kitchen staff plays a vital role in this process.

The bus drivers are in constant contact with parents and staff, for example, to discuss a child's reaction to being transported in a group and his behavior on the way to and from school. Children often go to the office to deliver messages, help with clerical tasks or as part of a special privilege. The kitchen and house-keeping staff interact with them around snacks, meals, and house-keeping chores, and the social workers as well as the speech and language consultant, the administrative staff and the medical director move freely among the children, interact with them whenever an opportunity presents itself, and consult frequently with each other both formally and informally so that all aspects of the various programs can be coordinated. The schedules of the daytime and evening staff members overlap. This is an additional important component of the program that ensures continuity and consistency of treatment. Different staff members are also trained in respite care and sometimes babysit a child on weekends or evenings to give parents needed time off.

The fact that staff tends to stay at Linwood for long periods of time despite the difficulties of working with autistic children and despite relatively modest salaries, is proof that this approach benefits not only the children but also the staff. And the many former pupils who maintain contact with Linwood over the years, who write or visit, all seem to remember and cherish the total Linwood experience. They do occasionally ask after a particular staff member or former friends, but mostly it seems to be Linwood itself, the building, the yard, the activities and outings, everything that made it a safe and central place in their lives, that they want to touch base with. Linwood not only nurtured them, it gave them the strength and the skills to function in the outside world.

One boy's letter reads in part:

Dear Miss Simons,

If you are still alive, I would like to see you when I come to Linwood. If you are not, I would like to come anyhow and see the building, the trees and my old room . . .

In contrast to many other programs where services to parents are minimal, Linwood also emphasizes the importance of close cooperation between parents and staff. In fact, admission to Linwood is generally predicated on the willingness of the family to actively participate with the staff in the ongoing work with the child, since the child's ability to grow and to carry over what he has learned at Linwood to the outside is a critical part of the success of the educational process.

The social work staff is therefore in regular contact with the parents. They keep them informed about the child's progress and in turn are kept appraised of anything that happens at home that might influence a child's functioning at school. Parents are offered help in dealing with specific problems that arise at home and those who are interested are also taught something about the Linwood philosophy and therapy techniques, such as limit setting without a power struggle or how to deal with compulsions or temper tantrums. General support during periods of stress, individual or group meetings, and discussion groups are part of the attempt to help families cope with the many-faceted problems of having a handicapped child.

The parents are also involved in admission review and dismissal meetings (ARDs) and in the yearly evaluation process, which includes drawing up an individual educational plan (IEP) required by law for every child not in a regular public school class whose education is publicly funded.

The ultimate aim is to make the parents as knowledgable and competent as possible so that they are not only able to live with their child when he is home and contribute to his growth but can be a continuing support to him once he leaves Linwood. Not all parents are able or willing to take an equally active role in the education of their children, but most of them feel the need to be informed, are eager to be involved, and want to do everything possible to ensure their child's progress and well being.

The ongoing dialogue with the home is an integral part of treatment at Linwood. At the same time, there is a conscious and deliberate distinction made between Linwood and the home environment. Something that a child is working on at school, like speech, for example, is not automatically transferred to the home. It is only once a particular skill or behavior has become securely anchored and is a well integrated part of a child's functioning at Linwood, that parents may be asked to work with the child on the same skill.

In fact, it is almost a policy not to share a child's progress at Linwood with the parents until it is firmly established or until they themselves can see progress at home. This ensures that there are no demands made of the child before he is ready for them and that the parent's understandable eagerness to see results does not lead to unrealistic expectations or to disappointments, should the child's progress be uneven or should he temporarily regress. Sometimes the children generalize spontaneously, but more frequently they apply what they have learned only in the situation in which they have learned it. We have stressed repeatedly that autistic children resist progress. To carry over a task or a demand prematurely to the home might make them resist the task, even at school.

The children themselves often separate Linwood and the home. Some of them will not let their parents come to school, others do not want staff members visiting at home. For some children the home situation may provide an opportunity to relax away from the demands of their group or their teacher. This sometimes results in more mature or advanced behavior. One parent reported that a child who is essentially mute at Linwood occasionally uses speech at home, for example. In other cases the home environment may result in an increase of behaviors like compulsions that have virtually disappeared at Linwood.

But the home situation also imposes certain natural restraints not found at Linwood. Behaviors that may be encouraged, accepted, or appreciated at school might cause chaos in a family setting. Children might be less free to roam or to make noise, or the parents may be less tolerant of certain things like spitting. Added demands and limits at home may make a child more negative, tense, or tired so that he might be unable or unwilling to demonstrate skills he already exhibits at Linwood, like asking for food, for example.

At Linwood, all children are accorded a right to their individuality, but the staff also know that eventually they have to fit into an existing world. Their task is to observe each child and to structure the environment in ways that make it supportive, responsive to his needs, and conducive to growth. As Jeanne Simons put it:

> And that's why we walk behind the child. He feels your protection when you walk behind. If you give him a chance to go any direction, he may be wrong when he goes this way or that. Just follow him. If it's a dead end, pick him up gently and bring him to the main route. But never think that you know the answers, because you are dealing with an individual who may want go very different routes which for him may be better. That's why I feel more comfortable behind the children so I can see where they are going.

Jeanne Simons

with Dr. Kanner, Students, and Staff in 1970

with a Linwood Child

with Linwood Graduates

Linwood

Reaching Out

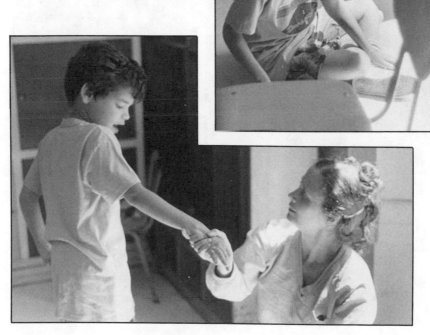

"Walking Behind the Child"

Blowing Bubbles

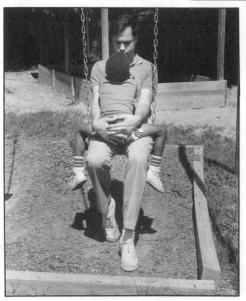

Touching

Beginning Relationships

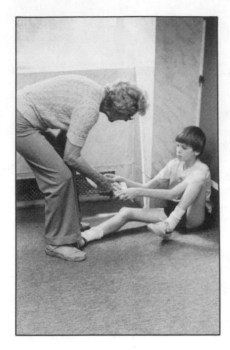

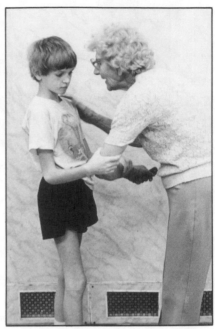

Jeanne Simons
Reaching the Hidden Child

Bibliography

1. Felicetti, T., Parents of Autistic Children: Some Notes on a Chemical Connection, *Milieu Therapy*, 1981, Vol. 1 (1), 13–16.

2. Funderburk, S.J., et. al., Parental Reproductive Problems and Gestational Hormonal Exposure in Autistic and Schizophrenic Children, *Journal of Autism and Developmental Disorders*, 1983, Vol. 13 (3), 325–332.

3. Torrey, E.F., Hersh, S.P., and McCabe, K.D., Early Childhood Psychosis and Bleeding During Pregnancy: A Prospective Study of Gravid Women and Their Offspring, *Journal of Autism and Childhood Schizophrenia*, Dec. 1975, Vol. 5 (4), 287–297.

4. Kagan, V.E., Nonprocess Autism in Children. A Comparative Etiopathogenic Study, *Soviet Neurology and Psychiatry*, Spring-Summer, 1981, Vol. 14 (1–2), 25–30.

5. Ritvo, E. and Freeman, B.J., National Society for Autistic Children, Definition of the Syndrome of Autism. *Journal of Pediatric Psychology*, 1977, Vol. 2 (4), 142–145.

6. Deykin, E.Y. and MacMahon, B., The Incidence of Seizures Among Children with Autistic Symptoms, *American Journal of Psychiatry*, 1979, Vol. 136 (10), 1310–1312.

7. Ritvo, E.R., and Ritvo, E.C., Genetic and Immunohematological Factors in Autism, *Journal of Autism and Developmental Disorders*, 1982, Vol. 12 (2), 109–114.

8. Folstein, S. and Rutter, M., Genetic Influences and Infantile Autism. *Annual Progress in Psychiatry and Child Development*, 1978, 437–441.

9. Damborska, M. and Stepanova, P., Some Behavior Characteristics of Institutionalized Infants. *Psychologia a Patopsychologia Dictata*, 1981, Vol. 16 (2), 109–122.

10. Susz, E. and Margberg, H.M., Autistic Withdrawal of a Small Child Under Stress, *Acta Paedopsychiatrica*, May, 1983, Vol. 43 (4), 149–158.

11. Delong, G.R., Bean, S.C., Brown, F.R., Acquired Reversible Autistic Syndrome in Acute Encephalitic Illness in Children, *Archives of Neurology*, March, 1981, Vol. 38 (3), 191–194.

12. Coleman, M. and Gillberg, C., *The Biology of the Autism Syndrome*, N.Y.: Praeger Publishers, 1985.

13. Schopler, E. and Reichler, R.J., *Individualized Assessment and Treatment for Autistic and Developmentally Disabled Children*, Baltimore: University Park Press, 1978–80.

249

14. Ferster, C.B. and Simons, J., Behavior Therapy with Children, *The Psychological Record*, 1966, 16, 65–71.

15. Ferster, C.B., An Operant Reinforcement Analysis of Infantile Autism, *Unpublished Paper*.

16. Selfe, Lorna, *Nadia: A Case of Extraordinary Drawing Ability in an Autistic Child*, N.Y.: Harcourt, Brace Jovanovich, 1979.

17. Arnheim, R., The Puzzle of Nadia's Drawings, *Arts in Psychotherapy*, 1980, Vol. 7 (2), 79–85.

18. Kanner, Leo in collaboration with Simons, J., Evaluation and Follow-up of 34 Psychotic Children, *Childhood Psychosis: Initial Studies and New Insights*, Washington: V.H. Winston & Sons, 1973.

Recommended Readings

Bemporad,J.R., Adult recollections of a formerly autistic child, *Journal of Autism and Developmental Disorders*, June, 9(2), 1979, 179–192

Copeland,James, *For the Love of Ann* (based on a diary by Jack Hodges), London: Severn House Publishers, 1976

Donnellan, A.M. (Editor), *Classic Readings in Autism*, New York: Teachers College Press, Columbia University, 1985

Delacato, Carl,H., *The Ultimate Stranger; The Autistic Child*, Garden City, N.Y.: Doubleday, 1974

Hundley, Joan Martin, *The Small Outsider, The Story of an Autistic Child*, N.Y.: St. Martin's Press, 1972

Lovell, Ann, *In a Summer Garment: The Experience of an Autistic Child*, London: Secker and Warburg, 1978

Park, Clara, Clairborne, *The Siege: The First 8 Years of an Autistic Child, With an Epilogue Fifteen Years Later*, Boston: Little, Brown, 1982

Rothenberg, Mira, *Children with Emerald Eyes*, N.Y.: Dial Press, 1977

Rutter, M. (Editor), *Autism—A Reappraisal of Concepts and Treatment*, N.Y.: Plenum Press, 1978

Schopler, E. and Mesobov, G. (Editors), *Autism in Adolescents and Adults*, N.Y., Plenum Press, 1978

Wing, Lorna (Editor), *Early Childhood Autism: Clinical,Educational, and Social Aspects*, Oxford, N.Y.: Pergamon Press, 1976

Wing, Lorna, *Autistic Children: A Guide for Parents*, London: Constable, 1980

Index

The Special Needs Collection

Woodbine House is pleased to offer these fine books for parents of children with special needs and the professionals who assist them.

CHILDREN WITH AUTISM:
A Parents Guide

By Michael Powers, Ph.D. Woodbine House, 1988. 275p. charts. graphs. index. resource guide. reading list. glossary. appendices. paperback (0-933149-16-6).

CHILDREN AND ADOLESCENTS WITH MENTAL ILLNESS:
A Parents Guide

By Evelyn McElroy, Ph.D. Woodbine House, 1987. 230p. charts. graphs. photographs. index. glossary. resource guide. reading list. paperback (0-933149-10-7).

CHILDREN WITH EPILEPSY:
A Parents Guide

Edited by Helen Reisner. Woodbine House, 1987. 230p. charts. graphs. photographs. index. glossary. resource guide. reading list. illus. paperback (0-933149-19-0).

CHOICES IN DEAFNESS:
A Parents Guide

Edited by Sue Schwartz, Ph.D. Woodbine House, 1987. 212p. charts. graphs. illus. resource guide. reading list. index. paperback (0-933142-09-3).

LANGUAGE OF TOYS:
Teaching Communication Skills to Special Needs Children: A Parents Guide

By Sue Schwartz and Joan E. Heller Miller. Woodbine House, 1987. 160p. charts. graphs. photographs. illustrations. glossary. resource guide. reading list. paperback (0-933149-08-5).

THE HIDDEN CHILD:
The Linwood Method for Reaching the Autistic Child

By Jeanne Simons and Sabine Oishi, Ph.D. Woodbine House, 1987. 250p. illus. index. bibliography. paperback (0-933142-06-9).

BABIES WITH DOWN SYNDROME:
A New Parents Guide

Edited by Karen Stray-Gundersen. Woodbine House, 1986. 237p. charts. graphs. index. resource guide. reading list. illus. paperback (0-933149-02-6).

	Quantity	Price	Total
Children with Autism		$12.95	
Children and Adolescents with Mental Illness		$12.95	
Choices in Deafness		$12.95	
Children with Epilepsy		$12.95	
Language of Toys		$ 9.95	
The Hidden Child		$17.95	
Babies with Down Syndrome		$ 9.95	
		Subtotal	
	Shipping/Handling ($1.50 per copy)		
	Tax (5% for MD residents only)		
		TOTAL	

SHIP TO:

NAME _____

ADDRESS _____

_____

_____ ZIP _____

TELEPHONE _____

VISA/MasterCard # _____ EXP. DATE _____

Return Order Form to: Woodbine House, 10400 Connecticut Avenue, Kensington, MD 20895. Or **Order Toll Free 800-843-7323** (outside Maryland), 301-949-3590 (in Maryland). **Also available in fine bookstores.** • **Thank you for your order.**